INSTANT REPLAY
the day that
changed sports forever

For information contact:
Creative Book Publishers International
269 S. Beverly Drive, Suite 1442, Beverly Hills, CA 90212.
www.bookpubintl.com

Library of Congress Control Number: 2008922439

Tony Verna

INSTANT REPLAY
the day that changed sports forever
ISBN-13: 978-0-9779131-4-5

Typography & Cover: Kirk Thomas, www.kirks-graphics.com
Editor: Ron Kenner, www.rkedit.com

This book is dedicated
to my granddaughters,
Taylor LeClair
and
Sophia Soiseth

ACKNOWLEDGMENTS

December 7, 1963 – Instant Replay "The day televised football changed forever"

PITTSBURG TRIBUNE

Tony told Lindsey, "We may do something different today, so watch for it." We were totally shocked.

JIM SIMPSON

What? You're going to do what?

LINDSEY NELSON

After all these years, I still remember how exciting it was to see that scoring play coming back at me, instantly on the monitor.

TERRY BRENNAN

My Boy, what you have done here will have such far-reaching implications we can't begin to imagine them today.

TEX SCHRAMM

You're a legend now.

ROGER STAUBACH

People who watched the game on television were honestly confused.

ROLLIE STICHWEH

Tony Verna has left a legacy of greatness to the industry. Believe me, the Instant Replay was all Tony's baby. I ought to know. He had to get my permission to use it.

BILL McPHAIL

Action in the Army-Navy Game was shown again immediately after it occurred.

ROONE ARLEDGE

Instant replay became instant success in '63.

WASHINGTON TIMES

Contents

PREFACE

Throughout this book you will see photographs of Tony Verna with sports stars, movie stars, presidents, dictators, Pope John Paul II, Mother Teresa.... How does a young kid from South Philadelphia get to make such a splash on the international scene?

Tony is more than "The Man Who Created Instant Replay." He received the Directors Guild of America's "Lifetime Achievement Award" in 1995, and before that he'd directed five Super Bowls and twelve Kentucky Derbies. He has traveled to Mexico to direct its Soccer Championship and to direct its national rodeo, the Charreada. Then he was off to France, to direct the Grand Prix and transmit it to the Mexican Network. After that, he was in Russia to direct The Mike Douglas Show live from Moscow.

Then it was off to London to direct the "World Circus," to Montreal to produce a daily report on the 1976 Summer Olympics for Saudi Arabia, to Las Vegas to become President of Caesars Palace Productions, to Ronald Reagan's home to direct an interview with the President-Elect, to the White House to direct President George H.W. Bush in a series of public service announcements.

In 1985 he filmed a "Christmas Special" with Mother Teresa. That year he co-produced and co-directed "Live Aid," Bob Geldof's 16-hour fund-raiser for Africa, seen by 1.5 billion people worldwide. He then created an international program for Pope John Paul II, "Prayer for World Peace." What Verna created was seen by a billion people, breaking the record for the most viewers to witness a television program at the time. He also produced and directed the live transmission that linked five continents. Another first.

In 1987 Omni Magazine chose Verna as one of "14 Great Minds" to predict the future. In 1990 he was the executive producer/ director for Ted Turner's Goodwill Games. And that list is merely part of the remarkable career that began for a 19-year-old Tony Verna at WCAU-TV in Philadelphia. In addition to fashioning a global career, Tony found time to get married, divorced, and remarried. He has three grown children: Tracy, Jennifer, and Eric. He's written four books. And, yes, he gave us the Instant Replay!

Through all the years Tony Verna has always—and is always— roughing out some new idea on taking the latest technology down a different path so as to create something it wasn't intended to do. Thus it comes as no surprise that he has currently patented a live tracking football widget for the Internet.

It's called the 'InstantFootballer' and, like the Instant Replay, it uses current technology to do something that never existed before. The InstantFootballer can spot the football during a live game. Yep! The ball is placed on the exact yard line and the image is immediately rendered to your computer or cell phone screen. It updates itself and it provides the latest game information as you continue with what you were doing on your computer or cell phone.

Reading the way Verna thinks about life may spark something in the way you should be thinking about life. So check him out. As Bette Davis once said, "Buckle your seat belts. It's going to be a bumpy ride."

Join me and meet the man who invented the Instant Replay— and accomplished a heck of a lot more. Tony Verna has an incredible story to tell.

CHAPTER ONE

BIRTH OF THE INSTANT REPLAY

I'd like to set the climate in which I invented the 'Instant' part of the Instant Replay, back to 1959 in the days when only technicians in the studio were able to record and play back the highlights of a live football game. Before December 7, 1963, the only tape machines servicing live sports pickups were miles away, anchored in some studio's tape bay. So between 1959 and 1963 this delayed process of replaying from the studio didn't change. In fact I had been hearing half time highlights two years before Roone Arledge got into sports.

The only improvement came when Arledge used a new type of recorder at an ABC studio to capture a football highlight and play it back awhile later in slow motion during the halftime. But during those four years from '59 to '63 there was always a lengthy delay before the airing of any replay, either in regular speed or in slow motion. And that remained the case until December 7, 1963, when I successfully aired the first recording of a previous play immediately following the live transmission of that play.

The first question I'm usually asked is: Why had the Instant Replay concept eluded everyone else? I suppose it was because those Ampex videotape machines weren't invented to provide Instant Replays. There was nothing instant about them, so I guess nobody thought about 'instant'.

But the first Instant Replay was no accident of history—I was ready for it, even if the tape machines weren't. Ampex had invented its machines mainly for time-delay broadcasting so that the networks could play back their prime-time programs whenever they wished, not instantly but in the different time zones across the country. The first airing of a time-delayed program came on November 30, 1956, when CBS broadcast a West Coast delayed broadcast of "Douglas Edwards And The News." By using videotape recorders in each time zone, the show was time-delayed.

Seven years later, in 1963, the first Instant Replay aired on December 7th, the 22nd anniversary of Pearl Harbor. But prior to my airing that first Instant Replay, let's go back a few weeks to November 24, 1963, when there was a live television transmission of Lee Harvey Oswald being shot by Jack Ruby in the basement of a jail in Dallas, Texas; and this led to an attempt at the time to immediately playback a significant event that had aired live. The 'shooting' was captured live on two TV cameras by NBC's WBAP-TV, but recorded by CBS's KRLD-TV.

In July of 2007 I contacted Ed Barker, KRLD's former news chief, and he told me, "We were in a church remote on location and had to break in and play a tape."

Meanwhile, before airing that first Instant Replay I had recently contacted the Curator of The Sixth Floor Museum at Dealey Plaza in Dallas, Texas. I must credit the curator, Gary Mack, for supplying key information I am about to pass on. Mr. Mack verified the amount of time lapsed before the first replay. He personally timed the sequence of events on the tapes, which are now in the possession of the museum. It was not an easy job. He had to deal with the different points in time in order to match the Dallas raw tape to the network tape. He confirmed that the first replay, fast for the time but hardly 'instant', took nine minutes from the time Ruby shot Oswald to the moment it aired as a replay.

The shooting occurred at 11:21 a.m. Central Time, and the first tape replay came later on NBC at 11:30 a.m.; and two minutes after that, approximately eleven minutes having elapsed, CBS aired its replay with Harry Reasoner saying, "We are back at headquarters in New York. We have... we got our tape. We have re-racked the videotape that shows that whole scene of confusion. We will now roll it and see it as it happened."

The videotape played without audio; not too surprising considering that those machines didn't like to be rushed before rewinding a tape back to its starting point. They were always in need of some prior navigational assistance and set-up by the operator. As well, there were several film cameras that captured the shooting by Ruby. I mention this because in those days 16mm sound film still played a significant role. Video machines weren't quite portable yet, and certainly not always reliable even for providing small clips. That meant that all major events were backed up with film coverage, and that's why the jail basement was so heavily lit; so that it could accommodate the needs of film.

By 1963 the news departments of the three networks, along with some local stations, had one or two video machines in a TV trailer. Gary Mack points out that KTVT, a Dallas Indie station at the time, rolled a delayed playback from its truck not only after the Oswald shooting but also after the JFK assassination. They rolled the tape as they approached Parkland Hospital, but the tape's video levels dropped dramatically when the truck stopped at a traffic light and then brightened to normal levels when the truck started up again. So the bottom line is that only NBC had the shooting "live" and that NBC aired the first replay nine minutes later, two minutes before CBS showed what happened when Oswald came down the hall flanked by Texas lawmen.

As I noted, tape machines weren't quite reliable and all major events were backed up with film coverage. Not only that, but during the first use of tape the engineers were filming off the monitor when CBS used the Ampex VR-1000 monochrome Video Tape recorder to capture the delayed broadcast of "Douglas Edwards And The News."

When I worked on the 1960 Rome Olympics, three of the engineers, Dick Sedia, Bob Zagoren, and George Zavales recalled making backup kinescopes of Douglas Edwards, just in case these were needed. And there was another factor. During the first year of operation, the videotape machines could only play back tapes that had been recorded on the same machine. This was due to the mechanical differences in the high-speed, rotating head assemblies. In short, the first recordings were not interchangeable. Thus countless hours of news and entertainment recorded during that first year couldn't be played back unless you found the same head that had been used in the initial recording. Even when the problem had been corrected, after the second year of operation, producers weren't eager to rerun their shows and had to deal with payouts for all the residuals.

CBS may have had several policies in place for saving shows that had been videotaped, but the only one I was aware of was the policy to erase and record over. So I have to assume that's what happened to the first Instant Replay. I wasn't allowed to keep the tape. That was the policy. Engineering controlled the tape and it had to be returned. As well, the storage was limited and that meant constant erasure. Like the first Instant Replay, they never found a recording of the first Super Bowl. My thinking is that since the first Super Bowl was called a Championship Game and not a Super Bowl, it got erased like all other prior NFL Championship Games.

Without anybody telling them differently, the tape guys probably thought that this was just another one of those championship games, like the ones I had done, and they automatically erased it. You have to remember the label "Super Bowl" didn't come until the second one was played, and the Roman numerals weren't affixed until the fourth Super Bowl. I directed both of those Super Bowls, the second and fourth, but first I'd like to take you back to 1960 when I was in Rome putting the Olympics together on videotape, and explain how that eventually led to the concept of the Instant Replay.

Rome was my training ground with the Ampex VTR-1000, the first commercially sold videotape recorder. I spent my days and nights with those big machines, and I really got to understand what a big pain-in-the-ass they could be—what they could do and what they couldn't do. But there was one part of their limitations that remained with me and became a factor in thinking of a method to replay instantly.

Because the tape machines couldn't synchronize immediately, the engineers spliced a test-strip of a prerecorded tape to the front of the newly recorded material they were about to put on the air. What they used was an old "I Love Lucy tape"—they called it 'Lucy Leader'—as the pre-roll so that they could tweak the images of Desi and Lucy into synchronization to get the new recording up to speed and ready for airing. A couple of years later the thought of that pre-roll came back to me as an idea that a pre-roll could be the key factor in creating a system whereby the tape could talk to me just like Desi and Lucy did on that test strip. Maybe the left side of my brain came up with doing something in sequential order while the right side of my brain related that pre-roll to the whole of a new idea. Or it could have been just a brain fart. I don't know. But if it was a mental gas problem, there was a good reason. I'd been having a hard time digesting some of my bad experiences.

The first bad memory that stuck in my craw went back to those days in Rome when I was recording my voice onto the cue track of the videotape before jetting the tape to the New York Control Room. The cue track being the second audio track on the tape, the one that the viewers couldn't hear when the tape was played back. I thought that putting my comments on the cue track of the tape jetted to the States would be helpful to the director in the New York control room, since those playbacks would be the key ingredient to the live programs being hosted by Jim McKay, who was hosting from Studio 41 in Grand Central Station.

My suggestion was intended to give the director and his engineers a heads-up before they aired the tape inserts. For example, on the cue track, I'd warn that certain portions of the tape had lots of video dropouts, or that another tape had a better angle of Wilma Rudolph sprinting to her gold, or I'd warn the director not to cut out of the recording of Cassius Clay, after he won the decision, since Cassius Clay's best reactions came as he left the ring. But the result of my efforts was bubkus. The asshole director and his smug crew made it a point not to listen to the cue track. Who the hell was this 'dago kid' to tell those 'pros' what to do?

For some reason the anger from those frustrations came flooding back to me three years later. Or maybe it was because I knew it was time to stop beating myself up for not covering a game better than I was doing for the home viewers. I knew there had to be a better telecast to show them. The shots were right there on the monitors in my truck but they were happening at the same time that my main camera had to stay with the movement of the ball, so I couldn't let the audience see what I was seeing.

Many times all that I could show them on their home sets was a lame shot of the receiver trudging back to the huddle after a long incomplete pass.

I remember times when Tommy McDonald of the Philadelphia Eagles would miss one of quarterback Norm Van Brocklin's bombs but we didn't see why he wasn't there for the catch. All the viewers got to see was the players' reactions, McDonald with his head down, and the Dutchman fuming. But the viewers didn't see why the pass wasn't caught. I wanted to show them what I had seen on another monitor, that McDonald had been tripped leaving the line of scrimmage.

By the fall of '63, some of the press started to make a big deal out of me being a live director in sports. But to myself I was also the biggest failure since I was directing the biggest game and yet I wasn't able to show what was happening away from the ball. And that frustration latched itself to my earlier frustrations and anger when my cue track commentary had been totally disregarded. So as the fall was turning into winter in '63, my mind was turning on how to pull off an Instant Replay. At nights I'd be at the bar of P. J. Clarke's, and when I'd be staring out into space my date would be asking if everything was all right. How could I tell a girl I wasn't concentrating on her, that I had problems deep in my hippocampus?

I knew better than to tell my dates about that. But now I think it's time to explain how I solved my problem and figured out how to make the replay instant.

So it's 1963, meaning that when I wanted to roll a tape there was nothing to see up on the tape monitor. There was no 'still frame' (the way there is today) to be seen before I ran my tape. When I hollered, "Roll it," the nothing that appeared on the monitor was replaced by a ten-second blizzard of shit they called video hash. The ten seconds of scrambled video came for the pre-roll portion of the tape that was needed so that the machine had time to synchronize it.

Problem One: The tape machine didn't possess the brains to be precisely cued. It wasn't conceived or built with those components. So where the hell was I supposed to mark a precise starting point on-the-fly? I couldn't rely on the numerical counter on the machine as the answer to immediately rolling back a tape and finding its correct starting point. What starting point would that be? How would the machine know where the exact starting point on the tape was, so that on playing back I could hit the start of a play on the dime and squeeze it between live plays? The tape machines had numerical counters on them, but they were highly unreliable for a machine pulling its tape at 15 inches a second. And if I ever got a machine with a reliable counter on location, I wouldn't be able to see the rotating counter, anyhow. It would be in another truck.

Problem Two: I had to know what was happening during the pre-roll and the advancement of the tape during those 10 seconds of jumbled crap. If I didn't know what was going on, how would I know what the tape would be showing me when it locked up?

Problem Three: The Ampex machine had no balls, no way of doing something different. I had to devise a system to compensate for what was missing within the hardware. So I turned my thinking from the machine to the tape itself. I figured that if the machine couldn't do the job, my only hope was the videotape itself. And that's when I thought of the unused cue track, as being my guide.

But how was I supposed to be talking to a tape machine while I was jabbering away a mile-a-minute calling the shots in a live game? And even if I could speak on the cue track, that meant that when the tape played back on the pre-roll my words would be just as distorted as the video. I wouldn't be able to pick them out from the rest of playback noise.

Then it came to me. When radio began, they used a 440-cycle burst of audio tones as a time check for their stations and a lead-in before the start of the day's broadcasting. Hmm. What if it were an audio tone that was being distorted? What if, instead of listening to my words being mangled, I'd be listening to a tone's changing pitch as it was tightening to its original distinct sound?

I inputted my commands as 'beeps' directly onto the cue track; and by focusing on the tape rather than the hardware I was able to do what the recorder couldn't do.

Now as the inventor of the new process, I also had to be the innovator of the invention. Only the director of a live game could be the one capable of giving the instant commands needed to accomplish an immediate playback of the videotape; especially when the rest of my crew had no idea of what I was doing. First I had come up with a system to code the videotape and that meant I had to have the tape machine on location with me at the game. It was the only way I could personally overlay the electronic cues exactly where I wanted them onto the tape as it was recording. And, as I noted, only a news department would have a video machine in a TV trailer; and the one at CBS News in New York never left Manhattan.

Back in those days these twelve-hundred-pound monsters were the size of big deep freezers. And they recorded on heavy metal reels in an open reel-to-reel alignment. They were called 'Quads' because of the four-head wheel, which rotated 240 times a second to record and playback, and the components inside those machines were regarded as too sensitive to be allowed to leave the tape center in Manhattan. The news department had enough trouble bouncing them around from block to block, let alone thinking about city to city.

And there would be problems other than the equipment. I had to deal with the bosses, co-workers, and the protocol. Somebody like me wasn't supposed to have invented the Instant Replay. You can't help but notice how little credit I get for coming up with it. Through the years, even CBS, the network where I worked for more than twenty-five years, ignores the fact that I created the Instant Replay. On the Internet, the network takes credit for the accomplishment in its chronological listing of achievements without ever mentioning me. Like it just happened.

But the invention of the Instant Replay was always a ticklish subject back at CBS. The invention certainly wasn't supposed to come from that young 'dago-kid,' the term lots of them called me behind my back. Those days, I was the only Italian-American with major credits in live television production. And to make matters worse, all of a sudden I had come up with something that could put me on an even higher plane. Certain people went about making sure that didn't happen. There's the same type of prejudice still going on today, and there's nothing I can do about it. But who knows? Maybe today's bloggers will go toe-to-toe with those spineless creeps and set the record straight. Bloggers have dealt with CBS on truth issues before, as they did when they turned Rathergate into a scandal.

In the old days, technical achievements were supposed to come from the engineering department so they could bring them up to the top brass so somebody there could take the credit. I had to get around this. I had to be able to get a videotape machine on location so that I could experiment with it.

First of all, I figured out to stay clear of the CBS Lab. They operated on development funds. And that meant I would have had to submit a bunch of memos on what the idea was, why it was needed, and how much money would have to be invested in research, research being the Lab's bloodline.

Next I had to end-around the CBS Engineering Department. I went directly to my boss, hoping to get his okay before anybody else heard about it and could nix the idea. I went to Bill McPhail, who was the VP of CBS Sports, and he loved the idea of using an immediate replay of the action during the Army-Navy Game. For years, even after he left CBS to join Turner Broadcasting, he was quoted as calling it 'Tony's baby'.

Those days, CBS kept its fourteen Ampex VTR-1000s housed on the seventh floor in the main terminal building of New York's Grand Central Station. Since a tape on a news van wouldn't be available to me, I had to get my hands on one of the machines. And there was more than just that Ampex VTR-1000 machine that had to be transported. Each machine came in two parts: the huge recording machine and the large electronics cabinet that housed the racks of large vacuum tubes, which supported it.

I conveniently forgot to mention to Bill McPhail that the machine I wanted came in two huge parts. Anyway, the whole setup ended up weighing more than a ton and it took a whole team of loaders at Grand Central Station to get the equipment down from the seventh floor to a loading platform and into a Hertz rental.

When the truck left the dock heading for Philadelphia, I looked over at my EIC (Engineer-In-Charge), the late Walter Pyle. He raised his hand to show me that his fingers were crossed. The machine was driven the ninety miles to Municipal Stadium in South Philly by the late Joe Tier, our best maintenance engineer. Luckily, Joe was smarter than any of us. He brought along plenty of spare vacuum tubes, which would eventually come in handy.

When the truck arrived, it also came with some serious electronic issues. As predicted, the machine arrived badly shaken from the trip. Sometimes it wouldn't want to record. Sometimes it wouldn't want to lock-in on playback. Sometimes it didn't do anything. In fact it wasn't until the day of the game before Pyle and his crew got it recording and stabilizing on playback.

Walter Pyle being my EIC, was responsible for the total pickup of the Army-Navy Game. Walter thought doing an Instant Replay was ingenious—but he warned me, "They didn't give you the best, most reliable machine in the bunch. In fact, you got the one that's been giving the guys the most trouble."

Walter didn't have any concerns with my adding something like the Instant Replay to the load the crew normally had in carrying out their assignments. And that was one of the few uncomplicated advantages of my conception. It didn't involve a separate set of logistics for the crew. I needed only five people to perform outside their normal assignments: the announcer, Lindsey Nelson; the cameraman, George Drago; the audio man, Dick Livingston; the tape operator, John Wells; and our ace maintenance man, Joe Tier.

I didn't get any comments from the heads of the Engineering Department at CBS. They ignored me. I still don't understand this kind of thinking. I worked for CBS, like they did, and that meant anything I created belonged to CBS. Period. And that's the way it should have been. I still can't fathom why they didn't follow up on having a form of the creative process, what I had invented, patented for our network... their network.

I had based my invention on a cuing system. Over some martinis I got to thinking—what if I overlaid a pattern of timed audio tones on the tape's cue track as it went about recording the live play. With the tones being put on the unused audio track, the home viewers would not hear those beeps when the tape played back. Next, I needed to figure out where the tones would be placed so that I would have a systematic way of relating to the game in progress.

Since I was isolating the quarterback, I decided to mark the offensive team's movements with my tones. I transmitted one tone to the recording tape when the offense huddled. And two tones when the quarterback came to the line of scrimmage. When the tape played back, the sequential tones I had placed on the pre-roll came back at the same variable speed as the video. At the time, nobody else was attempting to harness videotape so that it could be played back as an Instant Replay. I was the only one in the race. And despite CBS thinking of it as an accident of history, I knew I was the one who could pull it off.

The day I did pull it off was December 7, 1963. It was the twenty-second anniversary of Pearl Harbor Day. The Army-Navy Game had been scheduled fifteen days earlier, but President John F. Kennedy was assassinated in Dallas, Texas, on November 22, and the game was postponed to December 7.

The day before the game, my boss, Bill McPhail, asked me to come up to Manhattan to have lunch with him. Originally he'd loved my idea of airing the first Instant Replay on what was probably the greatest of college rivalries, but now he was worried since there was an emotional cloud hanging over the nation. He cautioned me that if I did get to use the Instant Replay that I should air it without any razzle-dazzle. It had been just fifteen days since the President's death, and with all the patriotism involved at the Army-Navy game, he said, the atmosphere would be intense. And screwing this up by saying there would be an Instant Replay and then not airing it, he added, would be like screwing up Cardinal Spellman's funeral.

Recently, I thought back on that lunch and I phoned the producer of that game, Bill Creasy, and asked him what he remembered, back those forty three years ago. Bill had joined me on the train ride back to Philly. This was the night before the game, Bill recalled, adding that it was the first time I told him what I was attempting to do.

Creasy got to the stadium extra early the next morning so that I could pick up the announcers Lindsey Nelson, Terry Brennan, and Jim Simpson at the hotel and bring them out to the stadium and tell them about the experiment.

Years later I had a chance to go back over that conversation with Lindsey. It was back in 1995, a month before Lindsey passed away, I gave him a call knowing he was seriously ill, and at least we got a laugh about how I held off briefing him—until we were in the cab on the way to the stadium.

In his biography "Hello Everybody, I'm Lindsey Nelson," Lindsey recalled, "You're going to do what!?"

I remember that after I told him what my plans were he fell silent. My guess was he was trying to figure out how he would explain something to the viewers that they had never seen before... that what they were now seeing was not a new play but a replay of what they had just seen.

Then I gave Lindsey a key restriction. He couldn't promote it in advance since I didn't know if it would work and the viewers would never see what he had promised them. He said he understood, and he was comfortable with that.

When it happened, though, Lindsey got pretty excited. He never mentioned it in my last conversation with him, but in his autobiography he wrote that he didn't realize how excited he was that the thing had worked until he heard his own voice rising till he was practically screaming.

Let's go back to the actual telecast. I opened up panning a hundred thousand people standing at attention, with the symbolism of the occasion weighing down on them. As soon as the West Point Band ended the National Anthem the crowd began cheering. The Navy fans for the Heismann Trophy Winner, quarterback Roger Staubach—and Army fans were shouting their approval of their quarterback Rollie Stichweh, that is, those who could pronounce his name (it rhymes with which way).

I recently spoke with both Rollie and Roger. We went back forty three years in our conversation, and how I couldn't have Lindsey pre-warn the viewers on what we'd be attempting because our boss, Bill McPhail, didn't want us to promote something I wasn't sure I could do. I told Roger that I had tried all game to playback him in action, but the only opportunity came with Rollie scoring. Both of them said it was an honor to be part of it. These are two great men who have had two great careers.

It was a great game. And that meant I was extra busy switching cameras to follow the story line of the game while at the same time I was going through the routine of trying to ready an Instant Replay. I had tried to get it working a half dozen times, but damn, something would always go wrong. Either the recording head was giving me a 'venetian blind effect', or the machine was changing speeds because the vacuum tubes were consuming too much electricity and burning out.

The news department mobile tapes never had this problem. Their window of operation was seldom more than an hour. I was using the same type of videotape they were using. It was the same kind of tape we all had been using since day one, 3-M's original number 179. It was 300 dollars a roll and I couldn't get my hands on any of it. But Walter Pyle was able to get us a little roll that had a previous recording of an old Lucy Show still recorded on it, the same 'Lucy Leader', I spoke about earlier; and it also had several Duz soap commercials which for some reason were razor-spliced into footage of that show. My guess is that they let me have one of their experimental tapes. Then to top it all, the rollbacks were showing flashes of Lucille Ball or a Duz box. Holy Shit! The damn machine wasn't always recording over the old video. Hell—either Lucy or the soap box could pop up at the line of scrimmage!

The game was almost over, and still no replays. It was the fourth quarter. Navy was ahead 21-7. In terms of the on-air game, everything was normal. Lindsey was doing his usual play-by-play. Terry Brennan added the color.

Recently, I phoned Brennan, we also hadn't been in touch since the game. He told me that throughout the telecast he kept wondering when the hell was that Instant Replay coming. And now, forty-three years later, he still remembered being stunned when the playback of the last play appeared instantly on his monitor.

I discussed that memorable day with Jim Simpson, our sideline reporter, when we got together at Ted Turner's 1990 Goodwill Games. Jim said his eyes were fixed on his field monitor. He too was waiting for that great invention I spoke about during our cab ride to the stadium. In the truck, we weren't surprised that Staubach and the Navy team would be leading, but we also expected Stichweh and the Army team to never give up.

Sure enough, Army didn't quit. They started a drive that went fifty-two yards. When they got in scoring position, Rollie Stichweh faked a handoff to his tailback, went off-tackle, and scored the touchdown himself.

It was an isolation that George Drago had caught on his camera and which John Wells immediately rewound and then hit the play button. And during the seven to ten seconds while the pre-roll played back, I heard the tones strengthen, and, lo and behold, clean video came up. My technical director, Sandy Bell, punched it up while I shouted into Lindsey's ear, "This is it!"

And when that Instant Replay hit the screen, we got Lindsey's famous on-air shout, "This is not live! Ladies and Gentlemen, Army did not score again."

In all fairness, we have to remember that those black and white video recordings playing in normal speed were indistinguishable from live video. Video recordings could be very, very deceiving. They played at the same speed, and there was no way to tell live from a clean recording.

Immediately after the Instant Replay, Army did score again, when Stichweh ran the ball again for a two-point conversion. For the record, let me point out that there was confusion at the end of the game. Stichweh couldn't communicate his audible to the team because of the unbelievable crowd noise. Rollie stepped back to signal a time-out, but the clock had already run its course. The game was over: the final score: Navy 21, Army 15.

Recently, over the phone, I asked Rollie if he was ever bitter that the game clock ran out on him because the referee had bollixed-up the time-out by starting-up the clock while Army was still in the huddle. Rollie laughingly said, "No excuses sir," knowing I was aware of the West Point answer that was given by a cadet if he failed to complete an assignment.

Well, if Army didn't win even after Stichweh's memorable run, CBS certainly did, despite their failure to give me the acclaim. I had to look for it elsewhere. ESPN Classic Moments recalled: "In the fourth quarter of Navy's 21-15 victory over Army, history is made. Not by the Cadets or Midshipmen, but by CBS."

After Stichweh's score from the one-yard line, "CBS immediately plays back an isolated look at Stichweh to the national audience. Instant replay is born." And Joe Starkey of the Pittsburgh Tribune-Review called December 7, 1963, "the day televised football changed forever."

Those evaluations, though, came later. About the only one who immediately foresaw the impact the Instant Replay would have was the late Tex Schramm, who was directly under Bill McPhail. Schramm was the one who first hired me to work for CBS. Tex had scouted me while I was a director in Philly and brought me to New York. Soon afterwards he left CBS to become General Manager of the Dallas Cowboys. It was Tex who was the first to congratulate me.

In the Dallas Morning News, sports columnist Barry Horn quoted Mr. Schramm as saying that he phoned me in the truck while the game was still being played and said, "My Boy, what you have done here will have such far-reaching implications we can't begin to imagine them today."

Tex Schramm was instrumental in my career and I was lucky to speak to him again just before he passed away in 2003. It gave me the chance to say thanks. As mentioned, I spoke to Roger Staubach recently, and we got to talking about Tex and his vision. Roger said Tex had that kind of head, and that, of course, would lead a guy like Tex to be instrumental in the use of Instant Replay for officiating in pro-ball.

Other accolades followed over the years. In 1999 Entertainment Weekly Magazine recognized the first airing of the Instant Replay as "One of the hundred great moments in television history." And in 2004, in their 50th Anniversary Issue, Sports Illustrated dubbed the Instant Replay "Deja View"—v-i-e-w—and listed it as Number Eleven of their "20 Great Tipping Points."

What I appreciated especially about the Sports Illustrated

citation was that they stressed the idea, not just the mechanics. They called it a "technical breakthrough and a conceptual one." The magazine noted that TV could now "improve upon the experience of watching a game in person," a shift that certainly qualified Instant Replay as one of "the most important events in sports over the past fifty years."

The next time I used the Instant Replay was a month later at the '64 Cotton Bowl when Navy, now ranked #2, lost the National Championship to #1 Texas, 28 to 6.

It may be interesting to note that Pat Summerall made his national debut on that game supposedly being viewed by the largest TV audience in college football history. And to the best of my memory, this was the game that the succinct Pat Summerall referred to the 'Immediate Video Replay ' as an 'Instant Replay'.

The key Instant Replays in that game were of the University of Texas wingback Phil Harris who had lined up just outside of the ends and raced down field to catch the bombs. The replays weren't spectacular. The best I had were a couple of wide shots coming back at the viewer immediately after the action. The weather was great. The bright sunshine gave me some crisp-looking replays but once again none of them featured Roger Staubach scrambling. Unless you were rooting for the Longhorns, the game was a dog.

But what was important to me about that game was that a system had been worked out to mark the videotape without having to rely on me to cue the audio track. The techs recalibrated the footage counter to be more efficient so that an assistant director could be in the truck to relay the numbers needed for the machine operator to execute the playbacks, instantly.

At the Cotton Bowl, in '64, by halftime Navy was in a hole. Texas was leading them, 21 to nothing. And Staubach hadn't done squat. The Longhorn Band was parading all over the field and blasting its music in all directions. I tried Summerall's earpiece but ended up using the booth phone so as to be heard. I told Pat that all my isolations on Staubach had been just as worthless and disappointing as Navy's performance in the game. Navy didn't score until the last quarter when Staubach took it in from a couple of yards out.

As a side note, when I spoke to Roger Staubach, we discussed the buzz going around after the game, that maybe Texas had scored so easily because they knew Navy's defensive signals in advance. Roger explained how it could have happened. Someone could have charted Navy's defensive signals on previous games and matched them against the game films. If that was so, then on game day the Texas quarterback knew what to expect since he was being flashed the same defensive signals that the Navy sideline was flashing to their defense.

I told Roger that I met up with Texas coach Darrel Royal again, a couple of years after the bowl game, when he came East to appear on a live studio roundtable of football coaches that included Fritz Crisler from Michigan and Bear Bryant from Alabama. After the show, I asked Coach Royal about his offensive team's stellar performance in the '64 Cotton Bowl victory, but now even with two years having gone by, there was no mention of the possibility of his team having known Navy's defensive signals. A film camera in the press box would have been used back in 1964 to capture the defensive signals, but in 2007 the NFL confiscated a videotape camera on the New England Patriots sidelines for illegally taping the defensive signals of the New York Jets across the way.

The Cotton Bowl I've been discussing was played on a Wednesday and on that following Sunday, January 5, 1964, I was directing the now-defunct NFL Playoff Bowl from the Orange Bowl Stadium in Florida. Bart Starr led the Pack over the Cleveland Browns 40-23. This would be my third use of the Instant Replay. Bill McPhail asked me to do something different to spice up this poorly conceived game that pitted the second-place finishers in the two divisions.

MacPhail wanted me to flex his CBS muscles now that the Instant Replay seemed destined to become a cornerstone component in televising sports. So I went in close, using isolations of the receivers and the linebackers and got in about a dozen isolated (ISO) Instant Replays, which I thought a pretty good effort on my part at the time. But the press didn't pick up on that. The Cleveland Press, for one, praised the sideline reporting for having diagnosed the game in a manner that took the TV viewers further and further into the machinery of a football game. But there was no mention of the Instant Replays.

Then it occurred to me that the Instant Replay was now being taken for granted. 'Next ball game', as the expression went. It was if they were always part of the telecast. In fact, when Bill McPhail couldn't get Instant Replays on all of the 1964 NFL games, the directors of those games, which were being telecasted without the ability of instantly rerunning the action, were being blasted for their poor coverage, even though it wasn't their fault.

In the next chapter I'll discuss how inventing the Instant Replay changed not only the way we televise sports but how it also changed my expectations of life. In more ways than I could have imagined—both good and bad. And we'll get into how creating the Instant Replay affected my career and led me ultimately out of sports and into globalcasting. I'll discuss my interesting experiences when producing and directing shows like "Live Aid," "Sport Aid" and the program I created especially for Pope John Paul II, "Prayer for World Peace."

I'll also let you in on my working experiences with Mother Teresa, Presidents Ronald Reagan and George H. Bush, Yugoslavia's Marshall Tito—plus all of the Super Bowls, Kentucky Derbies, Olympics, and MBA, NBA and NHL Championships. And then there are my friendships with sports legends and movie stars. And how the media visionary Marshall McLuhan linked Instant Replay with nostalgia. But before we get to all that, I want to lay the foundation. I want to look at the people and programs that shaped my life and my career, going from being the son of Italian immigrants in South Philadelphia to meeting the Pope and meeting presidents—and dictators—and Princess Grace, Grace Kelly. Actually, I met Grace Kelly a few years before she became Princess Grace. I knew her father and brother and went to school with one of her sisters, so we had a really easy conversation.

The Academy of Television Arts and Sciences Foundation has said that I've led an amazing life. Recently they videotaped a six hour interview with me. So let's take it in sequence, beginning with my television career in Philadelphia in the 1950s.

CHAPTER TWO

THE FIFTIES

My early life paralleled the early life of television. Television and I grew up together. I also grew up in South Philadelphia, the youngest of five in a family of professional photographers. And with my family came a large case of curiosity—how did one brother take a photo of himself playing poker with five other himselves—how did a second brother photograph himself in exotic places he'd never been to—and how, back then, did my third brother photograph the other two and put himself along with our sister in the same shot? So a lot of my growing up was in the family's photographic studio.

It came as no surprise to my family that I created something like the Instant Replay, knowing that my interest in cameras and recordings started from the cradle. It was a challenge as a kid to get the upper hand on the huge large-format 16x20 camera in my father's studio. Early lenses and films required the use of a sizeable negative—which in turn led to a large-format camera which was mounted on a sizeable tripod on wheels. The wood and brass housing of the camera ran on double rails and was geared to a focus knob, with the image projected onto a ground-glass viewer at the back of the camera. To make it harder, the image was upside down and backward.

Once you were satisfied with the framing and focus, you inserted a heavy holder with a single sheet of film. The part I liked best was putting the black cloth over my head to block out all the light except for that coming in through the lens. I liked isolating myself with my subject. And I became familiar with the dark room in the basement, too.

Under the red light bulb I soon was able to use the chemical trays, the developing tanks, and the contact printers to open up my brothers' bag of tricks. That's when I began my long-term commitment to being creative.

In 1939, my family moved to one of the taller houses on Broad Street, leaving 9th Street where the fictional Rocky Balboa once ran through the Italian market area and where the real Freddie Cocozza grew up. He was one of the much older guys who horsed-around with us kids and later became the great tenor known as Mario Lanza. Our parents had emigrated from Abruzzi, a small region in central Italy, fronting the Adriatic Sea, as did the parents of Dean Martin and Perry Como who settled with other Abruzzi immigrants in areas of Ohio and upper Pennsylvania.

I mentioned Lanza's success in particular because it was the first time I became aware that great achievements were not enough, that even a star like Lanza could be harassed just because he was an Italian-American from South Philly. Mario was being called a wop by the gutter press, with the papers printing that the section where he came from, and where I lived, had more murders in that square-mile portion than in a similar-sized area anywhere else on earth. But none of that made me less proud. I never believed that where I was born decided my destiny or my future. No way! No How!

Let me digress. As a kid, I sold programs at the 1945 Army Navy Game because it was the only way I could get in and see what was going on.

World War II had ended only a few weeks earlier, and the cover of the program I was hawking had a cadet and a midshipman painting a 'V' for Victory on a brick wall. This was the Army-Navy football game held December 1, 1945, in Philadelphia and broadcast live regionally to New York City, Schenectady, and Washington, D.C. There were more than a hundred thousand people inside Municipal Stadium, but I was one of the few kids who hadn't sold all his programs, and I didn't have a dime to waste.

At halftime, I figured I'd make my way down to the field level. I told the cop I needed to unload the rest of my programs to the soldiers who were down on the field, right in front of the box seats in their wheelchairs. These were wounded World War II vets dressed in their old uniforms, with some resting on crutches or leaning on canes.

The cop left me standing there without an answer. A whistle blew, and he took off. President Harry S. Truman was on the move, and that meant that police had to form a double line to protect the President, who had been sitting on the 50-yard line of the Army side, the Broad Street side, but now was ready to cross the field, over to the Navy side. Without anybody to stop me, I walked down to the field and stood near the end zone on the Army side. In fact, it was that same end zone where later I would capture the first Instant Replay and the same end zone where, later yet, I would position the stage for the Bob Geldof's "Live Aid" Concert.

When the game was over and I was leaving the stadium, I was still amazed that I got to stand by all those Army black jerseys in gold numerals that I had seen as black and white in the newsreels. But damn, I never got to see Truman.

A few years earlier, I did get to see President Roosevelt when he was riding in an open black sedan down Broad Street. There were a couple of secret service agents on his running board, but I managed to get a wave at the President, who was seated behind a rolled-up bulletproof glass window. And I was completely stunned that FDR waved back at me.

But with Truman it was different. All I saw when he got close enough to shake hands with the vets were the flashbulbs going off.

Years later, after I got into the business, I read that the director of the game was Burke Crotty and that he had used NBC's new image orthicon cameras for the first time and that the pictures were dramatically better than those of CBS' older orthicon and iconoscope cameras. I also learned that Crotty, at General Sarnoff's request, had one of his four cameras isolated on the President throughout the game.

And for the record, it was Crotty who, six years earlier, had directed the first live sports event on American TV, the 1939 Princeton–Columbia Baseball Game, using one camera with Bill Stern doing play-by-play. The game was seen on about 400 sets. But Crotty wasn't the first live sports director. Two years earlier, somebody at the BBC had televised the 1937 Wimbledon Tennis Championships to their home viewers.

Let's pick up my story back at the 1945 Army-Navy Game. President Truman must have enjoyed being there. He showed up at Municipal Stadium three more times to catch the rivalry. Also, for the record, Army won the game 32 to 13 with Doc Blanchard scoring three times.

When the game was over, I made a quick dash to beat the crowd to the subway entrance. To get there, I went through a dozen blocks where, corner after corner, there were streets of row houses intersecting each other. The last stop in those days was at Broad and Snyder, the corner that had our largest movie house, the Broadway Theater. Two years later I'd be in that movie house to see Doc Blanchard and Glenn Davis play themselves in the movie "The Spirit of West Point." The film turned out to be just an excuse to playback their game footage. I was more impressed with the fact that Blanchard and Davis were each paid $20,000 for their bad acting.

Earlier I mentioned about how the clock was running out on Rollie Stichweh and his 1963 Army Team. Well, same thing in this movie. The clock was also running out on the 1945 Army team. Be it 1945 or 1963, the clock on the scoreboard was not official. But Hollywood had an answer for that. The Army coach merely checked his wristwatch and told his team, "Two minutes to go." That's friggin' crazy, I thought. Even the stadium scoreboard clock wasn't official, so how could the coach's wristwatch be in sync with the stopwatch in the pocket of the back judge, the timing-official on the field?

I turned away from the screen like somebody not wanting to see Barry Bonds hit a juiced home run. But when I looked around, I could see that the rest of the movie audience was eating it up. They were cheering their team on before the time on the coach's wristwatch ran out. How could they believe that shit? Then it dawned on me that fans could experience 'blind adoration' on seeing their 'heroes' in action and were ready to 'forgive' whatever went with it.

I'm sorry to be jumping out of the chronology, but my memory is somehow tied to what's stored in my noggin; it isn't just 'stuff' floating around, it's situational storytelling. Somehow my past comes back to me best in a story format. For the record, the 1945 Army Coach was Colonel Earl 'Red' Blaik, played by the veteran actor, Robert Shayne. And the scoreboard clock did not become the 'official game time' until 1970.

My family didn't have a TV set back in 1945, but I did get a chance to see some TV at a friend's home. In those days, sports was the big time-filler. There were three nights of wrestling, two nights of boxing, a couple of nights of roller derbies, and lots of bowling. But I also remember watching a quiz show—I think it was Dumont's "Charade Quiz"—and there was this female panelist sweating her tits off because she was wearing a fur coat inside the studio which seemed to be unbearably hot from the bright lights. I was too young to figure out that by wearing the fur on camera she made it tax-deductible.

On my 13th birthday, I won an essay contest held by the Philadelphia Bulletin and got to travel on a historic tour through Washington, DC, Virginia, and Maryland. It gave me a huge bolt of confidence as I began my high school years. Up until then my only glory had been winning a contest for naming a Philadelphia Zoo camel 'Hannibal,' and having Ed McMahon mention my name on his WCAU-TV Charade Show when he used my mail-in suggestion, "Diamonds Are A Girl's Best Friend."

But now that I had won the city's essay contest, I was feeling my oats. I thought, hey, I might have a writing talent. I was still on a buzz from the sight-seeing tour I had taken from Washington DC to Williamsburg and Monticello, and I was itching to write something related to it.

Back in the forties I was always listening to the radio, and one of my favorite programs was, "You Are There." It featured historical reenactments hosted by John Daley. This was before Walter Cronkite did the same program on television, starting in 1953. For some reason the "You Are There" series hadn't reenacted the Hamilton-Burr Duel on the radio show, so I

decided to write my own radio version of what took place in
1804 at Weehawken, New Jersey.

I typed up a script in no time. Now what? In my high school,
if you weren't inclined to take performing arts, you didn't have
to take those courses. And that was because there weren't
any. None. Zip. Nothing. The closest thing we had was fancy
footwork at the Saturday Night Dance held in the gym, where
you're hoping to get lucky by having the roaming spotlight land
on you and the girl you were trying to impress.

Back to the Hamilton-Burr reenactment, why is that relevant?
Because the outcome of that incident turned out to be negative
and yet became a major positive. It turned into the big Yes I Can
factor throughout my career.

So here's the story. I was using one of the school's old
portable audio tape recorders, the ones with an open reel-to-
reel mount on spindles. It was my first experience with a tape
recorder, and I got two of the football players in my history class
to be the radio broadcasters who would be covering the famous
duel. I told them to talk into the empty wastepaper basket so
as to create a back-in-time echo effect, and then when the time
came, to slap a book on the tabletop to provide the sound of a
flintlock pistol being fired.

The two of them were all smiles. These were the same guys
who were thoroughly bored with history in the classroom but
now they were all jazzed up because they were going to be
part of history in their own way. I positioned them in front of
the microphone and asked them to look over what they were
going to read, and no ad libbing. They nodded okay, but I knew
they were going to goof around and screw with it.

Word got around, and the room began filling up with
wannabe actors.

It was starting to get really loud in there, and I began
worrying that one of the priests would come charging in and
bust me. So I rolled the tape to get things started.

My first actor did the color. He announced the arrival of
Hamilton and Burr. "They 'crawst' the river." And then. "Down
the 'tray-ul' right in front of me."

The other actor did the play by play: "They's handin' em the pistols, and askin' if they's ready."

This is not what I wrote. But I didn't care. These were my guys, even though they were deliberately ad libbing ala South Philly. Everybody in the room was enjoying the hell out of it. I kept the recording going and gave them a 'thumbs up'. Lunch break would soon be over. I kept my eye on the empty take-reel to make sure the cellulose acetate tape was passing through the recording head as "Hamilton was fixin' his eyeglasses so he cahn see better."

Then came the book slapping on the table as Hamilton fired the first shot, missing Burr. Then down came a second book as Burr fired back.

"Hamilton, he goes down," was followed by a room of laughter. Today that wise-guy call still reminds me of Howard Cossel's 1973 call when Foreman knocked Frazier to the mat and Cossel yelled, "Down Goes Frazier!"

The recording ended with "Burr, that 'bastid,' he's shot Hamilton in his friggin' liver."

The duel and the firing of shots had ended, but the book slapping continued. Everybody in the room wanted to take a crack at it, and it sounded like the Shootout at the O.K. Corral.

The doors swung open, and in came our pint-size principal, Father Polini, acting more like Tony Soprano than Wyatt Earp as he attempted to restore order. Polini knew he could never control this 'corner gang' of students, but he knew I could. A fact he disliked big time.

Father Polini showed his displeasure at my imaginative effort by telling me, in front of everyone, "You don't have a creative bone in your body." Even today I still wonder what kind of person would say that to a student.

To make matters worse the other priests were telling me that, even though I had top honors in the school, I would never be able to pass the West Point Entrance Exams. I didn't like the way they said it. And it helped to seal the Yes I Can factor in my life. I was pissed that I didn't have the math background needed to take the USMA Entrance Exam. It was like they had set me up for failure. The school wasn't teaching Linear Equations, Inequalities and Absolute Values, Polynomials and Rational Inequalities and

Quadratic Equations—all of which were listed as necessary for a cadet to start out on his engineering courses.

So I went to the head of the Math Department, Father Cannon, and asked him if he would teach me after school hours. And teach me he did. God bless the man. I took a West Point competitive exam and won an appointment, and then, luckily enough, I aced the USMA Entrance Exam.

On July 3, 1951, I entered West Point, and those past victories didn't seem to be so lucky anymore. At the Point, I experienced racial disparities that changed my expectation from graduating at the top of the gray line to becoming the most dispensable of the guys, and the first to be sent out to get his ass blown off.

Usually two cadets occupied a room, but I hit the trifecta. My room had three...a Wop, a Pollock, and a Black. But God wasn't asleep. A month later, 90 of those bigoted upperclassmen got theirs. They were caught cheating on their exams and were dishonorably discharged for violating the Honor Code.

Now, let's jump to June 18, 2007. I received a callback phone call from Rollie Stichweh, the 1963 Army quarterback who I featured on my first Instant Replay. I asked Rollie if, during his time at the Point, he was aware of any prejudice. Rollie said there probably was discrimination, considering that his graduating class had very few minorities.

I'd like to jump to 1972 and bring the great black running back Gayle Sayers into the story. Gayle Sayers was an NFL Football Hall of Famer who had just retired from the Chicago Bears. He was to audition as a sports announcer at CBS, and I was asked to fly out to Chicago to see if I could help Sayers with his speech. Gayle told me a lot of people talked the way he did; that is, with a trace of a 'black accent'.

Gayle had a point. He had an accent. I have an accent. I still speak Philly English, and I plan to die with it. But I explained that our accents were one thing and entertainment was another. In other words, if you don't speak the way management wants you to, you have to be entertaining with what you're saying. For example, Rocky Graziano, the former boxing champ, told me that the movie of his life "Somebody Up There Likes Me" was believable because Paul Newman had captured his Italian

Neighborhood accent perfectly, and it made for an enjoyable movie.

The same was true of another boxing champ I knew, Jake LaMotta. Robert DeNiro sported his tough-guy accent, and the movie, "Raging Bull" went on to be another big hit.

In baseball, Dizzy Dean spoke 'Mangled English' and yet Diz was one of the most successful announcers ever, and that was because he was entertaining, 'podnuh'. The same goes for Don Meredith, the Dallas Cowboy star. Don would thicken his Texas drawl when he scrimmaged with the pompous Howard Cossel. Dandy Don and Humble Howard turned Monday Night Football into a huge hit.

Again, digressing to finish my point, John Madden had once asked me if I had any advice to give him before he went on the air for the first time as a CBS sports announcer.

I told Madden to just "be yourself." And now with his Biff!–Bang!–Pow! –Delivery! Madden has become a mega-star. But I still prefer Frank Cilendo, the impersonator. Cilendo not only does it better, he's a lot cheaper. I knew some pretty tough guys—Rocky Graziano, Jack LaMotta and, as we'll discuss later, Rocky Marciano. The only thing 'cookie cutter' about those guys was how rough they had it growing up. And that brings us back to me.

In the late '40s I walked to and from South Catholic High, along with half a dozen other Italian-American teenagers. You had to be careful walking though other neighborhoods. All the kids traveled in packs for protection. Jack LaMotta once told me that when he was going to school he'd walk around with an ice pick in his pocket.

Anyway, sometimes the guys and I would stop to view TV in a store window, looking between other people's heads at a seven-inch TV set.

As I've said, we didn't have a TV set in my home, but sometimes I watched the set in the appliance store window, down the block. On Tuesday evenings I tried to catch 'Uncle Miltie' on the small tube. I had no idea that someday I would hire Milton Berle to host a CBS Network show that I would create and sell to the network, one that I'll talk about when the time comes.

Those days the black-and-white pictures were fuzzy and jumpy, and sometimes they rolled over, but I remember being awed by the way "Captain Video and His Video Rangers" used live video effects to let the Captain travel in space. I remember, too, that during the 1947 World Series the window was mobbed.

At the time, I read that AT&T had run coaxial cables, linking cities in the East and Midwest, and that TV stations were using a movie camera to film images directly from a television screen. They were called kinescopes. Having grown up in a family of photographers, recording something like a TV image on film really impressed me.

I was interested in TV but wasn't thinking of it as a career. Not yet. After graduating high school in 1951, I wanted to go to West Point. That was partly because they said it was the hardest college to get into at the time, but I probably wanted to go because an older brother had been a highly decorated war hero in World War II. Joe was assigned as the photographer to the famous news correspondent Ernie Pyle. Like Ernie Pyle later, my brother Joe was killed in action. Pyle, a thoughtful guy, used to write my mom letters. Like my brother, Pyle, too, was killed in action.

So I entered West Point in 1951, into Company M1. The Academy, in those days, sized the corps, putting taller cadets and shorter cadets in different companies so they'd give the impression of uniform height in assembly and marching. In fact, when I recently spoke to Rollie Stichweh on the phone, he recalled being in the taller Company B2, the most notorious for hazing plebes like me in the smaller Company M1.

Soon enough I got to dislike the Academy. I began thinking of it more like a prison you attended with honor. Unfortunately, one of the major occurrences that year was the cheating scandal of 1951, which caused the expulsion of ninety cadets. I got to know the real facts and kept them to myself. I developed such distaste for the way things were handled that, even today, I have the same mistrust of authority.

My reaction to the '51 scandal did not lead to my leaving West Point.

It was personal. I incurred an injury during a training mission, and so readily accepted the alternative to resigning: a Medical Discharge. And that led to my upperclassman Edward H. White having me report to his barrack's room.

Fourteen years later, Ed would become the first American to walk in space, Two years after that, in 1957, Ed White and two other West Pointers, Gus Grissom and Roger Chaffee, died in a tragic flash fire in the Apollo 1 command module during a launch pad test at Cape Canaveral.

That time in 1951 when I reported to Cadet White, he looked over my records and said he thought I should continue at the Academy. But I knew myself then, and I know myself now—I wasn't going to thrive under that type of authority. I told my upperclassman Cadet White that I'd decided not everyone was meant for a West Point life. I couldn't see myself being satisfied with a military career. And I think it soon became obvious to him that the others in his M1 outfit were better suited to take out a machine gun position or to squeeze themselves through the hatch door of an eight-foot Mercury Capsule.

I didn't give up on school, though. In 1952 I won an academic scholarship and entered the University of Pennsylvania and studied Metallurgical Engineering.

I was always interested in science. I may not have had 'the right stuff' for West Point, but I had the right math skills to win a few more college scholarships, thanks to Father Cannon's tutoring. So at eighteen, I tried my hand at studying the physics of metals with hopes that one day I'd find an innovative method for chemically extracting metal from ore. My interest in chemicals probably came about from my experimenting while developing the sheets of films I had shot when I was a kid shooting weddings on a handheld Speed Graphic. And that meant chemical trays and developing tanks. Plus I was always at the library reading up on scientific things. I still do that today.

Growing up in my home you'd find plenty of long-play records of opera singers, but no books. In the library, I found myself particularly intrigued reading about Charles Martin Hall and his process of deriving aluminum from bauxite. What interested me was that Hall established relationships that hadn't existed before. This really fascinated me. And I thought maybe someday I could do something like that—discover something that would change the way things were perceived. That kind of thinking is still with me today 24/7.

"A relationships that hadn't existed before," that's what's always fascinated me. In 1963 it was the Instant Replay and now in 2008 it's my creation of the computer widget InstantFootballer, which I'll discuss later. But for now, let's go back to the 1950s and to how I recall my mind shaping at the time.

As I've mentioned, my father and brothers were professional photographers, so in photography I knew the ins and outs. But already in 1948 something else new had arrived: Doctor Edwin Land invented the Polaroid Camera. The Instant Camera went on sale the same day as my birthday. Instant. Holy Crap! What could be better than 'instant'?!

The camera was to be my birthday gift. No sooner had the wrappings came off than the camera was taken apart with the help of two of my older brothers, Carl and Sevy, to see how the hell Instant Photography worked. We were intrigued with how the film process could spit out a print in less than a minute. We peered into the sealed compartment of the Polaroid to analyze how its rollers were spreading the chemicals on the photo paper.

Thus my introduction to Instant Photography came when I was fifteen years old and at eighteen I found myself studying Metallurgical Engineering at the University of Pennsylvania.

But the laboratory life wasn't the right chemistry for me, either. In life, I believe you always have to set a goal, and I soon discovered that engineering wasn't mine. I was more interested in reading about early television and about the first handheld camera. Some called it the Creepy Peepy. NBC called it the Walkie-Lookie, and their cameraman had to wear a fifty-pound backpack when he covered the 1952 Political Convention.

So by 1953 I had studied at two of the highest ranked universities and concluded that the military and metallurgy were well-traveled paths, and that I wanted something new. I dropped out of college and was trying to figure out how I could break into TV. I was living with a well-known singer who was starring at the Latin Casino, a Philadelphia nightclub. Mae West was also appearing in the late show at the same club. Her entourage of strongmen included Steve Reeves.

You know, Mr. America in '47, Mr. World in '48, the first Mr. Universe in 1950. When I knew him he hadn't yet become "Hercules" or "Hercules Unchained" in the late fifties "sword and sandal" movies but he still had a 29-inch waist, a 52-inch chest, eighteen-inch biceps, shoulders just barely short of two feet wide, and he had a crush on the singer I was living with. And the singer didn't like me seeing other girls, and Reeves didn't like me seeing her.

All of these complexities turned out to be a blessing in disguise. Steve Reeves didn't break my jaw. And, secondly, I decided to go out and find a job and live on my own. That's when I started looking at TV as my way out.

These were the days when a timepiece was attached to a ball and hurled over Niagara Falls, when Dancing Old Gold Packs had women inside the boxes so that their shapely legs could stick out. I liked it that TV was pursuing such outlandish gimmicks and I wanted to be a part of it. The thought of entering a new frontier like television was exhilarating. I never wanted a repetitive career. I always wanted a life that required imagination and then more imagination. And the most powerful image in my mind at the time was the spontaneity of Live TV. I believed I was a unique individual and a career in television would be right up my alley. I felt it to be my destiny. But even destiny needs contacts. Unfortunately I had no contacts, but fortunately I still had a lot of girlfriends. One of them showed me a want ad for a new show, "American Bandstand," over at WFIL-TV. The show was expanding to an hour and forty-five minutes and they needed help with crowd control.

I'm talking about pre-Dick Clark's Bandstand. Dick Clark came later. When it started, American Bandstand was a radio show that had been turned into an inexpensive television studio show by having teenagers dance live to pre-recorded music. The program began at 2:45 p.m. to coincide with the time nearby high schools let out and so they'd have teenage dancers close by, no matter what the weather. The show was hosted first by a local disc jockey, Bob Horn, who preceded Dick Clark. When I showed up, Horn said he liked my young looks and hired me on the spot. He handed me a key to the front door of the studio, and I was told to lock the doors as soon as a certain school filled the quota.

But it looked to me that the plan was to shut out the late arriving black kids. So I handed him back the key and quit just as fast as he'd hired me. I should note that three years later Dick Clark replaced Horn and immediately integrated the show. But in 1953, there was no Dick Clark, and once again I had no job.

Happily, my unemployment didn't last long. As I was leaving Bandstand one of the girls working the show suggested I try WCAU TV. She'd heard they were hiring roustabouts for their circus shows. That was good enough for me. Maybe I'd have to pick up some elephant droppings to start, but it would be a foot in the door. Was destiny calling? Over at WCAU, I met with a guy named Jesse Schooley as he was just putting down the phone receiver, ending a call. He said I had the job because the guy he was going to hire had just told him he'd decided to become a priest. That was a thought that had never occurred to me.

I began my television career in May of 1953 at the same time that the so-called 'golden age of television' began, when almost all of the shows were broadcast live. The medium was just six years old and I flourished in that hectic atmosphere. From the first day I entered a TV studio and saw the cameras and how it all went together, I knew I wanted to be a director of Live TV. That's where the innovations were to be had. I wanted to grow with the business, the coverage, and the changes. I set my goal and began to work on what I needed to know to get there. I was learning as much as I could, and a lot of it would be on my own time. I spent an incredible amount of time in the workplace and with the people. I also found out that if they liked you, they'd help you climb the ladder.

I entered television in the summer of '53, and my first job was helping the circus roustabouts to rig the high wires for some of the aerial acts. A circus shows for kids, it was called "M&M's Candy Carnival," and the set-up was small enough to originate from one of the television studios. There were three acts; usually a juggling act, a balancing act, and the topper—a high-wire act. On-camera during the circus shows, I wore a gray roustabout uniform. While it was hardly as honorable as the cadet uniform I wore as part of the Long Gray Line, I was at least beginning to answer, shall we say, my own 'call to duty'.

I also worked on another big circus show, "The Sealtest Big Top," where Ed McMahon was the chief clown. Big Top, a much bigger production than Candy Carnival, had to be held in an armory. It involved lion tamers, horse acts, trapeze acts—and an audience of hundreds. And all this circus experience came in handy later, in 1968, when CBS was looking for someone to direct the Florida State Flying High Circus—and again in 1978 when I was asked to direct World Circus from London, where I worked with Karl Wallenda, the famous high-wire daredevil. I'll talk more about that later.

There was a lot of live television being produced at local stations in the '50s. To fill up the almost round-the-clock air schedule, 90 percent of the programming originated live. At WCAU we were originating as many as nine programs a week for the CBS network, including "Action in the Afternoon," the live-outdoor western, and "Candy Carnival" and "Big Top," the shows I started on.

During my first year I moved up fast. By the end of the summer I was assigned as one of the dozen assistant directors who tried to lighten the load of the half dozen directors who often worked until midnight setting up the show that would air the following morning.

I thrived on all the creative tension. There was a spontaneous quality that made live television fun to do—and fun to watch. It was like we were partners in an experiment, and nobody was sure what would happen next.

Some of the station's directors wanted me to appear on camera. Live television in those days had a lot of unknown females belting out love songs, and during this period in the early fifties we had some of the most starry-eyed love songs of all time, not least with "Mister Sandman," "Young At Heart," "Three Coins in the Fountain," "Hey There." The male vocalists were covered by Frank Sinatra, Dean Martin, Perry Como....

But the female vocalists needed male props to make their love ballads more believable. So I was the guy wearing the mittens and hat, throwing fake snowballs under the hot studio lights. Or I'd be the guy who faked rowing a boat or driving a car while the vocalist sang how much she loved me. I'd be a lifeguard, a cowboy, or just some asshole superimposed over her dreams.

In those days Ed McMahon—later, since the late 1950s, Johnny Carson's sidekick from the late '50s until Carson retired—was doing a morning show on WCAU-TV. We became lifetime friends and I appeared in many of Ed's skits in front of the WCAU building. I still recall that on Oct. 19, 1953, CBS star Arthur Godfrey fired Julius La Rosa, the singer whose rendition of the party song "Eh, Cumpari" was a big hit. Godfrey said he fired La Rosa because the singer had "a lack of humility."

Ed understood live television and the importance of letting the viewer in on the joke. On an outdoor set, Ed had me working under the hood of a car. He approached me with a hand mike and asked for my reaction to the La Rosa firing. I became furious and waved my wrench at him, answering in Italian, with subtitles below saying that we shouldn't forget that LaRosa was getting more fan mail then this guy Godfrey. When Ed disagreed, I chased him across City Line Avenue with my wrench until the fade out to commercial.

Meanwhile, what looked like threatening action drew the attention of a passing police car, and I had some fast explaining to do.

The following week we did another outdoor skit. This time Ed had me dressed up as a cowboy from Fort Worth and then joined by another cowboy supposedly from the city of Dallas. When Ed said I was from the 'town' of Fort Worth, I drew my gun and said Fort Worth was a 'city' just like Dallas. This was in front of the building. The other cowboy drew his gun, and I shot him 'dead'.

Incredibly, the same passing cop car on the beat comes to a screeching halt and the same cops come after me. I ran in through the side door of WCAU and hid in a men's room until the cops quit searching.

Not long afterward I had yet another brush with the police

when the news department filmed a prime-time documentary on the Philadelphia Police Department. In addition to asking me to direct the hour-long program, Charles Shaw, head of news, asked me to star in it. Shaw had worked with Edward R. Murrow as a CBS correspondent in London during World War II. Later I found out that Shaw was also a good friend of Winston Burdett, the CBS Rome-based correspondent whose 1960 Olympics credentials I had been using for the Games until mine were processed. When the armed carabiniere would check my credentials they'd see a photo of a man who bore no resemblance to me and looked at least twenty years older. They thought that was funny and let me pass through anyway.

That was in Rome in 1960, but first let me go back to Philadelphia in the 1950s, when I was directing and acting in a primetime film special that covered all aspects of the Philadelphia Police Department. And the question being: Why did the station want to air such a show?

This was immediately after the quiz show scandals, especially when Charles Van Dorn, a young, personable and 'great-for-TV' professor, was exposed as having earned more than $100,000 in a game show after being fed answers by the TV producer. Professor Van Dorn eventually admitted the deception.

WCAU thought that a police documentary in primetime could help to improve their network's image with the public. The script called for a guy who got by solely on his looks. But in addition to his romances, he robbed, killed, and led the police through the streets of Philly, with squad cars and motorcycles chasing after him. In the end, I was captured off the waterfront by the Police Marine Unit and ended up being jailed at Eastern State Penitentiary.

The show was such a local hit that Mayor Richardson Dilworth wanted it to have a continued life. I was unaware the city went on to use the documentary as one of its police training films—after I had left town.

I was now working with the network and living in Manhattan.

One night, about a month after the show aired, I returned to visit my Mom, when a policewoman, doing undercover, recognized me from the documentary. Thinking I was a cop killer, she called in backup and suddenly I was surrounded by police cars.

I phoned the Mayor and requested the film be removed from training before I got killed. To make matters worse, I got a call from Warden Banmiller of Eastern State Penitentiary. He wanted to know if the real-life prisoner I'd used in the film had contacted me. His helping us on the film enabled him get enough merits to be paroled. I knew the guy had done twenty years as a bank robber. What I didn't know was that he was the only one in his gang they had caught and that the police had never found the money. The next day Warden Banmiller called me again and said they found the guy, dead. Evidently, when he left jail, he was followed, and when he went to retrieve the money, the others in the gang, who'd been waiting for his release, killed him and presumably recovered the cash.

I started at WCAU the first week of the summer in '53, and on the first weekend of November of that same year I made a gutsy move that led me to become a director by the age of nineteen. Here's how I pulled it off.

My shift as a floor manager ended at midnight when the station signed off. As I headed to the parking lot, the weather didn't look too good. Jack Essig, one of the news writers, came by, hustling to get into his car. He said that a major snowstorm had been predicted and he was going to get home as soon as possible. That's when I made my move. Instead of leaving, I returned to the studio and slept on the sofa in the lounge, knowing that if a big storm hit, the early Saturday morning shows could be affected because the directors who put them on might not be able to get to work.

By 6 a.m. on Saturday, November 7th, 1953, close to a foot of snow had been dumped in the Philadelphia's City Line area, making it one of the biggest November snowstorms on record. WCAU-TV's Saturday morning entertainment was for kids, mainly cartoon shows with a live host.

That morning the station signed on at seven with me taking a seat in the director's chair. Of course, I needed somebody to work the projectors. Fortunately, the late swing of technicians was snowed in at the station, so they manned the equipment. Charlie Wright manned the projectors, and John Demas handled the transmission. There was no need for anyone to man the cameras. There was no talent in the building. While the shows didn't necessarily need the on-camera cowgirl in buckskin or the Indian Chief with a feathered headdress to introduce the roundup of old cartoons, they did need a director in the control room to lead everyone through the sequence of films.

When the front office management arrived later in the morning, they set out to check how much money they'd lost from the early shows not airing. They were told that they'd lost nothing, that this kid Verna went up and played director. The seed was planted, and management set out to make the kid a director.

So my advice for young people aiming to get ahead is 'Look for signs. Always keep your eyes open for opportunity'. It could give your destiny a kick in the ass to get moving. Also, I'd add, 'Act as you eventually want to be'. I thought and dressed like a director. Every day I came in wearing a shirt and tie, and I stood out from the rest of the crew as if I was supposed to.

The quickest available assignments were live shows that were coming to the end of their run because they were losing their sponsors. And most of those live shows included live commercials since we had no videotape back then. Major advertisers, like the auto and cigarette companies, could afford filmed commercials, but live commercials were cheaper for local sponsors to produce, plus most of the ad agencies weren't geared up to do quality film commercials.

I directed quite a few live commercials in 1953. These live commercials were all exactly sixty seconds long and usually took place in a quiet corner of the studio, away from the main action. But because they were located in the studio—and live—everybody else had to freeze in place and remain silent for that minute. The announcer would be cutting into a Horn & Hardart pie being pitched as less work for mother, or he would be shooting a 'six shooter' for Quaker Oats while pitching it as 'shot from guns'.

The talent not only had to learn their lines and hit their

marks, they also had to keep an eye peeled for the red tally lights that lit up when the camera was on since, without Zoom lenses, there was a lot of cutting between closer and wider shots on different cameras. The worst thing a director could hear was the ad agency saying they didn't like the way their product looked on the black and white TV.

I remember being assigned to direct a live commercial that no director wanted to do. What they feared was a bowl of ravioli. Black and white television couldn't distinguish the different shades of color that made the pasta look so appetizing in person. In black and white, rich red tomato sauce turned pillows of pasta into a black blob.

That ravioli commercial was one of the sponsor's accounts on their way out the door, but luckily I found the answer in the network children's show "Winky Dink and You."

Those black and white shows encouraged the kids who were viewing at home to color on an acetate sheet that they were to place over the television screen. It was a highly successful gimmick, and the kids loved doing it. So with 'Winky Dink' in mind, I reversed the thinking. I took up a paintbrush and highlighted the overlapping pasta squares with gray and white paint. I brushed away until I got the proper separation from the overlapping squares. Then I added my own grayscale blend for the sauce. It looked terrible to the human eye, but the camera loved it. The ad agency ate up the results, and the account was saved thanks to Winky Dink and me.

The hardest live commercials to direct were during pickups away from the station. We'd have to wait on site for the studio cameras to arrive since there were no cameras used just to do remotes. Lots of times the cable runs were too long to go from the production truck parked outside the building, so they'd set up a separate control room which they called a 'load out'. That was usually the case in the early fifties. I didn't always have a remote truck to direct from. They'd put a canvas top over the makeshift control room, but the friggin' wind would whip the rain on the monitors while I was trying to punch up a shot.

Another part of my frustration at those live games came from the restrictions they put on my camera set-ups. A lot of ballparks were hostile to televised sports, thinking that TV would cut their attendance. So our camera placements were limited in baseball, and especially so in football. We were given only one space allocation in football, and we chose mid-field, and that's why I had to cover most of my football games from the fifty-yard line. That was the only spot I could get. Today camera positions are available up and down the field so you can pretty much cover the line of scrimmage straight on.

In most basketball games, I had good camera positions. But with a bad game, it didn't' matter. Sometimes you can't flatten out the memory of your efforts. Take the 1957 NBA Eastern Conference Finals. The Philadelphia Warriors were playing the Boston Celtics in Boston. It was a big deal locally since an away game hadn't been seen back in Philly.

I had our best basketball announcer, Bill Campbell, and the best cameramen in Boston. I was right on top of the Boston center Bill Russell, who was a rookie back then, so that I could cover his quick passes to his key man Bob Cousy—but it didn't help the telecast. The problem was the game I was covering. The Celtics were making quick work of the Warriors, somewhat like what the 2007 San Antonio Spurs did to the Cleveland Cavaliers. Looking back, I think the only thing that could have improved my game would have been to use ESPN's Colin Cowherd's suggestion of putting trap doors into the floor or having someone like Tim Donaghy ref the game and telling Philly fans how to bet.

At halftime we interviewed the NBA commissioner Maurice Podolof, but I don't remember him making any excuses about why the game was so bad, or anything about how the changing times affected the game. The next day, back in Philly, the basketball fans had nothing to talk about. The station had wasted its money. They should have let the fans watch the new Perry Mason series. The game was a waste of our time; the outcome was never in doubt. Maybe I could have corrected that by cutting to black before the game ended a la The Sopranos.

By the way, I recently chatted with my old friend Bill Campbell about the non-televised game he broadcast when Wilt Chamberlain scored 100 points. " 'Give it to Wilt, give it to

Wilt', Bill quoted the crowd as cheering. "But Tony," Campbell said to me, "Even though Wilt's Philadelphia Warriors crushed New York, after the game three of the Knicks hitched a ride in Wilt's car, from the arena at Hershey, Pennsylvania back to Wilt's nightclub in Harlem, Small's Paradise."

And there were problems with the lenses, as well as with the camera positions. Most of the time I had three or four cameras, all with fixed lenses. I seldom had a Zoom lens, and if I had one it usually didn't zoom smoothly. Sometimes they'd add a field camera, but it wasn't allowed to move and so it became worthless when the play moved up or down the field. As well, with directing live boxing matches in the early fifties, I had to do them with a load-out instead of having a control room. Plus I not only had to direct the live prime-time fight but I had to direct the live commercials between the rounds.

The load-out control room and the barroom were both in the basement of the arena, with a partition dividing us. The commercials revolved around the supposed patrons in the fake barroom, on the other side of my partition, enjoying the live fight on the television monitor as they drank the sponsor's beer—even though an Alka Seltzer pill might have been dropped in the glasses to keep the beer foaming.

These were live sixty-second commercials, not sixty-one second commercials, and that meant I'd be giving speed-up or slow-down cues to the bartender so that I wouldn't miss the start of the next round as Kid Gavilan came out swinging with his famous 'bolo punch'.

I had to learn the tricks of a trade that hadn't been a trade before. Back in 1953 I would always show up in the control rooms after my shift was over. The control room seemed to be my second home. For most of the directors, being in the control room doing things that had never been done before was a nail-biting experience. But it didn't bother me. And that would lead to the guys kidding me about having 'brass balls'.

I always liked sitting in the director's chair. It always felt right to me. It seemed to fit the rhythm of my thinking. Live television was growing up fast and becoming more adventurous. Maybe I wasn't afraid of directing live because of my tough beginnings, or maybe I didn't know better. I was always moving ideas around in my head figuring out what to do next if this happened or that happened. As you know, in live television you always have to ask, "What if?" But central to all my thinking was not only the element of improving what had been done before, but what hadn't been done before.

The sports columnist Michael Hiestand, in his 'USA Today' review of the 2007 Kentucky Derby telecast, mentioned that the blimp coverage used wasn't the first aerial shot used on a live horse race. Back in the sixties there was a strong demand for a live director to come up with something new so that the network could brag about the upcoming telecast in the newspapers. They knew they couldn't get any print with 'same old, same old'.

In the fifties there was something new always going on for me. I'd be assigned to direct interview shows, kids shows, cooking shows, exercise shows, gardening programs, news reports, musicals, variety shows. There was no such thing as a routine day.

Since we're tracking my career leading up to the invention of the Instant Replay, I should probably touch on the mechanical wizardry I came up with after I was assigned to direct WCAU-TV's late news 'money strip' headed by the late John Facenda, the legendary newsman who became 'The Voice of NFL Films'. John Facenda was the King of Philadelphia television news. He was a wonderful man with a wonderful voice, and viewers tuned in every night to hear his final report to feel reassured before going to bed.

I mentioned how a major snowstorm affected my early career, and how it led the brass to speed things up and promote me into their pool of directors. Now another snowstorm came along and the way I covered it moved the brass to bump me to the top of the list.

Let me tell you about that 'dark and stormy night' when the viewers were worried about another major snowstorm hitting Philadelphia. What I wanted to do was to contrast the severity of the storm with the inside peacefulness of John seated at his studio desk. A contrast like when the legendary Don Hewitt, back in 1951, split the screen with the Brooklyn Bridge in New York and the Golden Gate Bridge in San Francisco. I knew that the split screen could be an effective device. But WCAU-TV didn't possess an electronic split screen like the one Hewitt had in his Grand Central Station Control Room in CBS Studio 41. So I had to think of a way to get the effect without the needed electronic components in my switcher. The WCAU-TV control room switcher I was using was designed to put the images from two cameras together—we used it all the time to superimpose white-on-black titles over regular video. But the switcher wasn't designed with the built-in intelligence to split the screen. Electronic-blanking was needed to feed parts of two cameras together.

I had to come up with the mechanical application, a matte, to make the machine smarter. I wanted to show John Facenda comfortably seated at his desk inside the warm studio and next to him on the screen the bitter storm as it raged outside. I thought up a non-electronic split screen by unscrewing the bayonet lenses from two of the cameras. On the camera in the studio I inserted a piece of cardboard to mask the area over John's shoulder. On the street camera I put a cutout on the other part to mask John and show the snow. Then, as you may know, in those days we directors actually punched the buttons to switch between cameras and could use the 'fader' to dissolve from one camera to another. We could also 'split' the fader, to show video from two cameras at the same time.

That night I split the fader and brought the two cameras together as one, bringing the snowstorm into the studio over John Facenda's shoulder. As I reflect back on it today, it seems to have been a harbinger of what I would do five years later with a standard video recording machine when, once again, I used a mechanical method to achieve an electronic end. And you could say, in both cases, it was by default.

This was similar to what I would eventually do when I married my set of audio tones to a videotape machine that didn't have the built-in intelligence to make the first Instant Replay possible.

I might note, too, that John Facenda took personal pride in

the fact that someone of Italian-American ancestry was moving ahead behind the cameras.

In 1953 Perry Como was in town, and John took me to meet him. When I met Como, I felt as if I already knew him. Like John, he was pleased to see a person whose surname ended in a vowel getting recognition behind the scenes in TV. It wasn't easy being an Italian-American and traveling to less friendly cities where sometimes I had to work and socialize with folks who were hoping to make it tough on me by not giving me their best crew—and certainly not their best equipment. But then again, I met a lot of classy people who went above and beyond to help further my career.

Two months before the downfall of Sen. Joe McCarthy, chairman of the House Committee on Un-American Activities, I had the honor of working with Edward R. Murrow, the newsman who challenged McCarthy and the most distinguished and renowned figure in the history of American broadcast journalism. Mr. Murrow's CBS New York crew was in town to do a live pickup for his program "Person to Person" featuring a live interview with Eugene Ormandy, the conductor of the Philadelphia Orchestra, from his penthouse at the Bellevue Stratford Hotel.

Mr. Murrow was ninety miles away in a New York studio at Grand Central Station. He resided in Studio 41 whenever he was on camera.

In October of 1954 I was sent to head up the WCAU crew that would be supporting the New York crew. The technical crew ended up being sixteen plus the TD, the technical director.

When we arrived at the Ormandy Penthouse, the first thing was to take off the doors to get the cameras through. Next the mammoth backpack that came with wireless Budelman mikes had to be fastened to the backs of Mr. and Mrs. Ormandy so that an audio check could be sent to New York. During rehearsal we couldn't see Murrow in NY but he could see us in Philly. What we could do was hear him from a speaker box sitting in one of the chairs in the Ormandys' living room.

I was surprised that the Ormandys had been given a copy of the questions in advance. They told me that the answers were up to them. While they were looking over the copy, Mr. Morrow was familiarizing himself with the camera movements we'd be making in each room.

I was somewhat startled when his very recognizable voice came out addressing me. "Tony, why can't that camera dolly-in closer to that photograph?" I answered back politely, "Because of the rug, Mr. Murrow."

"So take out that rug."

"Uh, Mr. Murrow, there's a thousand pound piano sitting on that rug."

As Mr. Murrow pondered the problem, Mr. Ormandy's wife, Margaret Ormandy, a sturdy European, crawled under the piano, back first, and said to me, "I lift. You pull." As the rug came out, the cautious Murrow had one of his crackling-coughing fits, as he watched the fifty-year-old woman with a piano on her back being transmitted over his one-way video link.

I also worked with the famous and beautiful actress Grace Kelly, who had just returned from Kenya after finishing shooting the movie Mogambo. It was a 'July 4th Special' to celebrate the new renovations to Philadelphia's Independence Hall. Let me tell you about that hot July afternoon in the City of Brotherly Love.

This was three years before she became Princess Grace of Monaco. The beautiful Miss Kelly breezed in from Chestnut Street, into the stuffy old Hall, in a summer dress. She was unescorted, very demure, and cool as a cucumber as she sauntered across the creaky wooden floor. She headed straight to the Liberty Bell, where I was to meet her.

It's kind of funny to think that if she came through that door today, she'd have to wait her turn to go through a metal detector, and she wouldn't find the Liberty Bell in front of that entrance any longer. It's now housed in its own area, separate from Independence Hall.

Grace approached me, and we spoke about her sister, Lizanne, who had been in my English class at the University of Pennsylvania. I told her that her sister had aced me out of the top mark with a true-story essay. She had written about visiting her celebrity sister in Hollywood, thus relegating my true-life story of how I had saved the life of an injured lifeguard in Atlantic City to a second-place finish.

Grace had a laugh, and I spoke about being friends with her brother, Jack Kelly, and about meeting her father, the multi-millionaire John B. Kelly, when I directed his political pitches during the election years. What I didn't tell her was that her father—'John B.'— read his cue cards as if he were reciting an eye chart on an angle. When Grace went over her cue cards, she read so smoothly that I couldn't catch her reading. We went on the air live, and she gave a perfect reading. Better yet was the smile she laid on me when we left the Hall.

In January 1955 I directed one of the world's most famous scientists, the Scottish biologist Sir Alexander Fleming, who had discovered Penicillin in 1928.

Sir Fleming was quite a noble figure, in his early seventies. Of course, I treated him as a man of much dignity, but he looked tired and seemed almost to be dragging his reputation as he slouched down in his chair, waiting to be interviewed. So I lowered the camera to shoot up at him, to give him the 'look' he rightly deserved. But the camera angle wasn't the biggest problem I faced. The interviewer assigned came prepared only with a breakfast of Jack Daniels, and soon he was asking Sir Fleming how he had 'stumbled' onto his discovery.

Fleming bolted up in his chair and became momentarily headless in my shot, as he angrily fired back, "Sir, I did not stumble onto my discovery!"

It was an embarrassing moment. Fortunately, by the time I walked Sir Fleming to his chauffeured car he'd dismissed the incident and warmly thanked me for my efforts. I wished him a safe journey. He was on his way back to England, where he died two months later.

In 1955 CBS Sports began airing the "Baseball Game of the Week," and soon afterward I was hired on occasion to direct one of CBS' network games.

At times, I'd either direct the main game with Dizzy Dean or the backup game with Frankie Frisch and Jack Whitaker, in case of rain.

I could count on being freelanced if the game was originating from a city where a director would have to punch up his own camera changes, as I had to do in Philly. In New York, the CBS staff directors always had a technician, a 'switcher', to punch the buttons for their camera changes. And that always made the cut to first base a little too slow when the pitcher tried a pick off. With my fingers on the buttons, I could be a lot faster. Things like this didn't escape the eyes of the network brass. I was a young kid, but Tex Schramm knew that I could handle remotes and he sent a couple of his producers down to Philly to report back on how well I directed studio work.

In the mid-fifties CBS Sports was still under the auspices of the news department, and that meant that any network contract I signed would include doing news events as well, such as being available to serve as an immediate replacement for, say, Don Hewitt if for some reason he couldn't direct "Douglas Edwards And The News."

So Schramm sent two of his producers down to Philly specifically to watch me direct John Facenda's 11PM News— where I showed up at 10:40 p.m., half lit, not having seen the news script that included lens switches, slide changes and film rolls. Nor had I seen the commercial copy that included live beer-pouring shots, the changing of super cards, and the cueing musical jingles. But the show went on without a hitch and my ability to direct by the seat of my pants really impressed the two producers, Judd Bailey and Hugh Beach, who had come to town to scout me.

ABC had no sports department in the mid-fifties. And the main rival to CBS Sports was NBC. But people don't realize that many of the major live sports telecasts weren't being produced by a network. They were being put together by an advertising agency on behalf of a sponsor. Falstaff Beer owned the rights to the "Baseball Game of the Week." The Falstaff Producer sat up in the announcer's booth and controlled the telecast, in the same manner that a network producer does today from the control room.

Dizzy Dean and Buddy Blatner were the announce team, and neither of them wanted to wear an ear-piece, so I ended up talking to Gene Kirby, the Dancer Fitzgerald Agency executive, who sat next to them. Kirby was the Falstaff producer and the boss of the telecast. Period.

Dizzy was the first announcer to become bigger than the game he was covering. Dean was a big man in a ten-gallon hat who tipped the scale at 265 pounds. And he packed more backcountry expressions than Red Barber and Dan Rather put together. Dean was so colorful that a couple of years earlier Hollywood had filmed "The Pride of St. Louis" with Dan Dailey in the title role of Dizzy.

Dizzy was making a $100,000 a year and, on the air, told his fans about the added income he received from the movie. "They gave me 50,000 smackers for just living."

Dizzy always seemed to have a good-old-time destroying the King's English. Dizzy's secret in broadcasting lay in the way he dissected the game. He did it in such a manner that he made the viewers feel as if they were sitting in the dugout with him. The home viewers thought Dizzy was talking to them when he asked, "What do you figure he's throwing out there? You think those outfielders are playing too deep?"

Dizzy's color man, Buddy Blatner, had a hard time getting in his two cents. Even between plays Dizzy would interrupt Buddy and begin reading the telegrams being sent in from his fans. It got so bad that Pee Wee Reese replaced Buddy. Pee Wee was such a likeable guy that Dizzy felt guilty if he interrupted him.

One of the major problems I had directing those baseball games live in the early fifties was with the lenses. Those early television cameras, like the RCA TK-30A cameras, were modeled after film cameras and that meant they came with a fixed lens. By the time I was directing, the techs had already devised a camera turret that could rotate four different lenses.

Different lenses had to be used since the playing field was so wide and the players were so spread out. I had to work angles with the right lens to let the viewers be close enough to follow the ball. And to do that, I had to have my cameramen switch the lens on their turrets according to where the runners were in relation to the bases. It was also very difficult because I had to stay with the ball while it was in play, but Dizzy or Pee Wee could talk about whatever they wanted to talk about. For instance, one time there was a close tag at home plate, but Dizzy was telling the viewers that it was too bad they hadn't seen the outfielder fall down after he threw the ball to the plate. When I asked Dizzy why he did that instead of covering the slide into home, he said he wanted to let the viewers know what they had missed. And obviously what I had missed was having an Instant Replay to hold my own against the big man.

Between plays I'd feed all kinds of shots, but instead of commenting on them, Dizzy would spend most of his time plugging products. I'd have the bases loaded and he'd be talking about his new charcoal business or wishing Pee Wee good luck with his new bowling alley, or he'd be reading a telegram that just came in from his fans praising somebody who was now banking at a firm that he had recommended.

During one game I got so frustrated I called Western Union and sent Dizzy a telegram of my own. The messenger arrived at the booth and I could hear Dizzy and Pee Wee laughing. Dizzy read it on the air. "Dizzy, watch your monitor. Signed your director."

The two of them thought that was great. But I knew that Dizzy was also a bit of a prankster, and he liked to get even. He got his nickname Dizzy because of his erratic behavior, and later in that same game came his erratic request. On the air, Dizzy asked, "Tony, podnuh, can you pick up the guy and girl kissin' up there in the right field seats?" I had a camera swing around, and every time Dizzy made a reference, I swung the camera back around to the couple making out.

Finally Dizzy said, "I figured it out. He's kissing her on the strikes and she's kissing him on the balls."

Time to switch topics and plug my website tonyvernaTV.com because it will provide you with not only a quick summary of my career—and my current projects—but also a quick summary of the development of the television industry.

In the autumn of 1956, CBS Sports began telecasting a selected package of NFL Games. Before 1956 there was no unified NFL package. Before then, teams made their own arrangements to cover their games, many of which I directed locally. Now, with a 12 week/6 games-per-week schedule, the network desperately needed its own directors. So this was, literally, a new ballgame.

Early directors like myself were faced with the pressures of having to do network games from around the country. The first problem was handling those restrictions that the stadiums placed on the camera setups. Most times I had just three or four cameras. In baseball games we were usually above the bases. I seldom had a Zoomar lens, and if I had one, it was a gamble. It usually didn't zoom smoothly since the long bar inside the very long lens had to be pushed manually.

There was also a sunlight problem when the stands cast a heavy shadow over the field. If you panned into the shadow, or out of it, the picture would go black or flare out because of the nature of those early camera tubes. Sometimes I'd position a camera in the sun or shade that was already 'irised' for the light level, and I'd wait for the play to come that way before punching it up. In fact, the sunlight problem led to fewer and fewer post-game programs because of the fear that the late shadows would turn the interviews too dark for television. But when the sponsors wanted a post-game show, out came our studio lights onto the field.

Back in 1939, the first football game ever televised had to switch off the TV coverage and pick up the radio transmission because the darkness had blanked out the video images on the camera tube.

In addition to the game itself, The 1956 NFL TV Package created many new, inexpensive programs revolving around the games being played on the weekends. If a station carried the NFL, they got lots of free programming out of it as well. A key moneymaker was the mid-week highlight program showing film clips of the past Sunday's game. But a big problem I had was that there wasn't enough film footage to play back and insert during these programs.

Before NFL Films came into being, there was a firm named TelRa that filmed the games. It was a shoestring operation in North Philadelphia. Their cameramen were given only 15 minutes of film to capture a whole game, and that meant the camera had to be turned on at the start of the play and turned off at the end of a play. The film clips were so short that there was a tremendous lack of continuity on exactly what happened.

In 1958 I was delighted when the Philadelphia Eagles traded for Los Angeles Rams quarterback Norm Van Brocklin. I knew that Van Brocklin could chalk his diagrams to make the best use of my limited film snippets. The man was a born-coach. Years later, when I asked John Madden during his CBS audition where he learned his football, he said that when he was suited-up as a Philadelphia Eagle, he sat in the back of the room as Van Brocklin explained the game on the blackboard.

Back in the late '50s, the play-by-play announcers dominated the booth. The Detroit Lions had Van Patrick. The Green Bay Packers had Ray Scott, and so forth. In those early days a good voice was a prerequisite to being a play-by-play announcer. The game-caller was the one with the good enunciation, like one of my favorites, Jack Buck. Buck could sound like one of the guys, and yet he possessed the vocal clarity that was needed to talk over the game noise. In fact, Buck was so good, later I personally hired him to do sports for my company, to do a series of bowling shows. And he was terrific.

Before the Instant Replay came about, announcers like Chris Schenkel relied heavily on their color man. Schenkel shared the booth with Johnny Lujack.

And that came as a blessing. Before Lujack, Schenkel was working with another play-by-play man, Jim McKay, who was not a former player. What Chris needed was a former football great, someone who had the 'in' with the current players and coaches, somebody like Lujack.

Recently, Lujack and I got together with Tom Brookshier and our wives at Jack Whitaker's home. We got to reminiscing about the games when Chris chain-smoked even while on camera, leaving Lujack in a cloud of nicotine as Johnny kept the conversation going. Anyway, Lujack in the booth was a sensational improvement. He'd remind us what was important in the game we were televising.

When the Instant Replay came along it opened the gate for more of those former-athlete analysts, since they were the ones who could best tell you 'why' a play worked or didn't work. But having played the game wasn't enough. The brass wanted to match up the right analysts with the right play-by-play man, in hopes of delivering the same type of informal, folksy chat that Dizzy Dean had in pleasing the fans. Today there aren't many announcers using that kind of leisurely style. The only one I can think of is Bryant Gumbel who did it as the play-by-play on the NFL in-house Network. But today the fans want more.

Then there are those announcers talking about something other than the action that's taking place at the moment. These are the guys counting on today's technology to back them up. Strangely enough, with so many replay angles available these days, in some cases, a delayed call may be the best call.

Echoing my early comments about radio, it's interesting that this 'after-the-fact identification' dates back to early radio. The 1922 World Series was announced by Grantland Rice, a well-known sports columnist who spoke into his candlestick-shaped telephone (his microphone) only after the play.

You have to remember that Rice was a newspaper writer who had been using 'the past tense' all his life. Even in boxing, Rice waited for the action to end before reporting what he'd just seen, using the past tense, to say, "Dempsey just delivered Sharkey two foul blows."

Management soon began hiring announcers with better voices than Grantland Rice. 'Past tense or present tense', they wanted a deep, rich voice like that of former singer, Graham McNamee. A lot of those early announcers had been singers. When I worked with the late actor and director Tony Randall I asked him about the musicality of voices, since my uncles were gifted in that manner and I was not. Tony broke the bad news to me that voice-musicality is something you have to be born with and that I wasn't born with it. The same is certainly true of announcers. Either they were born with the rich baritone of a Chris Schenkel or Mel Allen or they weren't.

But most of those announcers weren't born with a knack for pre-game preparation. Back in the early days, some of the announcers just showed up with a sports program or a racing form. They'd arrive at game sites the night before just in time to go out drinking, and that was about the extent of their preparation. Many stayed in their hotel rooms, writing out what they would say the next day. Unfortunately, when those memorized comments aired most of them sounded like robotic speech.

Let me tell you about Red Grange. He was one of the first major sports figures to serve as a play-by-play broadcast commentator. Grange was a very humble man, so much so I'd forget he was a football great. Red had a one-tone voice, and I don't think he was proud of it. He shied away from talking, on or off, the air. During the game I'd have to remind him, in his earpiece, to say something. "Red, tell us what you're thinking."

But Red was aware he needed a talker, and he was smart enough to know he couldn't get away with who-I-used-to-be. So for his analyst he picked a good Irish yapper, George Connor, a former NFL star who'd been both an outstanding lineman and a linebacker. Red picked Connor so that George could tell the viewers how the defense was lining up according to how the offense had lined up. Red claimed that defense was the key to winning the game, but I think Grange needed George's defense-spiel to compensate for those viewers who figured Grange could only 'walk the talk' with the offensive game.

In addition to dealing with the on-air talent, I also had to work more closely with the NFL front office back in those days. In 1956 Bert Bell was the commissioner, and we had a few run-ins. Commissioner Bell was adamant that TV viewers would see only 'away games' because he wanted to protect the home gate. My run-ins came because Mr. Bell lived in Philadelphia and his NFL office was there, and that meant he saw only the Eagles away games, most of which I directed.

The Commissioner had a sharp eye and a sharp tongue. After every game he'd call me with some kind of complaint, such as why did I have to show the score so many times. I'd explain that a great many people were watching from noisy places, like the bars. I think the Commissioner would have loved the digital graphics being used today. Now a director can keep the game score on the screen in an unobtrusive manner, instead of pissing off Mr. Bell by having one of the cameras leave the playing field and actually shoot the stadium scoreboard.

Another thing that bothered the Commissioner, big-time,

was my violating his cardinal rule for TV directors: "Always cut away from a fight or an injury." Well, easier said then done. This ultimatum could be a problem since there were times that the outcome of the action was a lot faster than my reactions. When that happened, I knew the Commissioner would be phoning even earlier the next day. He'd be angry that I'd shown a player coming up, hobbling out of the pile or someone throwing a punch. He'd growl, "Verna, I told you to keep off that kind of shot."

I'll give him this. In the years when the Commissioner played football for Penn, thirty three college players had been killed from hurdle plays where the ball carrier was picked up and launched over the opposing line. I guess it left an impression on him.

Finally Commissioner Bell said that if I showed another fight on the field he'd be after my job. And I remember one time when he summoned me to his NFL Office in Bala Cynwyd. This was a very pleasant Philadelphia suburb just a few blocks away from my apartment and WCAU. But I was shocked to see how small his NFL office was, and it got me thinking about the phony Wizard of Oz. Yet Commissioner Bell was the real deal. He was an amazing man when you think of his unbelievable work load, considering he was staffed with only a couple of nameless guys and a 'Kelly Girl' who did the League's clerical work and didn't like watching sports on TV. Quite a cry from some forty years later when I visited the NFL in their Manhattan-Park Avenue skyscraper with two entire floors and several tons of TV sets devoted to offices.

Ironically enough, with all the berating I received from Mr. Bell on showing things other than the game, it turned out to be the Commissioner, himself, who would provide the most tragic distraction of any televised football game I'm aware of. It happened at Franklin Field, on October 11, 1959, during the fourth quarter of an Eagles' home game that I was producing and Frank Chirkinian was directing.

There was such a disturbing commotion in the packed stands that the game on the field had to be stopped for order to be restored. One of our cameras found the explanation. The fan who had suffered a fatal heart attack was the Commissioner, himself, Bert Bell. He died while watching the Steelers play the Eagles, two teams he once co-owned. Two years earlier in 1957 there had been another death in the stands at Kezar Stadium. Anthony Morabito, the co-owner of the San Francisco 49ers, had a heart attack, and died similarly during their home game against the Chicago Bears.

That ironic moment with Commissioner Bell—and most of the games I directed early on—tied me to Philadelphia, but in the early fifties my reputation as a live director brought me a lot of outside offers. I not only directed sports telecasts for the network, I was hired out to direct other programs and sportscasts for local stations around the country.

And that was because the local stations had to deal with L-I-V-E mobile telecasts throughout the country. Stations had begun deploying mobile units for location shooting. But they had a major problem. Who was going to direct these major events where the action was so spread out and so difficult to cover with that early television equipment? Their local directors weren't adequately experienced to handle shows like that. Either that or they were just plain scared.

Most directors could handle confined action. They had no problem directing a wrestling match—or any other show you could do with a single camera. All these directors had to do was to make sure that about five-hundred-foot-candles of light were poured onto the wrestling ring; enough so that the people in the first three rows had to wear sunglasses.

Let me give you some specific example of the shows I was hired out to do. Let's say that in Chicago, WBBM had to do a major horse race, or in Dallas, KRLD had to do a major football game. Those stations would phone me directly. They had sold the pickup to major sponsors, and management was on the line to deliver the goods. So why would they take a chance? Why not cover the station and fly in somebody like me and pay him a few bucks?

Plus the stations needed someone who could not only punch-up his own shots on the field switcher but who could also call out the different lenses in both millimeters and inches to their cameramen because of the mix of lens being used for the special coverage.

As I mentioned, the camera turrets had to be switched constantly so that the cameramen would be able to pick up wide shots or close shots as the game progressed. Many times, I'd travel with an extra luggage bag that held my own long lenses that were on loan because WCAU was a sister station. Without any Zoomars, I needed these longer fixed lenses to juice up the coverage with tighter shots. For a hired gun, the money may have been good, but the job wasn't easy.

The jobs I hated most were baseball games. The ballparks usually consisted of a double-decked grandstand that wrapped around home plate. Lots of baseball parks, like Philadelphia's Shibe Park, were awful places to watch a game in person, let alone on television. Most seats in the park were unbelievably far from the field. If you didn't have binoculars, you were dead. That's why I needed to use longer lenses. The cameras I had to use were riveted around the stadium because the ballpark didn't want them moved in, fearing they'd block a few seats.

Returning to football, the 1958 NFL Championship Game between the Colts and the Giants is known as the 'Greatest Game Ever Played'. It was the first-ever NFL game to go into sudden death overtime. I don't know who directed that game for NBC. I do know what I was doing that weekend. I was directing two shows. On Saturday I did the pilot of a new franchise show in Philly called "Romper Room," which consisted of a hostess and her group of children embarking on an hour of jumping games, dancing and more jumping. The only advice I had for the hostess was to do something about her breasts. They were bouncing all over the place and distracting the kids. I'm not sure how she took care of the problem.

The next day was a Sunday and back then those Sunday afternoons were reserved for serious programming. And they had me directing a half hour show for the network called "What in the World." It was an archaeological quiz show in which scholars tried to identify ancient artifacts and delve into the story behind them. I don't know what the historical pieces were that day exactly. One could have been something like an ancient carving of the great horned owls that were big hooters, but I'm not sure.

Then one summer, I'm not sure what the year was, the studio set had to be torn down so that they could film the movie "The Burglar," starring Jayne Mansfield, the buxomy bombshell. One day while I was standing in line at the studio cafeteria, Mrs. Mansfield's five-year-old daughter walked over to me and asked if I were her daddy. I said I wasn't. That much I was sure of.

For the record the little girl is now a grandmother. Jayne Marie Mansfield was only sixteen and was with her brother Mickey and half-sister Mariska Hargitay when her mother and companion/attorney Sam Brody and the driver died in a late night car crash en route to New Orleans. Fortunately, the three kids, asleep in the back seat, received only minor injuries.

Jayne Marie's half sister Mariska, a close friend of my daughter Tracy, is the television and movie star Mariska Hargitay. Mariska was also fathered by Mickey Hargitay, a muscleman who once appeared with Mae West along with the already noted muscleman Steve Reeves.

Let's go back to the 1958 Championship Game, which drew a record TV viewership and made a national celebrity out of Alan Ameche of the Baltimore Colts. Ameche had scored the winning touchdown with a dramatic 1-yard plunge. The final score was Baltimore Colts 23, New York Giants 17.

As I said, I didn't do that game, but afterward I got a call from Bill MacPhail's office to immediately put together a bowling show in Philly focused around Alan Ameche. To achieve the overnight miracle, New York sent down their best technicians; a crew nicknamed the 'Dead End Kids'. They were a tightly knit group, mainly single guys who preferred traveling and doing pickups rather than being stuck in the studio. At first, the crew was suspicious because of how young I was, but once they saw how fast I made things happen I was accepted. Speed was the important thing with that bunch of sharp pros. They liked fast thinkers. And they liked that I was one of them and hadn't come into the business through the back door—no nepotism, no political pull.

As far as Ameche's special bowling show, it was a nothing

special, but I couldn't wait to work with the crew again. The only thing I really remember of the show that day was Ameche appearing with his wife, Yvonne, and how they were more interested in talking about re-flooring the kitchen of their row house.

Needless to say, times were different in 1958. Players like Ameche had no trouble living among the fans. Today's sports stars are behind the guarded gates of their suburban mansions; even so, despite their security measures they can still be targeted and assaulted; as happened to Sean Taylor, the Washington Redskin's safety who was fatally shot in his suburban Miami home by a would-be robber.

Another show I directed in the '50s was called "The Big Idea." It featured inventors showing off their ideas and products in the hope of getting financial backing. One of the inventors on an episode I directed was the father of the multi-talented Carl Reiner and the grandfather of another multiple talent, Rob Reiner. On "The Big Idea," I directed Irving Reiner, a watchmaker who had invented a new type of clock. Later I directed Irving's son Carl Reiner in a match on "Celebrity Tennis," and still later I directed Carl's son, Rob Reiner, in an episode of "The Battle of the Sexes." Another trifecta!

Speaking of famous names, in 1959 Nelson Rockefeller, then the Governor of New York, praised me for my camera direction even though I really hadn't deserved it. I used a floor-mounted camera to merely separate the governor from the busy background during a talk show, but when Rockefeller saw himself on the monitor, he saw more than I saw. He claimed the lower angle showed his strength and dominance on the screen.

I had directed so many dog acts, tap dancers, and musical numbers that I was always moving cameras around. This caught the eye of a lot of outside producers who in turn offered me jobs. The producers of "Ted Mack's Original Amateur Hour" asked if I was interested in directing their network show. I had also directed so many circus shows that the booker of the acts, Leo Grund, invited me to join the Grund Talent Agency and become his heir apparent.

I remember during one circus rehearsal one of the female

bareback riders caught my eye; and as I went over to introduce myself, a sandbag came down with a thud next to me. Her boyfriend was on the high wire, and the bag 'accidentally' slipped out of his hand.

It was safer directing commercials. I had directed enough live commercials in which the products came off looking good that I was offered a directing position at a couple of major New York Advertising Agencies. I was even offered a college job to teach television production, but what I enjoyed most was to learn a lot more. And to do that, I was itching to work again with CBS, New York's number one remote crew.

So by the time the '50s ended, I made my decision. My aim was to be hired full-time by CBS Network Sports. Sports seemed the best opportunity for me to fulfill my twin agenda of traveling and trying out new things. For me, the unexpected was always a good teacher. It brought about the enthusiasm and the energy I needed to grow.

Ed McMahon once told me that my stories were like nobody else's.

We ran into each other recently at the Hollywood Turf Club. We got to talking about when Ed performed as a clown, with a blinking nose, and about a show I did with him before he went off with Johnny Carson.

It was a late night show at WCAU called "5 Minutes More" and it was nothing more than Ed sitting in the darkness on a stool. But the show commanded a strong following due to Ed's imagination and his utilization of the unexpected power of live television. For example, one night he surprised us all by having the massive, hundred-member sequined and ostrich-plumed Ferko String Band parade in behind him. While all that was going on, Ed, to the accompaniment of strings, percussion, accordions, banjos, and a glockenspiel, offered a simple goodbye as though unaware of what was happening around him.

One last story about the fifties before we move on to the sixties. In 1953 CBS aired a live western series called "Action in the Afternoon." They did it from the back lot of WCAU. The show went off the air a year later but the western town remained standing in behind the studio. And that led the station to put the ten-building façade of the Old West to use by having someone else direct their star cowboy, Jack Valentine, in what was supposed to be a live half hour mix of song and action. The show was called "TK Ranch," and it aired as a mix of musical laments and inactivity that turned Valentine into no more than a mumbling drugstore cowboy.

When I watched Jack on the TV monitor I wanted to place my two fingers over his lips like you can do with an iPhone and pull them apart. When the sponsor threatened to drop out, the station had me take over the reins. To add some action, I enlisted five of the old Action stunt men as bad guys to pursue Jack. Pursue how?

I couldn't have a horse chase on a set that was a half a football field long. And that meant that the bad guys had to be a 'chip shot' away from Jack and yet they'd have to eat up at least twenty minutes of the live half hour so that I didn't have to end up with Jack having to fill by doing his snoring medley of songs.

During the rehearsal, I tried having the bad guys walk slow enough so that I could get some anticipatory close-ups of them before they tried to shoot down Jack, who would be moving around ever so slowly. Then to kill more time, I tried adding some extreme close-ups. I told the bad guys to walk even slower and Jack to move even slower. I added some musical bursts from the Capital Q library of the station's musical director, Dick Lester. That didn't work either. The defects in this lemon were immediately apparent in rehearsal. The gunmen looked like they were walking on Vaseline, and Jack looked like he was swimming in Jello. Come airtime, I gave up. I had Jack sing a song and then shoot a bad guy off the roof. Jack did five songs and shot five guys.

After the show, Jack and his stuntmen went to have their usual drink. I went to answer a couple of phone calls. The first was from the station lawyer who told me we weren't insured to shoot guys off the roof. As I went to pick up the second call, I thought it might be Dick Lester zinging me for my crappy use of music. But the other call turned out to be from the TK sponsors, who said they loved the show and that they were renewing.

For the record, yes, that Dick Lester was the same Richard Lester who, a few years later, moved to London; the same Richard Lester who, among his other acclaims, was chosen by the Beatles to direct their films. And also for the record, in a few years, Sergio Leone would come along with his fluid use of his minimalist cinematography, his brilliant recognizable close-ups and the virtuosity of his editing that would be accompanied by the eerie scoring of the gifted Ennio Morricone.

In this business, you never know what will work—or what or who can make it work. So let's move on to the Sixties, which took me to Rome for the Olympics and back to Philadelphia for the invention of the Instant Replay.

CHAPTER THREE

THE SIXTIES

As we move into the sixties, It's as obvious now as it was then that you can't just walk into a network like CBS and get a job. You need a strategy, and—as I've noted—I've always had a strategy for getting ahead. In this case, my strategy included not only how but where.

Let's go to the summer of 1960 and my freelancing with the CBS Network during its coverage of the Rome Summer Olympics.

Those Olympics were televised by RAI-TV, the Italian state national television network. No previous Summer Games had ever been televised to the States. The 1956 Melbourne Olympics were too far away; and those days there were no jet planes or videotape machines in use. There was no satellite transmission in 1960. And that meant that CBS Sports had to operate from a makeshift control center at Fiumicino Airport so that the live events could be taped as close to the terminal before they were jetted to the CBS Videotape Center, located then on an upper floor of Grand Central Station.

A commercial jet made the trip from Rome to NYC in nine hours. Subtracting the six-hour time difference, that meant that the tapes arrived in NYC from Rome only three hours after departure time. Some morning events were seen in America the same day. Afternoon and evening events were seen the next day. Some airings were rescheduled due to the tapes showing up frozen from the long trip in cargo.

Above the tape center in Grand Central there were four studios, one of which was used for Jim McKay, who hosted a show at 8 p.m. every evening for almost two weeks.

In 1960, CBS Sports sent over a team of commentators, tape technicians, and a few in-house producers. They didn't hire any freelancers. So I had to figure a way to get involved with the network crew.

I had a discussion with Jack Schneider, who, at that time, was the GM at WCAU-TV and would later be President of CBS. I told Jack that I thought CBS Sports would find itself shorthanded since it always operated on a tight budget. I asked if could take a vacation leave and head for Rome.

Schneider, who was a savvy guy, thought it a good gamble on my part. "After all," he said, "the Olympics come only every four years." So I bought my own ticket to Italy with no guarantee of employment—and no place to stay.

When I landed in Rome, I called the CBS Executive Producer, Pete Molnar, whom I had known in the past when freelancing. Molnar had set-up headquarters at the Bernini Bristol Hotel on the Via Veneto.

I left Molnar a phone message saying that I was vacationing in Rome and was available if he needed me to help out. I couldn't leave a callback number because I was operating out of a phone booth. The next day, I found a suitable room with an unsuitable bathroom down the hallway.

I called Molnar again, and he told me he was not only understaffed but also under fire. The U.S. press had been panning the daily shows in the States because the commentary and the tapes didn't give a clear enough picture of what had happened in Rome.

As soon as I got the job, I made sure that events were more finely edited so that the studio anchor could have suitable video for his narration.

In those 'Good Old Days', since the audio preceded the video on the tapes, they had to be cut diagonally by a razor blade before splicing the ends together with cellophane tape. And that was a problem, a physical problem. It was August in Rome, and without air conditioning it was hard to keep those packaged stories from pulling away from their edits. We used 4800 foot reels of two-inch quad tape that held approximately one hour of recorded material. Each editor was given an aluminum block with a slot for razor-blade editing. But as I mentioned earlier, the racks of electronics that supported those early machines gave us trouble. They were filled with glass-structured cylindrically sealed vacuum tubes that had a tendency to blow out when you least expected.

For the record, all in all, the 1960 Games eventually turned out to be well received in the States. And that helped with my being offered a producer-director contract at CBS Sports.

The 'live TV' industry was centered in New York City, and that meant I had to move from Philly to Manhattan—a given if you wanted to master the coverage of live remotes. I knew I'd miss my family and friends in Philly, but I was looking forward to all the traveling and work that CBS Sports demanded. I never liked roaming, but I did like traveling in those days and being young was the best time to do it.

I found myself constantly sweeping into towns across the nation with a ton of equipment and an army of technicians. Network management knew we couldn't rely on the local stations to supply all of the hardware or to provide crews experienced enough to handle the demands of our telecasts. The traveling itself wasn't all that bad, but I did have to fork over two thousand big ones to join The Directors Guild of America, which, in turn, stipulated that I had to fly first class at all times.

My network contract allowed me to be non-exclusive, and that meant plenty of outside assignments since you were qualified, or, as they'd say, 'bankable', to direct all kinds of shows. This was an unusual arrangement, considering that most directors in sports did only sports, most directors in news did news, and so forth.

At first, Bill McPhail didn't like the idea, but I pointed out that I came into the business when TV directing was as diverse as the TV programming itself. And that, I said, was really the career I wanted; one with diversity. I explained that if I directed only sports my mind would eventually grow shortsighted; and finally, in my thirties I would have directed all the major sports events. Then what?

Eventually I would have to ask myself: Weren't five Super Bowls enough to do? Or a dozen Kentucky Derbies? How many Stanley Cups and NBA Championships does a guy like me have to do before he moves on with his life past sports? Come hell or high water, I was going to make sure that I didn't end up like a lot of those guys, feeling trapped in sports. I knew that even with the option of freelancing, the day of saturation would eventually come.

I was convinced back then, as now, that the best thing about television is live television. It was also a place where I always felt the most secure. I had to take the freelance approach, or else I'd never know how high was up.

Since my career had a way of soaring in so many different directions, I think I should mention that this book has involved several years of research—to avoid any form of 'making up' or 'making over'. Dependable biographical data is the cornerstone of research, and it's an absolute necessity when dealing with a life as diverse as the one I have led.

At the local level, everyone was impressed to see a director like me as a one-man show taking full command in those frantic control rooms during live telecasts. But that wasn't the case in New York. I found the directors in the Sports Department were different. They were also gluttons for work, yet I think they didn't necessarily feel, as I did, that they should be a one-man show.

As for the producers, I found them to be schleppers; the kind of guys who were more impressed that I had this metal key topped off with a rabbit's head that meant I was a member of the newly opened Playboy Club on North State Street in Chicago. Back then, the Bunnies I was dating didn't get off until 4 a.m., and the rule was that I had to meet them two blocks from the club. That fit in with my nocturnal habits.

In New York, the hottest club closed a couple of hours earlier, but the pickings were way better. The big deal in Manhattan was the Peppermint Lounge on West 45th. This was the headquarters for the revolutionary new dance, the Twist, and it was another hot spot the guys were jealous I could get into. The manager was a hard-faced guy named Frank Rocco; and unless you greased his palm heavily, you couldn't get in. I knew him as a kid when we had some knockdown street fights. He gave me a front-row table that would be a good place to meet a movie star like Ava Gardner, twisting the night away.

Okay, back to work. My first assignment took advantage of my past experience directing film. I was sent out to capture the record-breaking riding of jockey Eddie Arcaro as he went about setting the mark for the most consecutive victories in a stakes race. My aim was to catch Arcaro's every move, and using film was the only way to capture it from start to finish.

Before meeting Arcaro, I saw him circling around me. I waited for him to make his move. As I readied my first shot, he came nose to nose with me, mine being Roman and his being Banana, his nickname.

He was angry. He wanted to know why CBS hadn't flown in his good pal, Mervyn LeRoy, the famed filmmaker of such classics as "The Wizard of Oz" to direct the ten-minute piece? And he wasn't kidding. Even though Arcaro remained a little edgy, I was still able to film enough of his rides, 'up close', to show how involved he was in this very dangerous sport.

But when I tried to get 'personal', he shouted out, "Stop the interview!" I was getting too personal. How dare I ask him about the time he was once suspended for riding another jockey into the rail! He didn't want to talk about possibly trying to kill that guy. Period.

I could live with that, but my biggest problem with Arcaro was that he never told me what horse to bet on. By the end of the shoot, I had managed to cash a few tickets since I'd figured out some of the sign language going on between the jockeys. But I also learned that there was no such thing as a sure bet. Arcaro laughed. He told me that if he could book all the bets in the jock rooms he'd be rich.

In this twenty-first century, all eyes had been on controversial Barry Bonds as he went about breaking Hank Aaron's record, but at the end of July, 1961, when I was directing the Baseball Game of the Week from Yankee Stadium, the big story was Roger Maris and Mickey Mantle chasing Babe Ruth's 1927 Homerun Record of 60.

The M&M Boys were locked at 39 home runs, and I needed to be close up to see the pressure they were under on their home run chase. Normally, a director would have captured their facial close-ups with a handheld camera. I knew the key to reporting the record-chase was to have the right close ups. But I didn't have a live TV handheld camera.

If Mantle hit a homer, it wasn't a problem being close enough to catch his reaction. His big country-boy expression would be on one of my cameras. But what about Maris? That was a dilemma. On previous games I had directed, I could hardly see his face after he blasted one. Maris kept his expressions under deep wraps. He'd circled the bases with his head down and zip straight into the dugout and get lost behind the water fountain.

I needed a super-long lens to pick up a close-up as far away as that water cooler. I needed a telephoto lens like they had in films that made distant objects appear magnified. I recalled that my buddy, Harry Coyle, over at NBC Sports, had used an 80-inch lens in that same ballpark to 'steal' the catchers' signals. But I needed an even longer lens. A couple of months earlier, over at the News Department at CBS, Hal Classon had used a 100-inch lens to cover Astronaut Alan Shepard's sub-orbital flight launch. Fortunately, I had done some live news pickups for the News Department, and that meant Classon trusted me to borrow their lens.

We didn't have lens stabilizers in those days and the 100-incher was so long that it had to be wired to my camera. We just secured big lenses the best we could. Once the camera fired up, I started to have sugarplum dreams of finally catching Maris' mug behind the dugout's water cooler.

Maris was batting third, and because he was a lefty, I had my third-base camera pick him up at the plate. On my first base camera, I had Mantle, who was batting fourth and was on the on-deck circle. I intercut the two shots to pick up the tension. So far, so good. But the big lens wouldn't be any good to me unless Maris homered. And sure enough, he put one into the bleachers. And as expected, he never looked up while circling the bases. But I was ready for him. I knew when he hit the dugout the 'hundred-incher' was going to catch his face up-close and personal.

What I had hoped to provide the nation with was a privileged look at a meaningful expression on Maris' face. Instead, I violated the man's privacy. The long lens revealed a nervous guy lighting up a cigarette and puffing away like a chimney. That's why he hid behind the water cooler. Shit! I wasn't happy putting it on the air. But I did!

The following summer, I got a chance to apologize to Roger when I ran into him and Mantle in Fort Lauderdale, where they were shooting "Safe At Home," a phony movie to capitalize on their celebrity. I was having a liquid-lunch at the Jolly Roger with their 'supposed coach', the actor, Bill Frawley, "I Love Lucy's" Fred Mertz. The restaurant was packed with visiting college girls seeking adventure.

I noticed Roger and Mickey coming through the door. The boys noticed the striking blonde from Zeeland, Michigan, seated at the next table and chatting with me.

As they pulled up chairs to join us, I finally got a chance to tell Roger how sorry I was about showing him lighting up one of his Camels during the game. He shook it off as no big deal. Mickey laughed and offered Roger one of his Viceroys. As the 'boys' lit up, they gathered-up the unstable Bill Frawley and accompanied him back to the set. My thoughts went to accompanying the blonde back to Zeeland, Michigan.

The biggest thing missing in those days was a screen-splitter on my remotes. My announcers were making a big deal about the lead the first base runner had since the viewers couldn't necessarily see it. They thought that their comments gave them an edge over the director and a plus for the home viewer. So the only way I could get a matte shot of the pitcher and runner in the same shot was to offset the lens of two cameras and then switch to their superimposition.

Let's say Robin Roberts was pitching and Willie Mays was giving him fits at first. In preparation, the cameraman shooting Roberts would frame Robin to the left. Then by turning his turret slightly, his lens would be no longer directly in front of the camera, thereby leaving a shadow on Roberts' right side. On the other camera, the lens was off-setted the other way. Mays, the first-base runner, was framed on the right so that when the lens was cocked, the shadow portion would be on Willie's left side.

Then I'd punch up the superimposition of the two cameras as one shot, resulting in a crystal clear shot of Robin Roberts checking on Willie with a soft curved line between them. It worked very well.

The next show I was assigned to do was a Network Special featuring the West Point Glee Club and the Naval Academy Glee Club. Before the telecast, I was called in to discuss the show with the Academies' two superintendents, Admiral Davidson of the Naval Academy and General Westmoreland of the Military Academy. They liked the ideas I was going to implement and were quite surprised that I knew so much about the Academies. I finally had to confess that I was once a lowly plebe and, worse than that, a drop-out.

Recently, I discussed that 1961 show with Roger Staubach, who was a year away from attending. I told him I was surprised to meet (his soon-to-be good friend) Joe Bellino, the 1960 Heisman Trophy Winner, while I was rehearsing the glee club in the Rotunda of Bancroft Hall. But it was after the show that the host, Jim McKay, gave us the biggest surprise of all. He was jumping ship to work on a show Ed Scherick had created, "ABC's Wide World of Sports."

Soon afterwards came another surprise. CBS's top sports producer, Peter Molnar, took off without warning and left for NBC Sports along with announcer Bud Palmer.

Well, at least I had Chris Schenkel to host my next show, which was quite a stretch from covering the solemn body of military cadets singing lyrics such as 'To fallen heroes let us sing', to the raucous crowd chanting 'more barrels' as they spurred on the ice skaters for longer jumps during the "Barrel Jumping Championship" at Grossinger's Resort in the New York Catskills.

After the show, Chris and I took off from the hotel's private grass strip on a Comanche 260. Jenny Grossinger, a sweet lady, was thoughtful enough to stand there and wave us goodbye. Unfortunately, the pilot took off without compensating for the wind gusting over the top of the towering pine trees that surrounded the field. He clipped his right wing across the top branch which came flying back at me and sent us careening back down to the grass runway, to where sweet Jenny stood. Amazingly no one was seriously injured.

In September of 1961, directing NFL games got a lot harder. I also had to work the pre-game show, the "Pro Football Kickoff" which was originating from stadiums around the country. The show was formatted to give a comprehensive look at all the day's games, which I'm sure was intended to help the betting aspect of the sport. The host was Tom Harmon, the 1940 Heisman Trophy winner. 'Old 98' and I became fast friends. During World War II, as a pilot, Tom had survived three air crashes, and now he got me thinking maybe I had two more to go, before I'd be home free. Hmmm.

Next I headed for Planica, Yugoslavia, to direct the "World Ski Flying Championship." And I was able to tape an interview with Marshall Tito on the telecast, even though the dictator had no plans to attend the event. Here's how I pulled that off.

On arriving, I took my announcer, Art Devlin, a former Olympic ski jumper, with me down to Zagreb, the capital city of Croatia, to pay a visit to the prominent art galleries in Upper Town, in hopes of meeting some of their intellectuals who could leak a secret to the political elite.

Once we introduced ourselves, I made up this cock-and-bull story that questioned Tito's health, claiming that a U.S. newspaper had noted that the dictator hadn't been seen lately. And maybe his absence was due to poor health. Everybody smiled, and we made a toast and downed the slivovitz. Everybody but Devlin. He wanted a coke.

When I got back to Planica, I asked the event officials to point out the route that Marshall Tito would use if he were to enter the stadium. They said that there were no plans for their leader to be there but if Marshall Tito did attend, he certainly would only use the prominent main entrance. Nothing less! Now, as I said earlier, I had trouble trusting people in authority, so I set up a couple of cameras at a back exit, the least likely place Tito would enter through.

Sure enough, on the big day, a motorcade of limousines ushered in Marshall Tito and his entourage through the back entrance, the one that seemed to be the least suitable. He saw me by the cameras and smiled knowingly.

Marshal Tito, age 70 and leader of the Socialist Federal Republic of Yugoslavia since 1945, wore a simple gray-green uniform when he came in, walking in front of an entourage of bodyguards. There were no medals dangling from his chest, only the golden laurel leaves on the lapels, indicating that he was the Marshal of Yugoslavia. Alongside him was his wife in a full-length black mink coat with a mink hat to match. Behind Marshall Tito and his wife was a small army of secret police.

No sooner than his party was seated, the P.A. paged 'Mr. Tony' to report to Marshall Tito's box. Meanwhile, I'd made it clear to Art Devlin, who was going to do the interview, that in no way should he bring up the issue of Tito's health.

The interview went fine, but before Devlin could end it, Tito took over and pounded his chest, exclaiming, "As you can see, I'm in good health." Of course, the comment didn't make sense since it came from nowhere. But to Tito it didn't matter. He showed up to prove his point.

Tito's security head made it quite clear to me that I should send a copy of the program to Marshall Tito. Did I understand? I took out my pen and asked for an address. I was told to send it to: "Tito, Yugoslavia."

When I returned to the States and CBS, I had another surprise awaiting me: my second airline scare. At the last minute, CBS said they needed me to direct a "Sports Spectacular" swim meet in the Midwest. The show was going to air the next day, so CBS chartered a flight to get me there. This was nothing new. I was always getting a last-minute assignment. This time I was just glad that the assignment wasn't another one of those death-defying pieces of crap where somebody got shot out of a cannon or drove off a ramp into a head-on car crash—or that ever popular 'human bomb' act where some guy blew himself up.

This was a swim meet, and I figured the only danger could be too much chlorine in the water. I was wrong. It wasn't the show that was the problem. It was getting there. It didn't take long before the plane's wings began icing up. The pilot had filed a flight plan, but I guess it never occurred to him to get an updated weather briefing before the two of us took off. No pilot wants to be in ice for very long, and this guy didn't have any anti-ice equipment to 'buy time' in order to get us out of it.

We made a hairy emergency landing in Wisconsin. The pilot lost his license, and I lost my lunch.

Back in the '50s, I also had a lot of turbulence as a CBS director. While I usually had total control of the telecast, I couldn't always shoot an NFL game the way you wanted without getting on the bad side of Bert Bell, the Commissioner. Then in 1960, things changed. The decade came in with a new NFL Commissioner, Pete Rozelle, a young guy who would encourage us to capture the game to its fullest. For me, that meant getting closer on the tangle of bodies.

And that brings me to the game played between the Eagles and the Giants, November 20, 1960, at Yankee Stadium when I tried to capture one of the most ferocious hits in the history of the NFL. That game was also hard to forget because it was such a cold day, something like 18 degrees but feeling like 18 below. It was late in the game, and my freezing crew knew there'd be more freezing, since the Giants were losing and wouldn't be running out the clock.

The Giants quarterback, Charlie Conerley, threw a quick flair over the middle to Frank Gifford, his halfback, but when the ball arrived so did Chuck Bednarik. The Eagles linebacker had leveled Gifford with a crushing blow that left him with a deep concussion.

I knew the longer I waited to play the 'hit' again, the more I'd piss off the viewers. I hit my intercom linking me to the tape operators to tell them to bust their ass, that I needed the play now. The tape operators weren't accustomed to getting that kind of request. They knew that I'd usually wait until halftime to run a play again, because if I reran a play that happened minutes ago it could really screw-up the announcers. It wasn't easy for them; they had to dial back into an old play when their commentary had moved on with the game.

But with Gifford almost being murdered, I needed to play the tape back now. As I waited, I put Giff on the screen. He was flat on his back with Bednarik leering over him, pretending to be Spartacus. This moment was one that needed to be immortalized, but I wasn't the one to do it. The technology to freeze the frame didn't exist in '60. But a press photographer did freeze that classic shot and, for years, Bednarik would autograph a copy of that photo and joke about Gifford as "The guy I put to sleep." The line was only funny because Gifford eventually woke up.

Let's move on to a happier part of the early sixties. This was when CBS assigned two crews of announcers to cover an NFL game. Why did the network have two sets of announcers calling the same game with the same video feed? In those days, every team had its own regional network of stations. And that meant that the game being broadcasted had a visiting-team audio-feed and a home-team audio- feed. And that, in turn, meant two sets of 'signature' voices that would basically plug their own team, no matter how the action unfolded. What was in the best interest of the team was what shaped each of those audio feeds.

The word 'biased' took on a new meaning in those booths. Recently, Tommy Brookshier told me that he still gets a laugh remembering when I used to ask the announcers on their headsets, "What game are you guys looking at down there?"

Let me give you an example on how the announcers were assigned in double booths. Let's say the Philadelphia Eagles were playing the Cowboys in Dallas. With the game being played in Dallas, the Eagles announcers, Jack Whitaker and Bosh Pritchard, would be in the visiting booth, feeding the Philadelphia Network, which stretched all the way up the state by using hard intercity connections called AT&T long lines.

The Cowboy announcers, Lindsey Nelson and Dave O'Brien, would have been in the home booth, feeding the Texas Network. Their audio would have been broadcast over the 'common video' with their broadcast being sent out to the cities nearby, once again by using AT&T long lines. So a key component was knowing what landlines to order for what network of announcers.

Okay, one more example. Let's say, the Packers were playing the Bears at home. That would have meant that Ray Scott and Tony Canadeo would have been in the visiting booth feeding the Green Bay Network while in the booth next to them Red Grange and George Connor would be announcing over the same video, feeding the Chicago Network that covered a few states like Illinois, Minnesota, Ohio, Kentucky and Tennessee.

The Chicago Network was interesting because it fed a big hunk of the Midwest and didn't go unnoticed by Falstaff Beer. Their distribution pattern basically matched the football linkup, and Falstaff was more than happy to also pay for those AT&T long lines along with the cost for the game rights.

So basically, at times back in 1960, there were two sets of CBS announcers covering the same pro football game. For St. Louis it would have been Jack Drees; for L.A., Bob Kelley; for Detroit, Van Patrick; for New York, Chris Schenkel; for San Francisco, Bob Fouts; and for Washington, Jim Gibbons. And each of them would have been assigned a 'color man', usually somebody who had played on the team. The question from me became, which announcing tandem woud I listen to while directing the game.

I never did come up with an answer. I'd flip back and forth but usually I preferred listening to the home announcers, thinking I'd get a better insight. In 1962, I was curious how well Pat Summerall would do replacing Johnny Lujack on the Giants game because Pat had just retired and had closer ties to the Giants.

I should point out that, at times during 1960 the two sets of announcers covering the same pro-football game could also be from two different networks, with one set from CBS and the other from NBC. That's because back in the '50s the Colts, Steelers, and the Browns were being broadcast by NBC. Cleveland had Ken Coleman. Joe Tucker was in Pittsburgh, and Chuck Thompson was in Baltimore.

Let's say I was producing and directing a game that had NBC's Cleveland Browns at the CBS' Philadelphia Eagles Game. That would mean I would be calling the commercials for both CBS and for NBC's 'away producer' Perry Smith who would be in his own truck, next to mine. Perry and his announcers would be feeding the Browns Network that extended from Texas to the East Coast, while I fed my announcers to upstate Pennsylvania.

In 1962 Pat Summerall signed on as an analyst replacing Johnny Lujack. It meant that Chris Schenkel and I got a new drinking partner. The brass had asked Pat to be more analytical than Lujack. But after a couple of games, Allie Sherman, the Giants coach thought Pat was 'too analytical' and got him bounced off the Giants telecasts. Pat was calling the plays before the ball was even snapped. In some ways it was good news for McPhail. He was able to assign Pat to the Washington games where they needed some help to improve their Redskins telecasts.

Let's move away from sports briefly. In 1962 I was commissioned to stage a live aquatic show billed as "The Theater of the Sea," and it was to be held at a newly constructed Aquarama on South Broad Street across from the football stadium. And there were porpoises! I had some experience with actors, but who knew from porpoises!

It was an offer I couldn't refuse. The call came from Ike Levy, a very prominent Philadelphian. He had decided that the city needed an aquarium and a commercial show to go with it, so he went about rounding up a group of his cronies, and they spent a few million to make it happen. Mr. Levy asked me to stage it and I wasn't going to say no to Mr. Levy. You see, he also happened to be William Paley's brother-in-law. In fact, it was Levy who had once convinced Paley to get out of the cigar business and to purchase some radio stations, which Paley eventually networked as The Columbia Broadcasting System.

The main auditorium was filled with palm trees, there was a variety of glass displays filled with aquatic creatures along the walls, and in the middle of the building there was this huge circular pool surrounded by bleachers. I usually worked by the rim of this large fish tank looking at the porpoises that had their heads poked out of the water looking back at me. They had flown several Atlantic porpoises in from the Keys in South Florida to a water tank in South Philly.

It didn't take long before I realized these were remarkable creatures who could learn to do their tasks quickly and—just as quickly—be begging for their reward.

I knew that Mr. Levy was bent toward symphonic music, so I didn't want anything common or corny, like having the porpoises rescue some clowns who had fallen into the water. I told the porpoise trainer, Dell Winders, that I wanted something theatrical with the full orchestral treatment so that the porpoises would appear balletic as they went splashing, twisting, and tail-standing. Then, to top it all, I wanted them to leap through hoops of fire, timed to the syrupy melody Tara's Theme.

Winders was a smart guy. He understood what I wanted immediately, but, of course, it took the porpoises a few weeks to learn their 'behaviors', as he called them. As the days went by, my human mermaids were finding it difficult to look graceful swimming next to animals that could perform with such consummate ease. The biggest problem for Winders, though, was cueing the porpoises as a team and adjusting the hoops for the leaping animals so that they would be in better sync with the music. I told Winders that I still wasn't happy with the timing.

When I was at WCAU-TV, I had directed several shows in front of live audiences where I could exercise some control over an actor's timing by having the floor manager give hand signals to slow down or speed up. But these were porpoises.

Also, when I rehearsed a live studio show as the director, I'd have a lot of stopping-and-fixing to do, to change what the 'dry run' had uncovered. Winders advised against doing that with the dolphins. He said that these animals weren't like your pet dogs. Their temperament had to be watched at all times. In particular, he didn't like the way the porpoises were behaving and said we should take a break until they stopped splashing around so much. I had begun to tire of the commutes from Manhattan and wanted to get on with it. But I found the trainer was right. As soon as I cued the lights, music and fire, the porpoises came at me, slapping away at the water with their tails and soaking me from head to toe.

I learned my lesson. Porpoises could get temperamental when it came to working with directors. By the way, the mermaids also learned a lesson. The girls found they could only swim with the animals while wearing wet suits, no bathing suits. Porpoises could get sexual when it came to working with girls. This show that I directed was years before the satiric writer Karl Hiaasen would write his best-selling novel Native Tongue, replete with a shocking scene involving a beautiful television reporter and a porpoise at a Florida amusement park. I'll leave the scene to your imagination.

The show ran seven years. It surprised me that it lasted that long. The trainer deserves all the credit. He was never taken aback by his job. For the record, Dale Winders went on to stump the panel of the hit show of the time, "What's My Line?"

Next I was off to London, England, to cover a soccer match. Bangu of Brazil was to play Everton of England at Wembley Stadium. The match was to be taped for a later playback in the States.

My only memory of substance comes the day after the game. I was being interviewed while having lunch with a British sports writer at a noisy old college hangout in the vicinity of his office. He kept shouting over the loud students to give me his take on the 'inside' of yesterday's game, how Brazil had 'grooved' its offense so as to work the ball closer while his Brits, on the other hand, based their offense on the stamina and daring of its players. I didn't get it, but I nodded as if I understood. Where I grew up, I didn't spend any time learning to control a ball with my foot or head. But to keep the conversation going I shouted back at him over the noise. I told the British sportswriter something he didn't know. Earlier that morning I had phoned my office in New York to report that the game had been recorded successfully when I was told the latest, that Walter Cronkite had replaced Douglas Edwards on the Evening News.

As I looked over at the table across from us, I saw this young girl staring at me. At that point I realized that she had overheard me. She introduced herself as Douglas Edwards' daughter; Lynn Alice, I believe. My unintentional blurting was the first she had heard of the news. I sort of apologized, but I was soon to discover that this lovely girl was more grown up and understanding about the nature of the TV business than I was.

On my return home from England in 1962 I received a phone call from Televisa, Mexico's largest media company. The call came from Rene Anselmo, one of their key executives. He had seen a tape of my TV coverage of the Brazilian game against England and asked if I'd come down and direct a soccer game the following month from University Stadium in Mexico City. Rene was very involved in the Latin American television market and planned to have the game broadcast as an international special.

Rene and I agreed that there would be no commercial

interruptions, nor would there be any interviews while the ball was in play.

The first thing I did after crossing the border was to take a look at some of their tapes to see how they had been covering their games. The camera coverage was a little too wide but acceptable; however, I couldn't figure out what the Spanish announcers were babbling about so much and why they were expressing themselves with such a childlike exuberance.

As far as my coverage plans, I told Rene that I would be avoiding any shots that made the continuous action appear too distant and that I'd be using a couple of raised platforms with which to get better angles, especially on the corner kicks which needed to include the attackers on the near post, the middle, and the far post.

I learned enough Spanish words to deal with my crew of forty, who were as passionate about the game as the 70,000 who were in the stands. As far as the commentators were concerned, I told them that I didn't speak or understand Spanish and that meant they had to call the action from what they saw on the monitor and to do it without screaming their heads off.

The telecast was okay, but it did not look exceptionally different from what I had seen of their regular coverage. Their chief engineer said I shouldn't be disappointed. He brought to my attention that when certain directors, like myself, were getting talked about on and off the air, top executives like his bosses wanted to hire one of us simply to give their international telecast more credibility. Rene was delighted with my simple telecast and so was his boss, Emilio Azcárraga, and that was amazing since he hadn't even seen the telecast.

Mr. Azcárraga proceeded to invite Rene and me to join him for dinner at his private club. The size of the club was quite impressive, as were the décor, the paneling, and the paintings. On stage a very large Mariachi orchestra provided our dining music. As I looked up from the large-choice menu, it dawned on me that we would be the only three dining in the club. Mr. Azcárraga's private club was, indeed, private.

Come the fall of 1962, I began directing an NCAA College Football game every Saturday and an NFL game every Sunday.

At the end of the season, on December 30th, I directed the 1962 NFL Championship where the Green Bay Packers beat the New York Giants 16 to 7 at Yankee Stadium.

A couple of days before the game, Green Bay was working out, and as I moved closer on the sideline, Vince Lombardi singled me out. His face turned gorilla, and I knew he would lay a little leafy-shoot, ass chewing on me. The big man had been on the cover of Time Magazine earlier in the week and I figured he was probably feeling like King Kong. I showed him no signs that I was afraid of gorillas. When Lombardi got side-by -side with me on the sideline, he became fierce, yelling about a close-up I had taken of him during my last telecast. He was pissed that I had taken this one shot of him. "Verna, you made me look like a madman."

Hmmm. I guess he could say that—since he seemed to be cursing and screaming on the sideline. But there was a reason for the shot appearing on TV. I told Lombardi that I hadn't deliberately singled him out to catch that specific reaction. "Coach, I go where the ball goes. That ball rolled by your feet and as the official came over to pick it up, you let loose on him. The ball was under your feet, Coach. Fair Enough?"

Lombardi didn't acknowledge my clarification on why his ranting had appeared on TV. He just growled and walked away from me.

By 1963 I had been directing NFL Games for almost ten years, first locally then with the Network. As I reflect back, the biggest difference over time was that in those earlier years, cabling the stadiums was especially hard on the crews. It was a tough job pulling those heavy cables over their shoulders and up those stands. But by the sixties, things got somewhat easier for them. Drop-cable had been left in place throughout most of the stadiums, and all the crews had to do now was roll up the remote truck and plug in.

Another thing, back then there were no 'cable extenders' and that meant we could only run our cables about 200 feet from the control truck, so a lot of baseball games didn't have a centerfield camera and some football games didn't have an end zone covered. The cameras themselves weren't dependable either. If they gave me four cameras to work with on a baseball game, I had to put two of them behind home plate so if one of them went out, which it would, I'd have the other camera for my basic coverage. The same was true for football's fifty yard line and horse racing's finish line. Sometimes I'd end a game with just one or two cameras working. I would go on to direct NFL Games for the next twenty years, so we'll get back to that. For now, let's switch to the other sports I was covering.

In June, 1963, I directed the Harlem Globetrotters in Rome, but the taping was halted by Abe Saperstein, the owner of the team. Saperstein and I had a fight that couldn't be resolved. He insisted that I put one of his ideas into the show. Abe wanted to have the black athletes stop a watermelon wagon in the streets and whip out their switchblade knives to carve the melons, and then he wanted me to get in close on the all-black team faces munching watermelons. I flat-out refused. I said it would take away from the players' dignity and that I had never portrayed them that way on television. The year before, I had taken the team to London where they played 'Pied Piper' to English school children and delightfully interacted with the workaday crowds in London. It came off great.

Now, in Rome, I had already taped a visit to the Boys' Town of Italy. I knew the founder, Monsignor Carroll-Abbing, having met him in Philadelphia when my family helped to raise funds for his orphanage. The taping at Boys Town was just what I wanted. It showed the other side of these clowning athletes. These were also serious guys who understood about kids being given 'a second chance in life' and how they could help them rebound by giving them their first chance at ball handling—to the tune of "Sweet Georgia Brown."

I can still hear those happy kids whistling and clapping with the Globbies as they circled around the court, trying to bounce the ball off their head, or roll it up their arm and around the back of their neck. When I think of today's NBA, maybe the Globbie's trick of twirling the ball between the legs of the ref could be helpful to get our minds off the 'under-and-over', the wager set on the outcome of the game. Anyway, Saperstein remained pissed that I wouldn't incorporate his idea, and he kept his players on hold. A couple of days passed, and he didn't give in. Bill McPhail had to fly in and straighten things out. Saperstein wasn't happy when McPhail agreed with me that no watermelon shots would be taken.

The show aired on CBS in 1963 even though books written on the history of the Harlem Globetrotters have their TV games airing on TV on different dates. I know it was 1963 because that's when the Rome Cavalieri Hilton opened up, with me being one of their first guests. On opening day, I found out that phoning-in room service meant my going down to the kitchen to pick it up.

As I continue with the accounts of my life, unfortunately I've found that cross-checking has exposed a lot more erroneous facts that others have printed. For now, though, 1963 was the Globetrotters' 13th annual tour of Europe, and after the show I accompanied the team for an audience with Pope Paul VI at the Vatican.

The audience was quite solemn, but that night things got a lot louder. I took the players to the new local nightclub to try out the latest dance to hit Rome, the Hully Gully. Basically a line dance with some exaggerated chicken movements, it was created in Florida by my old friend Frank Rocco from my Peppermint Lounge days.

On my return from Rome, in September, 1963, I was assigned to tape a tour of the newly opened NFL Hall of Fame in Canton, Ohio. The announcer Chris Schenkel and I got the assignment because it was one of those programs that should have been scripted but wasn't. I led Chris with my shots, and he found a way to handle it with his ad lib ability. He exuded such self-confidence that his mere being on the hollowed ground of Canton seemed to be enough in itself. Schenkel was a big part of the sixties.

The two of us spent a lot of time sitting at the front bar at Toots Shor's on West 52nd in Manhattan, a New York landmark frequented at one time or another by the likes of Frank Sinatra, Hemingway, Orson Wells, Jackie Gleason. There was always something going on and in one notable episode Toots Shor supposedly out drank Gleason to the point of leaving Gleason passing out in the men's room. The food wasn't anything fancy—standard steak and baked potatoes, shrimp cocktail—but it was the clubhouse away from the clubhouse. Baseball players were special favorites at Toots Shor's—Yogi Berra, Micky Mantle, Joe Dimaggio....

One day we met at the 21 Club, the more elegant former prohibition era speakeasy a few doors down at 21 W. 52nd. Chris Schenkel was happier than usual. He had just signed a deal with ABC for $250,000, a 70 percent increase in his pay. Chris knew a lot of people who could open a lot of doors for Roone Arledge and ABC Sports.

In September of '63, I was off to Mexico City to direct their National Charreada. A charreada is part horse show, part Mexican Rodeo, and part Mexican Mariachi. The charros were the cowboys and they used roping skills that no cowboy in his right mind would ever use on his ranch, like roping a calf from a riding horse and causing it throat and neck injuries.

I also had some experience covering American rodeos, and I found them to be just as cruel. They use a flank strap to bind the testicles of the bull to make it buck. Have you noticed that rodeo bulls don't stop bucking after they've thrown their rider, but only after the painful strap is pulled off their nuts!

The host of the show was a former steer wrestler, Lex Connelly, a real kicker. Strangely enough, his good buddy was an ultra-trendy Mexican guy who claimed to be the President's son. The guy had a collection of curved knives that he would mount on the legs of his fighting cocks so as to improve his chances of winning a bet. But he found out that I was only interested in his private stash of tequila that had been awarded double-gold medals.

That night I stayed at a fancy hotel in Mexico City. The next morning, while having a bit of the 'hair of the dog' at breakfast, I noticed that I might not be alone in combating a hangover. Sitting at the table across from me were two people sipping their water as if it were vodka. He was reading a newspaper and smoking like a fiend. She was casing the room with her violet eyes. The maitre d' told me that the twosome had just got in from Puerto Vallarta, where "Night of the Iguana" had finished filming. Looking outside the window behind me, I could see the herd of paparazzi waiting for Liz Taylor and Richard Burton to hit the public street and become fair game for them.

When I arrived in LA, I checked into the Beverly Hills Hotel to catch up on my sleep before flying back to New York. I got an hour's worth before one of my friends, Steve Bershad, Sheldon Leonard's son, roused me, telling me there was someone I should hunt down, a top model that I had to meet. Three months later I married the model I had to meet, Joanne Meyer.

But first I had to direct the 1963 Army-Navy Game. And that meant going down to South Philly to survey Municipal Stadium. The old stadium, never one of my favorites, was designed as a horseshoe of seats that surrounded a cinder running-track that ran around the grass football field, with wooden bleachers at the open end. The stadium had hosted lots of Army-Navy Games over the years, and it was there, twenty two years later, when it was renamed JFK Stadium, that I arranged, with Philadelphia Mayor Goode, for it to play host to the American portion of "Live Aid."

As was the tradition, President John F. Kennedy was to attend the 1963 game. The halftime plan was for him to leave his seat on the Army side and cross the field to sit on the Navy side so as to share his presence with both Academies.

Thursday morning, two days before the game was scheduled to be played, I went to the stadium to meet with the President's Secret Service inside the stairwells. They wanted to discuss which of my crew members needed access to the stairs since they would be sealing them off, as an added precaution.

Then, the next day, Friday morning, the day before the game, I flew to Boston with my E.I.C., Walter Pyle, to survey the following week's college game, the Harvard Yale Game. About quarter of two on that afternoon I was standing on the roof of Harvard Stadium, trying to figure out where to put a camera. Looking down below, I could see that the visiting side of the horseshoe would be the sunny side during the game, but I could also see that my E.I.C. was in the shade on the home side of the field and waving like a madman at me. I was wondering why he wasn't inside the field office watching TV and checking on the soap that he was technically responsible for.

The Harvard flags on the roof were snapping in the wind, so I couldn't hear what Pyle was saying until I descended closer. "Kennedy's been shot. Cronkite just broke in with a slide." Pyle explained he was just sitting there, watching "As the World Turns" and grumbling about why the lighting was so flat on the two actors seated on a couch, when Walter Cronkite broke in and said that three shots had been fired at President Kennedy's motorcade.

Pyle phoned his operations office and was told that the newsroom camera was still being lined up on a chip chart. We stayed glued to the set. Finally Cronkite appeared on camera, and eventually the announcement came of the President's death.

By the time we left for the airport, next week's game with Yale had been postponed. The athletic director who drove us to the airport was still recounting how President Kennedy had been in those stadium seats just a few weeks earlier when he watched his alma mater, Harvard, play Columbia to a 3-3 tie.

Biographies tend to be predominantly chronological since it seems to be the best method of compilation. So let's move to December 28, 1963.

And I'm on the West Coast to marry the model I had met three months earlier.

Unfortunately the marriage didn't work out, and we divorced three years later. Today, for the life of me, it is no longer quite clear why I married in the first place. Too bad I couldn't have married my second wife first. But it couldn't have been a mistake. From it came an important part of my life, my wonderful daughter Tracy Verna, the first of my three children.

Now let's go back so that I can tell you my thinking once the Instant Replay was under my belt. I was pleased that the Instant Replay had sped-up the tempo of the televised game. That was just what I wanted. It felt good that the game was now being viewed with a continuing anticipation that didn't exist before. As a director, you knew that the viewers were now expecting a second look at the action. But once the Instant Replay was used for officiating, it had the opposite effect on the playing field. It slowed down the game, big time. I remember when writing my other books that I always mentioned how the game of football was well suited for the television viewer.

So the question now is: How did the Instant Replay affect that basic premise? First of all, football didn't fall into the trap of repeating itself like soccer and hockey. Football has an opening curtain. The ball is snapped, and the action is covered by the play-by-play guy. After the play, the curtain comes down, and the color man makes his remarks. Then the curtain goes up again for the next play. How did the Instant Replay change that? Well, it meant the curtain stayed open most of the time since there always seemed to be some form of repeat of the last action. And that continuity overcame any respite between plays, since it served the game.

I was on new turf with this innovation, so I kept digging into the history of radio, hoping for something to jump out at me that I hadn't thought of. But the only thing I found out was that innovations didn't jump that much in those days. Meanwhile, Bill McPhail and his top assistants, Jack Dolph and Bill Fitts, were moving fast, working with the engineering department so they could make the Instant Replay a reality on all the games for the 1964 NFL Season.

And in 1964, Roone Arledge was moving just as fast, apparently trying to take credit for inventing the Instant Replay.

In the Coda Chapter at the end of this book, I'll point out that the press never questioned how Arledge could have achieved an Instant Replay without ever having directed a live game—or how he could ever have been in a position to make the rat-a-tat commands necessary for the 'instant' part of Instant Replay. As I've noted, to be the inventor of the Instant Replay you also had to be the innovator. History shows that Roone Arledge was neither.

But for now, let's move on to May of 1964 when I directed my first Kentucky Derby and how I got that assignment. The guy who directed the '63 Derby had missed the start of the race, not good when you're telecasting in black and white. It took a while to pick out the favorite, Candy Spots, a chestnut, who was running third and it became harder to pick out the eventual winner, Chateaugay, another chestnut, running in the back of the pack.

I ended up directing twelve Kentucky Derbies and at times I got a chance to visit with Pee Wee Reese who made his home in Louisville. I always thought of him the same way I had thought of the late Phil Rizzuto… a genuine guy.

When I'd get together with Pee Wee, we'd get to talkin' about the old days and how much tougher it used to be takin' the train rather than flyin', and about those hearts games he played on those long trips with Jackie Robinson and some of those other Dodgers. I told Pee Wee that something strange came up the other day. A couple of the guys on my crew said that they used to go to the Chock Full of Nuts on 44th and Lex, and that last week they had seen Jackie Robinson working behind the counter. Could it be? Pee Wee said that the executive offices for the coffee company were above the store and that Jackie, being a V.P., sometimes liked to go down and chat with the customers.

It was on the Kentucky Derby in 1964 that I tried using the Instant Replay on horse racing for the first time. But I isolated the wrong horse. I went with the favorite, Hill Rise, who came in second.

I immediately aired my isolated camera showing Hill Rise being bumped a couple of times and going into the stretch, closing ground to the finish line, but with Bill Shoemaker never getting him there. Bill Hartack went to whipping left-handed and won on Northern Dancer. I had one iso camera and one instant replay machine, and I'd picked the wrong horse.

After the race, my announcer, Bryan Field, was in the jock's room doing an interview with the winning jockey. Hartack was talking into Bryan's mike, and I was talking in Bryan's ear. I wanted Bryan to wrap it up and to interview Bill Shoemaker, the jockey who lost on the favorite, on the previously undefeated Hill Rise. That was the bigger story.

Time was running out and no Shoemaker. I kept hitting Bryan's earpiece with, "Get Shoemaker." Then in the middle of his interview with Hartack, a frustrated Bryan Field turned to the camera and said, "He's in the shower, Tony." The show was still on the air when the phones began to ring. The viewers wanted to know who was in the shower, and who is Tony?

Let me tell you about Bryan Field. He was a newspaper reporter who miraculously developed a British accent once he got a deal to be on television. We had met at a racetrack in New Jersey in 1953. And I quickly knew what he was about. I'd been working in TV for only a couple of weeks when I was sent over to work a show at Garden State Race Track that was being televised by the network crew. Looking around, I saw there were four cameras. Two were on the roof to cover the race, and there was another camera on the paddock where Bryan Field would be conducting interviews with the celebrities. Good luck finding celebrities in New Jersey.

My job was to work with the fourth camera, to pick up live color shots of the crowd. The show's assistant director would have normally done the job, but he was big-time now and had gone off to direct a dramatic show.

My cameraman explained that he needed my help in pointing out what to shoot since his Zoomar lens had him busy plunging the metal rod at the rear of the camera so as to move the multiple-lens assembly for magnification.

Come airtime, the cameraman plunged the zoom tight enough to eyeball the ladies and the fashions. Then a strange thing happened. Certain guys began holding up their newspapers to cover their faces so they wouldn't be recognized. Then it dawned on me: those guys were with ladies who weren't their wives.

As for Bryan Field, with no celebrities to be interviewed, he ended up interviewing any familiar face that came his way. And the youthful assistant director I had filled in for, he had left to direct the "You Are There" episode that covered "The Hamilton-Burr Duel." His name: John Frankenheimer.

In the summer of 1964, Bill McPhail held a CBS-NFL Clinic. He flew in all the producers, directors and announcers from around the country for a daylong session. Bill thought it important to have 'face time' with crews, many of whom had never met. In those days we arrived the day before the game, just in time to have dinner together and go out drinking. But now with the clinic, names could be put to faces. McPhail started things off by giving out some of the details on how CBS had won the two-year bid for the NFL TV package back in January, for an unprecedented $14.1 million per year.

What Bill didn't mention was that he had the bid-number covered going in.

He was counting on getting $14 million from his contacts at the Ford Motor Company and the other $14 million from Philip Morris with the help of his buddy, adman Jack Landry, creator of the Marlboro Man. In fact it was Jack Landry who asked me to direct the first Marlboro Cup in 1973 so as to take advantage of the enormously popular Secretariat being called the 'people's horse'.

Let's go back to CBS's 1964 NFL Clinic with all its producers and directors assembled at Black Rock. Bill McPhail started things off by giving out some of the details on how CBS had won the two-year bid for the NFL TV package back in January, for an unprecedented $14.1 million per year. CBS had also anted-up another $1.8 million per game for the rights to carry the 1964 and 1965 NFL Championship Games, both of which I ended up directing.

McPhail turned over the mike to Jack Dolph, his right arm. Jack welcomed two new pairings, Jack Buck as the new voice of the Bears, and Jim Morse, the new analyst for the Lions. Bill Fitts, our executive producer, explained that we'd be trying out a new announcer format, which he called 'half & half,' whereby the home announcers would work the first half and the visiting announcers would cover the second half. For the record, this idea bombed out. After the '64 season, the split audio feed was reinstated for the next couple of years.

McPhail came back on mike and told us that the 1964 Season offered another first for the network, that during the last five weeks of the regular season we'd be broadcasting double-header games. These would be games which I would end up producing and directing.

Then I was brought on to explain another first, the addition of the Instant Replay to our telecasts. I went on to describe the workings of the Instant Replay and how the production team should go about it and how the announcers should deal with it. I knew some of the talent would be blasé about using any new technique, so I specifically warned them that they'd learn real fast that a good instant replay from the truck could strangle a bad analysis from their booth.

Let me jump to the end of the '64 season and tell you how things turned out. We found that some directors got in only one or two key replays in a game, while other directors played a slew of them, mostly meaningless. We found that some play-by-players only accepted replays with an attitude, saying that the instant reruns were helpful when they had a dull game to cover. But we knew the BS was because the analyst had become the star of the team.

All in all, some analysts handled it better than others. And some never got the hang of blending in what they were saying with what they should be saying about the replay. Even years later, one analyst, Paul Christman, still couldn't get the hang of it. Paul asked me if his wife Inez could sit in the truck so she could give him a better idea on how the dang thing worked. All I can say is that Inez Christman was a lovely person.

When McPhail adjourned the 1964 Clinic, that meant closure at Toots with lots of drinks and lots of talk about the good old days. Some of the old-timers speculated on how past announcers, who had once hung out at Toots' bar, would have handled the instant replay. They were referring to the days when Ted Husing worked the mikes for CBS, and Harry Wismer was in the ABC booth. Then one announcer, I think it was Ray Scott, said that maybe he could get some Bill Stern type fan mail. That got a big laugh. He was referring to the early years when Stern was the announcer for NBC Sports and how the network would receive letters on how good Stern's play-by-play was. The only problem was that the letters came in two days before the event took place.

At end of the 1964 NFL season I tried another one of my experiments. Frank Ryan of the Browns threw five touchdown passes and beat the Giants 52 to 20. But I was interested in the field goal attempts, not the passing game. I always thought that a lot of the field goal calls were questionable, and I had this discussion with an official, Jimmy Tunney, who I got to know at the time. I told Tunney I was going to try a 'still frame' analysis. I wanted to try freezing one of those balls going over the uprights.

Tunney didn't react one way or the other. So be it.

I should note that back in those days the vertical posts that came up from the crossbar were shorter, ten feet shorter, and that there was only one official, a field judge, under the crossbar. So I put former kicking star Pat Summerall in the basement of Yankee Stadium to snap-away with a Polaroid I had strapped to the front of his TV monitor. Pat wasn't happy with the assignment, to say the least. When Pat got a Polaroid he liked, he brought it to me for my okay, then he mounted it in front of my live TV camera.

I aired a couple of shots that stopped the ball's pin-wheeling and froze it between the uprights; both stills were successful attempts by Lou Groza and Don Chandler.

As an aside, the field judge calling those field goals was the same Jim Tunney. In fact, two years later, it would be Tunney who would be the field judge standing alone under the goalposts in Green Bay's Lambeau Field and making a call so controversial that it caused the rules to be changed. The game I'm talking about is one that I directed on December 26, 1965, a divisional playoff game between the Packers and the Colts, with Tunney calling Packer kicker Don Chandler's game-tying 22-yard field goal 'good'.

After the game, Don Shula, who was the Baltimore Colts coach at the time, asked me what it looked like on TV. I told him the kick sailed wide-right, but it was so high above the upright it was too hard to tell. But when a film camera confirmed that the ball had sliced right, the league added ten feet to the goal posts' verticals, and they put a second official under the goal post which now would be painted bright yellow.

At the start of 1965, I almost bought the farm again; my third brush with danger. I was on a twin-engine seaplane flying my film crew to cover a hot-air balloon race that was to launch off Santa Catalina Island. The seaplane had left LA and in fifteen minutes was skirting the island channel. The pilot nosed the aircraft downward to make a power-on landing atop the ocean swells in the harbor. But he miscalculated the cargo weight of the film equipment, and the plane hit the water hard, so hard that it felt like the float struts had broken and the craft was going under.

As I started to release my seatbelt, the pilot pulled up the craft and put down the retractable gear. Luckily he landed safely in the center of the Island, but the bad news was yet to come. It would be the Santa Catalina Air Balloon Race that would experience a tragic outcome. Though the weather turned poor, they still launched the ships. No sooner had the balloons cleared the island's ridge than they began disappearing in the low overcast—and from my cameras' view. From above, the balloonists struggled to maintain the necessary visual contact with the chase boats. Eventually they aborted their flights and returned. Except for one.... The sole woman balloonist, Barbara Keith, whose balloon had gone into the ocean, died of pneumonia during the night.

On a happier note, on May 1, I directed the 1965 Kentucky Derby with close friend Jack Whitaker replacing Chris Schenkel as the host. Jack had never done a horse race before; so from L.A. we flew in Gil Stratton, an old pro with racing, to give Jack a hand.

All was going well until an hour before the telecast. Two of my cameramen had picked up some smoke coming from their left. When they panned over, I saw that flames were coming from the clubhouse at the top of the stretch. I knew that if the wind continued to blow in that direction, the Twin Spires would soon be the Charcoal Steeples. I told my cameramen to lock their shots and get the hell out of there. On their monitors in the truck, I could see the blaze advancing from the box area to the roof, but then, fortunately, the wind shifted directions and the fire department quickly put out the fire.

At 4 p.m. I went on the air with no producer in the truck. His last words were "Don't air any commercials until I get back." But he never came back until the telecast was over. I aired the commercials anyway. I figured nobody would be tuning off. I was right, and the sponsors ended up paying up.

Come airtime I faded up on Churchill Downs, but My Old Kentucky Home looked different that year. There were fire engines on the racetrack instead of horses. The phone rang, and the director of racing told me that post time would now be a half hour late. Hmmm? That would be 5 p.m., which was the time we were scheduled to be off the air.

Hmmm? I began wondering what else could go wrong. Then I was told that another fire had broken out. This one, unrelated, was in a Baltimore sewer tunnel that housed the audio lines running north from Louisville to New York. And that meant there'd be no audio leaving the truck. Hmmm? What about the announcers? I figured it best to keep them yapping away since I didn't know when the audio would be coming back. The audio never did come back, but at least I isolated the right horse this time.

Two months earlier, I had seen Lucky Debonair win the Santa Anita Derby, and now, once again, with Bill Shoemaker aboard, the bay colt made a dash to the wire and won by a neck.

Shortly after the 1965 launch of the world's first commercial communications satellite, Intelsat I—better known as Early Bird—I got a call from Fred Friendly, one of Ed Morrow's closest associates and then CBS News Division President.

As I entered Mr. Friendly's office, we shook hands. The last time I had seen a hand that big was when I met the actor John Wayne. Friendly was his own man, and as president of CBS News he had a fiefdom with its own budget. He spoke with flair about what the medium could do with the aid of a satellite. Obvious Mr. Friendly was looking forward to the day he could send out his anchors at the drop of a hat and have them report live from all over the world. He recalled once filming Edward R. Murrow when Ed was on the phone with someone in London who was also being filmed at the time and how he, Friendly, had later edited the two pieces together with a split screen. Mr. Friendly correctly predicted that the satellite Early Bird would be the forerunner of the era when live television could be linked up anywhere in the world. Friendly wanted me to produce and direct the 1965 Epsom Derby. My announcers would be the veteran Charles Collingwood and a new reporter up from Dallas, Dan Rather. I was honored that Mr. Friendly had selected me for the assignment. I got along great with Collingwood, but Rather was not my kind of guy.

I had the whole telecast ready to go: Cameras set.... Collingwood in his morning coat in the grandstands.... Rather in his boots, wandering in all his ego among the infield crowd. I had successfully pre-tested sending the signal from Epsom Downs to Goonhilly Downs in Cornwall. From there the signal was uplinked 22,300 miles to the satellite which was in a synchronous orbit above the equator with a line of sight-communications to the ground station in Andover, Maine, where it was downlinked. So far so good. But the show never got on the air. The EBU, the European Broadcasting Union, had to have the permission of all countries in the coalition before I could telecast by way of the satellite. France was the only country to decline. We never found out the reason.

Au contraire! Let's go back to Britain and to Epsom Downs. Notably, from that very site the 1931 Epsom Derby was transmitted as the first outside television remote. But that 1931 transmission was wired to a movie house and not sent to the homes, since people didn't own TV sets yet.

The first home transmission didn't come about for another six years when the BBC televised a tennis match from Wimbledon. Baird Television had placed a camera across from the finish line to catch the little colt Cameronian flashing by the post to victory. The feed was sent by telephone wire to London's Dominion Theater, where it was projected on a large screen to more than a thousand people in the cinema. The exhibit, which some called Distant Vision and others called The Eye of Radio, was a tremendous success, so much so that the BBC carried the race again the following year, and the cinema was sold out with crowds jamming the street.

By contrast, while England's Epsom Derby was televised in 1931, America's first Kentucky Derby wasn't televised until 1954. The Kentucky Derby was only on radio back when the colt 'Twenty Grand' won the 1931 Derby. The 1931 Epsom Derby had played to a paying cinema audience. Back in the USA the only horse racing you paid for in the cinema was to watch Clark Gable win the 1931 Kentucky Derby for MGM with his colt, the fictional "Tommy Boy."

Now let me take you to July 8th, 1965, two weeks after I returned from London. I was assigned to do a 'stop-action' test on an NFL game by using something brand new: an Ampex Disk

Recorder. The test wasn't successful.

The recorder's storage was too limited, and the bursts of slow motion and stop motion weren't airable. That was in 1965. A couple of years later, in 1967, Ampex came out with the HS-100 and ABC aired the first slow- motion instant replay during a downhill skiing event in Vail, Colorado.

Back in November of 1965 Pete Rozelle had informed Bill McPhail that if he didn't come up with the price he had in mind for the 66-68 NFL Rights, which was a 25 percent increase, he was prepared to have the League telecast its own games.

I thought it was strong talk since Rozelle knew that he had no other network to bid against CBS. The other two networks were committed to other programming. Late that night, I got a phone call from Pete, saying that he was thinking of setting up his own network if he had to. Then he asked, if it came to that, would I make a deal with him. I knew Pete well. I smoked, I drank, and I played cards with him, but I told Pete that our phone conversation didn't feel right to me. While he had to do what he had to do, I told him that he shouldn't count on me being a part of it. He thanked me and hung up. Maybe Pete figured I'd tell McPhail about the phone call and what his plans were. I didn't!

By 1965 fifty percent of CBS's regular primetime schedule was being broadcast in color. And on Thanksgiving Day, 1965, I directed CBS's first-ever color broadcast of an NFL game. Detroit and Baltimore played to a tie, 24-24. I wasn't that impressed with the addition of color. But when I was visiting The Masters in 1966 I was blown away by how color television could bring out the beauty of a golf course.

The day after Christmas 1965 I flew out to cover the New Year's Ski Jumping Championship from Garmisch-Partenkirchen in Germany.

But I left the country still wondering how the rights for the NFL package were going to turn out. I had to stop off in Paris for a meeting with one of my bosses, Jack Dolph. And it was there at the bar of the Hotel George V that a bartender told us that CBS had just purchased the 1966-68 NFL TV rights for $18.8 million per year.

In 1966 my career took another turn that was not accidental. I wanted to leave Manhattan and move to Los Angeles because I knew if I lived out on the West Coast I would have a wider range of opportunities in directing. I spoke to Jack Schneider, who was now the President of CBS-TV. Jack knew me and he knew my restlessness pretty well from my WCAU days. Jack made arrangements with Perry Lafferty, head of CBS West Coast Productions, to give me access to whatever else I might be interested in directing.

Along with my wife and daughter, I moved to Los Angeles, and soon I found myself observing how the directors were capturing the humor of "Gilligan's Island" and the action of "Wild Wild West." At that time a couple of reporters from Sports Illustrated were tagging along to do a feature story on me. In the course of events, they printed something that happened on the "Wild Wild West" set when I encountered one of the guest actors, Peter Lawford, who definitely wasn't my kind of guy. Lawford's attention was on the poodle he was holding and he was late on his cue from the renowned director Richard Donner. Lawford was to enter the scene on cue so as to coordinate his actions to that of the star of the series, the reliable Robert Conrad. In a panic, Lawford turned to me and said, "You, hold my dog!" I looked at the jerk's little poodle and said, "Shove it up your ass!"

S.I. printed the incident, and when my mother in South Philadelphia read the story she was shocked that her Anthony had said that to her favorite actor. But when I spoke to my mother, my main announcement was that I was getting divorced. It became obvious that my wife and I weren't right for each other and that things weren't going to work out.

So now I was what I would call between marriages. What turned out to be very strange was that I had lots of girlfriends, but I was lonelier than hell. They couldn't fill the void. I felt a profound sense of separation from my daughter Tracy.

I was a bachelor again, this time living the nightlife along the famed Sunset Strip. But Go Go girls suspended in a cage above the dance floor and the 10-block traffic jams began to bore me, so I began doing my drinking with my own Rat Pack at a quieter setting, like the small mirrored-bar at the newly opened La Dolce Vita that was co-owned by actor George Raft.

One night George, the movie tough guy, walked in and spotted me as the guy to answer his question: "Where are the girls?" That kidding remark started us talking—talking about the days when George ran the Capri, a posh gambling joint in Havana, and a time when I was dating a showgirl at the Tropicana Nightclub in the heart of Havana. I had turned twenty five there, but I wanted to get home before Christmas. George said it was a good thing I did. Right after the holiday, Fidel Castro's army came marching into the city and machine-gun sprayed his gambling tables, confiscated his bank account and emptied his pockets of $2800 in cash before he was able to leave the city.

George Raft had a calm way of talking. He said he spoke the same flat way in his movies if the director liked it or not. I liked it! He was a genuine guy, and he introduced me to a genuine gal, the headline singer at Dino's Lodge, a hot spot owned by Dean Martin and used as a setting for the TV series "77 Sunset Strip."

My next assignment was a 1966 NFL Monday Night Game, four years before the first ABC Monday Night Game in 1970. Rozelle had been trying to do a night game on TV since '64. His idea to do it on Friday got shot down because he'd be interfering with high-school-game attendance. Now, two years later, in 1966, he convinced McPhail to televise a game on Monday Night. But McPhail didn't want to spend an extra dime on the telecast. And it showed. The telecast looked and sounded just like any of our Sunday afternoon games.

After the telecast, Rozelle approached Bob Wood, CBS's President, for a regular Monday night schedule. Wood wasn't interested in more telecasting more football. He needed more first-run theatrical movies. When he couldn't find them, he put CBS into the feature film business.

Then, in 1966, Televisa, the huge Mexican media company I had directed for in the past, hired me again. This time Rene Anselmo contacted producer Hal Uplinger and me to produce and direct 24 Hours of LeMans Race and feed it back to Mexico.

Hal and I headed for France. We weren't much on tense diesel standoffs, but through our yawns we managed to cover the European powerhouses vying with each other. I was also able to pick up some unexpected color.

The cameras around the track couldn't avoid the sprawling campgrounds of the annual visitors along with their RVs and rivers of beer.

It was a race of endurance all right, and Mexico got every penny's worth from both Hal and me. As an aside, Rene Anslemo would go on to be the founder of the communications satellite company PanSat. His motto: "Truth and Technology Will Triumph Over Bullshit and Bureaucracy."

In 1966 Caesars Palace opened in Las Vegas, and I directed the first sports event there, USA USSR Amateur Boxing. That was a year before Evil Knievel was unsuccessful in trying to jump the water fountains in the front of the hotel. One of the vice presidents of Caesars, Harry Wald, was interested in establishing Las Vegas as the boxing capital of the world. He put the ring right in the middle of the casino floor. At the time there was no where else to put it. Harry thought of himself as a General Wald and, soon afterward, he invaded the back lot and built a pavilion to house Caesars' sporting events.

That was in 1966, but when I was in Vegas, in 1958, there were no Roman marble reproductions nor any fountains to leap over. Caesars was just a big empty lot next to the Dunes Hotel.

In '58 I was staying at a place up a stretch of the then-empty road that led into town. It was called the El Rancho Vegas, and the headliner in the showroom was Milton Berle. I met some of the female sheriffs who danced behind Milton with their pointy stars and rounded bottoms, but it wasn't until 1979 that I corralled Berle into hosting a network show I had created, "The Pete Rose Roast." That would be a decade and quite a few stories away. Right now, let's go to January 15, 1967, the date of the first Super Bowl.

I was getting ready to leave for Europe at the time to direct the 1967 Figure Skating Championship from Vienna, Austria. The taping took place during the same week as the first Super Bowl, though in 1967 it wasn't called the "Super Bowl." It wasn't named the Super Bowl until Super Bowl II, a game which I directed.

After the first Super Bowl, Bill McPhail called me and said the event was more hype than game and that the L.A. Coliseum was half empty even with the local blackout. I think he said that because he hadn't brought me back to the states in time to direct the game.

My next call came from Art Linkletter Productions to direct a Roy Rogers and Dale Evans Special.

As a kid, I had seen them ride the range in B-rated celluloid westerns, but now the world had changed and they were relegated to doing occasional guest appearances. Roy and Dale showed up in matching, spangled western outfits. They were teamed up with the New Christy Minstrels. Our rehearsal ended with a tricky musical number, "Ida Rose." While I was trying to figure out how to camera-cut the jumping lyrics, Roy gave me one of his squinty glances. No problem for him. He could hear a song once and knew it cold. All you had to do was put the words down on a cue card.

Roy was a pleasant guy and easy to get along with. Before we went on the air, everybody was more interested in what his wife, Dale, had to say so that the crew could make their final preparations. As we neared airtime, Dale returned all coiffed-up on horseback, waiting to make her entrance onto the stage. When I asked about Roy, she nodded to the area behind the hay bales away from the hot TV lights. As I drew closer, I could hear Roy talking to his horse, verbally reassuring his nervous mount. Roy caught me with another one of his squinty glances, mounted his horse, and joined Dale as they broke into the theme song she had written, "Happy Trails To You."

On April 16, 1967, I directed a CBS soccer game which would start off a schedule of Sunday telecasts that would cover the National Professional Soccer League. The CBS brass had picked the marketing slogan, 'Just for kicks!' And I said. "Just for the hell of it, can somebody tell me how I'm gonna get around not showing the thousands of empty seats?"

No problem they said. "When the ball is kicked in the air, just pan the field and don't have the camera follow the ball up in the air."

"Brilliant!" I told them. Just frigging brilliant!

Sure enough, come game day there were only 8,000 spectators in Memorial Stadium along with 40,000 empty seats as the Baltimore Bays, their home team, won a 1-0 'snore' with a one-kick score over the Atlanta Chiefs.

Jack Whitaker did the call with Danny Blanchflower, a former Irish Footballer, doing the color with what sounded like a strange negative attitude. But then I figured out the former star was the first guy to 'tell it like it is'. Danny never hesitated to be brutally frank about the brand of soccer he was covering for his employer, CBS. If the player dribbling the ball didn't boot it the way he liked, he called it a "horrible turn."

One time when the ball wasn't being advanced to his liking, he said something like, "The midfield isn't generating anything for the forwards. They're just waiting for them to die of boredom."

I found it all a bore, myself. I never looked forward to doing those games. The only consolation I had was that I'd soon be covering the Triple Crown of Racing and someone else would have to direct this drek.

In the 1968 Kentucky Derby, Dancer's Image crossed the finish line first but was disqualified when traces of 'bute' were discovered in his post-race urinalysis. Phenylbutazone (Bute) is an anti-inflammatory medication that also relieves pain. Second place finisher Forward Pass was declared the winner and he would also go on to win the Preakness, and my cameras would again feature Lucille Markey of Calumet Farm in the Winner's Circle.

After the Preakness, we departed Baltimore by train. Every year, Bill McPhail would charter a railroad car and have it joined to the 7:30 p.m. to Manhattan. During the trip most of our conversation included mention of the colt having won the first two legs of the Triple Crown.

The last stop was 'last call' at Toots Shor's. By then a quiet Heywood Brown, who had done the color commentary on the race, began to overflow with the thought of Forward Pass winning the Belmont and him having to explain that Mrs. Markey had won a tainted Triple Crown due to her horses Derby victory being achieved by a disqualification. So now with Forward Pass having won the Derby and the Preakness that brings us to the 1968 Belmont Stakes. I was worried, like Heywood, about disappointing or, worse yet, alienating Mrs. Markey, who had been so kind to me and our telecasts.

A month earlier Carol and I had visited Mrs. Markey at her beautiful 800-acre Calumet Farm with its rolling pastures and white wooden fences. The main residence was a roomy brick house with the servants quarters in the rear. As we viewed the trophy collection, and while lunch was being prepared in the main dining room, her husband, Rear Admiral Gene Markey, was descending the staircase in a velvet ascotted robe as if he were Clark Gable. Not a far stretch since they were best friends. Movie stars often visited and drank their bourbon there. Gene Markey had been a former producer whose previous wives included Joan Bennett, Hedy Lamarr, and Myrna Loy. Famous actresses, all of whom were accustomed to the attention of stage-door Johnnies.

Now guess what? I used my one iso camera on a horse called Stage Door Johnny, a long shot that hadn't run in the other two races against Mrs. Markey's colt, but a horse that stood out in my handicapping.

Stage Door Johnny was the fresh horse and he won Belmont's grueling mile and a half in record time, beating Mrs. Markey's colt Forward Pass who came in second, a length-and-a-half back.

Even though I had a great 'iso' of the winning horse, the highly rated telecast was a downer. The viewers' disappointment lay in the fact that the Triple Crown had eluded Forward Pass. That claim to fame wouldn't be accomplished for another six years when CBS Sports telecast Secreteriat's three victories, a Triple Crown that I covered.

Okay, time to change gears. I mustn't forget that I had three or four careers going at the same time. One was freelancing. I received a call from Four Star Pictures wanting me to direct a sports pilot hosted by Tom Harmon. Four Star wanted to do a half hour featuring the life of Gary Beban, the 1967 Heisman winner. I told Four Star that Beban was only 21 years old and he didn't have enough of a 'life' for me to make up a half hour.

I knew what I was talking about. I had written, directed, and agonized over filling lots of half hours featuring sports legends twice his age.

Tom Harmon, whom I've mentioned before, was the 1940 Heisman Winner. He really wanted to do the pilot. I could say no to Four Star but I couldn't say no to 'Old 98'. I filled most of the show with footage from the 1967 UCLA-USC Game when Beban's #1-ranked UCLA faced off against O.J. Simpson's #2-ranked USC. UCLA lost to USC 21-20, but Gary Beban still won the Heisman over O.J. Simpson. So an interview with the so-called 'Juice' was in order.

O.J. was a junior at the time, and he was married to 18-year-old Marguerite Whitley, a lovely young lady. When O.J. showed up, Harmon and I became a little reluctant about questioning him as being the 'runner up' when the footage clearly provided strong evidence of his greater playing ability.

Little did we know at the time that strong evidence didn't always work in the case of O.J. Simpson.

For the record, Gary Beban was drafted by the LA Rams, who traded him to the Washington Redskins where he ended up sitting on the bench. And the pilot Tom Harmon and I shot ended up sitting on the shelf.

In the winter of 1967, the sports department wanted to stock-up on some of their own surfing footage since surfing was being identified as the coming sport for the younger viewers. They sent me to Oahu, Hawaii, to film some of the action during "Duke Kahanamoku's Invitational Surfing Championship."

The waves were topping over twenty feet, and some of the world's best surfers were competing. I mounted my cameras on a surfboard and a chopper to get the usual slo-mo of the surfers running their boards diagonally across the water, in front of the break. My coverage didn't really thrill me. I hadn't done anything new. It was just a job I had to do. But what I found really interesting was comparing what I had shot with footage shot back when the Duke rode those giant waves fifty years earlier, before rock-n-roll and psychedelics influenced the surfing.

Duke was not his title but his given name. He was a handsome figure with his mane of white hair, his nut-colored skin and his glistening white teeth.

Duke showed me a photo of him on his old surfboard which was sixteen feet and weighed more than a hundred pounds. I pointed out another change of times. His shorts had a metal zipper while today's surfers were sporting the newly introduced Velcro on their fly. We had a good laugh at the time. Sadly, the Duke died soon after the surfing contest in January of 1968.

But let's move on to what was for me the most fascinating sports event I ever directed. It took place on December 31, 1967— The Ice Bowl.

It has been noted by reporters that I probably aired the first famous instant replay during the broadcast of the coldest game in NFL history, the 1967 NFL Championship, the game between the Green Bay Packers and the Dallas Cowboys. The Instant Replay I'm referring to is Bart Starr's quarterback sneak over his guard Jerry Kramer for the winning touchdown.

The official game-time temperature was 13 degrees below zero (minus 25 degree Celsius) with sharp winds and a wind chill factor of minus 48 degrees. Despite the frigid temperature, the game was a sellout with 50, 861 fans in attendance in the then ten-year-old outdoor football stadium. So that was The Ice Bowl. The term has since stuck, along with the Packers' nickname—borrowed from former player and long time head coach Curly Lambeau—"The frozen tundra of Lambeau Field."

These are my frozen memories of directing that New Year's Eve game. I guess the game and the telecast were the worst and best all rolled into one. It certainly was one of the coldest of days, and was probably the most dramatic game ever played in the NFL.

I was staying at the Northland, a hotel that the Packers recommended since they held a lot of their business meetings there. That Saturday night the temperature must have been about 30 degrees. Not bad. And the weatherman on TV didn't offer any kind of warning. Out the window, the sky was crystal clear.

The next morning the wake-up operator said something about the temperature being below zero. Well, okay, but when my car rental wouldn't turn over, I knew there could be trouble ahead. Luckily, I hitched a ride with the crew, who had returned to the hotel for the heating blankets we put over the cameras and some sponges to stuff in the 'field parabs' (parabolic microphones) to cut down the wind noise. It looked like it was going to be a tough day, but at least the best New York crew had been assigned to cover the game. Later, I learned that the doors at the Cowboy Hotel were frozen shut and some of the players had to kick them open. By that time, the temperature had dropped to eighteen below zero, and the wind was forty miles per hour.

When I arrived at Lambeau Field, a helicopter was hovering over the stadium and blowing the snow off the seats. Looking up at the announcers booth, it wasn't a very encouraging thought that they would be working in an open booth, battling the same weather as the players on the field.

When my crew came in with the electric blankets, Jack Buck and Ray Scott unfroze their smiles. I broke the bad news to them. The six electric blankets were going to be wrapped around my six cameras to keep them warm enough to operate.

Over on the sidelines it was slippery, and the wind biting cold. Blowers were shooting warm air in the direction of the benches but you had to be right next to them to feel the heat. I went over to talk to Jim Tunney, the alternate referee who would be handling the down markers. He was wearing three pairs of gloves and was happy his job didn't require the use of a whistle. The referee, Norm Schachter, was convinced his whistle would freeze. It eventually did, leaving Norman to holler at the players when a play was dead. Meanwhile, along the sideline heaters, still photographers were keeping their cameras warm under their parkas, hoping their lenses wouldn't crack.

I said hello to the father and son team of NFL Films Ed and Steve Sabol. Only half of their cameras were working, but they went on to record the game. And it's a good thing they did since the videotape of the telecast was erased just like the first Super Bowl and the first Instant Replay. The only thing that survived was the post-game interview with Vince Lombardi and Tom Brookshier. But thanks to the Sabols and NFL Films, the game was reconstructed from the painstaking footage they had taken.

As I headed for the remote truck, I ran into Tex Schramm, my former boss who was now the general manager of the Cowboys. Tex told me that Commissioner Rozelle wasn't going to postpone the game. There'd be no way to reschedule it for TV. On the field the grounds keepers were rolling up the tarp, but underneath there was more bad news: the playing field was frozen. The condensation layer underneath had iced. The weather was bizarre. The day before, the turf was in perfect condition.

Chuck Lane, the PR director, was the one who had to tell Lombardi that his field was frozen, but Lombardi came out of the tunnel to check the field himself. The previous summer he had paid $80,000 for electric coils to be laid six inches below the surface of the Lambeau turf. But the radiant system wouldn't work in the sub-zero weather. Lombardi looked pissed. Maybe people would think he was Machiavellian enough to let the field freeze so as to gain the advantage.

The players took the field for their warm-ups with most of them keeping their hands tucked inside their pants. This was a good time for a couple of security cops to escort me from the truck to the men's room. The passageways were totally jammed with people trying to get warm, and I didn't want to get stuck in the human flow.

Before we went on air, the control door was locked so that the icy blasts would stop cutting through me. I checked in with my two sets of announcers for the game. The telecast was to start with the announcers linked to the Cowboys, Jack Buck and Tom Brookshier. The Packer announcers, Ray Scott and Frank Gifford, would handle the second half.

We aired at one p.m., and I opened with the fans in their seats almost obscured by their own breath condensation. Rows of clouded breath came from bundled-up people in hunting jackets and hooded wool coats, some in ski masks, others wrapped in blankets and sleeping bags. During the game their loud and boisterous cheering would strangely pierce the surreal cutaway shots of the crowd.

When the Cowboys won the toss, the joke in the press box was, "Dallas won the toss and elected to go home." Up in the announcer's booth, Jack Buck set the tone by asking the audience to "Excuse me while I have a bite of my coffee."

In the first half, Green Bay scored twice with passes to Boyd Dowler, who I isolated from the end zone. The Green Bay quarterback, Bart Starr, wasn't using gloves.

Lombardi allowed the linemen to wear them but not anyone handling the ball since the ball had expanded to a rounder form due to the cold, and the quarterback needed to grip it as tightly as possible. Starr had a fur muff piece in his uniform to keep his hands warm, but his fingers still suffered frostbite.

Buck and Brookshier had a way of making you feel as if you were eaves-dropping on two of your closest friends, and when either one got excited you knew you should, too. And they did get excited as the game drew closer, with Dallas scoring on a fumble and then adding a field goal to cut the Packer lead to 14 to 10 at halftime. But there was no halftime show. The marching band couldn't perform. Their instruments had frozen. So I had to stall, and it was hard to resist panning the tens of thousands of puffs coming out in the incredible haze of breath. I ended up in the area around Section 20, to look at the players' wives who seemed to be frozen stiff in their heavy fur coats.

I dissolved up to the booth to check in with our second-half announcers. In all major sports cities a broadcaster is regarded as the voice of that team. Ray Scott was known as the Voice of the Green Bay Packers. And he worked well with Frank Gifford's low-key manner of analysis. There was no 'Biff! Bam! Pow!' approach to the game.

Before the second half got underway, I took some sideline shots of the shuddering players who had just returned from the locker room and were hopping up and down to keep warm. During the second half the field conditions worsened, and the third quarter went scoreless. In the fourth quarter I figured that Dallas had to come out throwing. I had been isolating the receivers with my end-zone cameras. Long passing plays were common with AFL teams. Don Meredith, the Dallas quarterback, shrewdly called a halfback option from midfield, and Dan Reeves

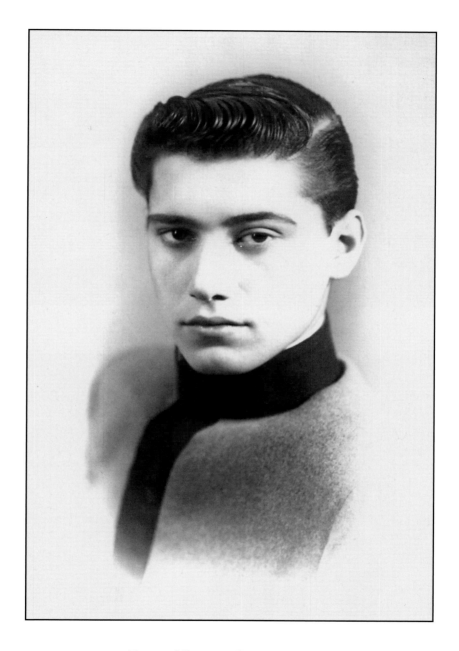

Tony while attending West Point

In the studio

Prepping Kirk Douglas

Directing Paul Hornung and Frank Gifford

Working with Jonathan Winters

In Russia with Mike Douglas

Ringside with Tom Harmon

Directing Paul Hornung and Mickey Mantle

Christopher Reeve, Carol Verna, Ted Turner, Faye Dunaway, and
Larry King

Tony with President Reagan

Congressional Record

United States of America

PROCEEDINGS AND DEBATES OF THE 100th CONGRESS, FIRST SESSION

Vol. 133	WASHINGTON, WEDNESDAY, JULY 8, 1987	No. 112

House of Representatives

TONY VERNA

HON. THOMAS M. FOGLIETTA

OF PENNSYLVANIA

IN THE HOUSE OF REPRESENTATIVES

Wednesday, July 8, 1987

Mr. FOGLIETTA. Mr. Speaker, on June 6, 1987, more than 1.5 million people in 16 locations on 5 continents joined with Pope John Paul II in a "Prayer for World Peace." A global television audience of more than 1 billion people watched this historic telecast, described by the London Times as "the most complicated live telecast ever attempted."

The producer and director of this telecast was Tony Verna, who last year produced "Live-Aid" and "Sport-Aid," global television events which used electronic technology to bring people together. Mr. Verna was born in my congressional district in Philadelphia, and it is a privilege to describe to my colleagues the enormous achievement this historic broadcast represents.

Immediately following his meeting with President and Mrs. Reagan in Rome on June 6, 1987 Pope Paul II led the "Prayer for World Peace," a recitation of the Rosary with responses coming live via satellite from congregations in the following cities: Lujan, Argentina; Mariazell, Austria; Rio de Janeiro, Brazil; Quebec, Canada; Lourdes, France; Frankfurt, Germany; Bombay, India; Guadaloupe, Mexico; Caacupe, Paraguay; Manila, Philippines; Fatima, Portugal; Dakar, Senegal; Zaragoza, Spain; Czestochowa, Poland; Knock, Ireland; and in the United States, Washington, DC.

Faces of people around the world lit up as they saw themselves on television screens along with people on five continents. Mother Theresa joined the Pope from Poland. In Manila, President Corazon Aquino prayed with the Pope, as did hundreds of thousands of people holding candles outside the cathedral. As his Holiness finished the Rosary, people around the world waved handkerchiefs at him and at each other, while church bells chimed. ABC News described the event as "an hour when the people of the world came closer together."

This historic broadcast event was made possible by U.S. technological ingenuity. Tony Verna, president of Global Media Limited, utilized 23 satellites and 28 transponders to broadcast the "Prayer for World Peace" in 12 languages—Latin, Italian, Greek, Portugese, Polish, French, Spanish, Russian, German, Dutch, Arabic, and English—to an estimated audience of 1.5 billion people.

In a recent interview, Mr. Verna explained what he sees as the vast potential of electronic communications: "In the beginning was the word of God. Satellites are manmade meteors—bits of wire, metal and silicon orbiting the Earth. They are still controlled by man, and the creativity God gives to man. When satellites give way to optical fiber, when new technologies replace the old, the word of God will still remain. Today, we are able to use the technology of these cold satellites in space to bring a lot of warmth to this globe."

Today, at the Vatican, Tony Verna will present a commemorative video and book of the "Prayer for World Peace" to his Holiness Pope John Paul II. I am pleased and privileged to pay tribute to Tony Verna on this important day.

On the set of the record-setting Live Aid Worldwide Telecast

Larry King between shows at the 1990 Goodwill Games

Pope John Paul II greets producer-director Tony Verna

Directing Mother Teresa

President George H. W. Bush with Tony Verna

Tony with Joe DiMaggio

Perry Como and his publicist chatting with John Facenda
and Tony Verna in 1953

Tony in the center with Bob Geldof to his right and surrounded
by an army of British producers.

Tony Directing the 1960 Rome Olympics

threw a 50-yard bomb to Lance Rentzel. The Cowboys took the lead 17 to 14.

I cut to Lombardi pacing along the sideline in his long winter coat and black fuzzy hat with muffs. I think it was too cold for him to look too angry. On the other side, the Dallas coach, Tom Landry, seemed almost motionless as if frozen in his long coat and fur cap. Strangely enough, back in 1956 I had shown both of these coaches on the same sideline when Landry was a defensive coach and Lombardi was an offensive coach for the New York Giants under head coach Allie Sherman.

The Pack marched down field, and the ball was now at the two-foot line. The next two running plays went nowhere. The running backs had no traction. Now the clock was down to 16 seconds left to play, and the Pack was still down by three.

Bart Starr called his last time out. I figured Starr wouldn't be running the ball since if they did they could run out the clock and lose the chance for Don Chandler to tie the game with a field goal.

Starr went over to the bench to consult with Lombardi. A couple of years later, when I was writing and directing a film that dealt with Starr being a sports legend, I asked him about that time-out conversation with his coach. He said Lombardi had asked if the right guard, Gerry Kramer, could get enough footing on the hard surface by the goal line. That's part of the story. The other part is what Gerry Kramer had told me after the game. He said that back on that Thursday he was watching films, and he noticed that Jethro Pugh, Dallas's huge defensive tackle, was staying high on short-yardage plays. Pugh was a mountain of a man at 6 foot 6, 260 pounds. He was so big he couldn't get all the way down when he lined up, Kramer had passed his observation to Lombardi, and the coach put a 'Brown 31 Wedge' to be used against Pugh in the playbook the next day on that Friday.

On the sidelines, Starr suggested they run the 'wedge', but rather handing the ball off to the fullback he thought they could run it in on a sneak. Lombardi nodded and said, "Then run it and let's get the hell out of here."

I panned the Cowboys' defensive linemen digging at the

ice with their cleats on the goal line. On the Packers' side of scrimmage, Kramer had found a convenient divot for his right foot and dug in.

In television, the best shots sometimes happen by mistake. I had directed my cameraman in the south end zone, Herman Lang, to shoot Bart Starr walking up to the line of scrimmage, then to 'pan right' and pick up the flanker, Boyd Dowler, before the ball was snapped. But when Lang tried to pan right to cover the wide receiver, his camera locked because of the cold. He kept his composure and kept his camera focused tightly on Starr, who was facing him.

Starr took the snap. Kramer came off the snap so quick that he was probably offsides. He slammed into Jethro Pugh hard and, with the help of Ken Bowman, the center, Kramer opened up enough room for Starr to go over his back and fall into the end zone. Umpire Joe Connell signaled the touchdown.

With Herman's angle from the end zone, I had a dream replay. And I reran it again and again. Gerry's name kept getting repeated every time I reran the touchdown, and he became the best known lineman in America with the 'Instant Replay' to become the title of his best-selling book.

The stadium went crazy. I broke Tom Brookshire to make a beeline sprint to the winning locker room. The fans stormed the field. The goal posts came down, the pennants were ripped off, the helmets affixed to the fence were unbolted and even the Packers' bench was stolen. I understand it was returned later and is now in the Canton Hall of Fame.

I had a camera preset in each locker room. During the game they worked the easels and flip-stands, feeding me title cards, commercial IDs, and players' names. In those days the locker rooms were full of smoke. There were cigarettes burning all over the place, and the cameramen had to keep shooing away the smoke.

No sooner had Brookshire arrived at the Packer locker room than Lombardi booted him out, along with my cameraman and soundman.

They had to stay in the hallway until Lombardi was done talking to his players, who were eager to defrost. Lombardi had a powerful way. I was familiar with that type of tight-knit bureaucracy, having experienced it first-hand at West Point. In fact, I first laid eyes on Lombardi when Army played Villanova at Michie Stadium and he was an assistant under head football coach Earl Blaik. Shortly afterward, thirty seven of those Army players were expelled for cheating, including Coach Blaik's son, the quarterback. Fortunately, they had Lombardi to help turn the Army team back to the glory days.

In 1959 he took over the winless Packers and turned them into a dynasty.

In those early days, there were major restrictions placed on the media by the coaches. Today's sport reporting is the way it should be, with athletes and coaches being interviewed before, during, and after the game. It certainly helps make the presentation more engaging for the fans.

In '67, things were different. A few weeks earlier, Lombardi had booted another one of our announcers, Jack Whitaker, out of his locker room.

Eventually, Brookshier and the crew were allowed back in. I readied the Kramer block on tape as Brookshier shouldered up to Lombardi for a two shot. Brookshier mentioned that we'd be showing the block, and Lombardi frowned, saying he wasn't sure he could see the monitor. But when he saw the play executed perfectly, he clapped, smiled, and cried out, "Atta Boy, Jerry!"

The telecast provided Kramer with a tidal wave of endorsements and business opportunities. The following week Jerry called and asked if I'd mind if he used Instant Replay for his book title. I told him I had no rights to the title and wished him the best. His book sale quadrupled expectations, and Jerry ended it with: "Thank God for the Instant Replay."

During 1968, in addition to being contracted by the network I was also extensively freelancing my services, and I was turning out various programs that I had created for my own company. I did a series of half-hour shows from Las Vegas featuring stars like Liberace who would lend assistance and accompany young want-to-be performers. Lee showed up with one of his sequined suits and a handshake that carried with it a 34-diamond candelabra ring. When I brought my mother to Vegas, another of her dreams came true when Liberace (also called Lee, or Walter Valentino) gave her one of his toothy smiles while performing.

During the sixties I also created quite a few promotional videos for corporations, organizations, and banking institutions. I directed several short films that I had written, a romance, "A Day at the Derby"; theatrical short, "The Hambeltonian"; and "Instant Quarterback," featuring Johnny Unitas, the Baltimore Colts star quarterback. I knew that every kid wanted to throw with Johnny's dead-on accuracy, so I knew it was important that I capture John's throwing mechanics close up. We had set up in a hangar-type facility, and as the camera tightened on Unitas I told him to pick up some targets around the studio since they wouldn't be seen in my close-up work.

That was okay for the short passes, but when I rolled to capture the bombs, Unitas got more inventive with his long-range targets. I had my eye in the eyepiece as he let loose with a series of bombs.

Once he depleted the rack of footballs, I hollered, "Cut!" and told him how realistic it looked to me. Johnny turned to me with one of his bashful smiles as he pointed to a row of colored gels hanging in the distant rafters. He had blasted a hole into the colored plastic framed in each of the clip-ons.

In 1968, 60 Minutes started ticking at CBS, and I was assigned to direct the second NFL AFL Championship which was now being called Super Bowl II.

Super Bowl I had two directors, and Commissioner Rozelle kiddingly asked if I could do Super Bowl II without a second director, as they had on Super Bowl I. Pete should have asked how could I help the game from being such a bore. The Packers took control of the game and won easily 33-14.

In May of 1968, President Richard Nixon would be the first sitting U.S. President to attend the Kentucky Derby at Churchill Downs. President Nixon was also a familiar voice on my broadcasts as he regularly placed a call to a winning locker room. Meanwhile, My producer, Chuck Milton, and I decided to take care of some of our buddies, hockey players from the New York Rangers, by getting them box seats behind the President. When my cameras cut to Nixon, he'd be sitting there in his trademark slouch, exhausted from the day's activities. Behind him our hockey friends sat in their trademark sprawl exhausted from the night before.

In another one of my creations I capitalized on the jogging craze of the sixties with a ten-minute film featuring Jonathan Winters and Rocky Marciano portraying two joggers on a beach who comically demonstrated the physical fitness benefits that resulted from jogging.

Rocky stayed at my beach house in Malibu. Of course, with Jonathan Winters popping in, there were plenty of laughs. Since I was living a life knee-deep in celebrities, I often created a short film that would wrap a star or two around a simple plot that could appeal to a wide audience. The script I wrote called for Jonathan Winters and Rocky Marciano, two enormously popular celebrities, to portray two lonely joggers and how their actions culminated with hundreds of people jogging along with them down the beach.

Rocky had been retired thirteen years. He loved being by the ocean. He was a real health nut, and I made sure I had a lot of vegetables on hand and a jar of honey to sweeten his morning coffee. He'd wake up and stroll around the deck in his robe, looking like the undisputed champ that he was. I'd call him champ. He liked that. And we spent a good deal of time talking about things like the computer fight, called Superfight, he had with Mohammed Ali and how Ali kept knocking off his toupee. Rocky told me how producers of Superfight had amassed the critical historical data on both him and Ali—their strengths and weaknesses, their abilities to take a punch, their tendency to cut, their fighting heart, and their skills. The producers fed it all into a computer and presented the mythical match up as a super fight.

I've always thought that Superfight was the true beginning of the merging of reality and fantasy in sports. The result of the computer match was a Marciano knockout in the 13th round. Rocky died before ever seeing the film.

I saw Mohammed Ali after Marciano's death, and he showed me the bruise marks on his body, the result of body shots that were for real.

While Rocky was staying with me, he also talked about being tired of having to travel around looking for business deals. He was now bound for Chicago with a connection on a free charter flight to Iowa. Before leaving, he opened his suitcase. Inside were hundreds of cheap paper brochures that highlighted his career. I don't think Rocky realized that the photo layout was poor and the print didn't always line up.

After he left my house in Malibu, Rocky flew to Chicago, where he boarded a small private plane to make a buck in Iowa. The pilot was not instrument rated, and as he approached their destination, Newton, Iowa, it was a stormy night with no visibility. The pilot tried to drop his Cessna below the low-hanging clouds looking for the runway, but he came out of the clouds two miles short of the runway and was less than one hundred feet off the ground when his plane struck a lone oak tree in the center of a cornfield.

Rocky had been flying in the front passenger seat, and the impact was so forceful that it completely crushed his jaw. His face was unrecognizable. The only way the state troopers realized that the passenger in the downed aircraft could be the champ was because of those cheap brochures, which were blowing through the cornfields.

On learning of his death, my then partner, the producer Hal Uplinger, and I flew to Florida to pay our respects to his wife Barbara, who he had been married to for 19 years. It was so sad. They had one daughter, Mary Ann, and an adopted boy, Rocco, who was in a playpen. She showed us the money clip that had been removed from the tangled wreckage. The large heavy money clip was bent and twisted.

Rocky Marciano grew up poor during the Great Depression. Money was tight in his working class family, and Rocky was tight with money.

Barbara Marciano, Rocky's wife, did not have a checking or savings account, so Hal and I gave her $25,000 to hold her over until she got things straightened out.

Hal Uplinger put together an all-star television tribute for Rocky Marciano. One of the performers was the retired legend Jimmy Durante, who played the piano and sang Rocky's favorite, the classic "September Song." My 35-mm cameras swung around on their giraffe cranes, and Jimmy ended up with the tearful lyrics: "These precious days I'll spend with you." It was a perfect ending. Durante had done it in one take.

But as I hugged Jimmy, he whispered he wanted to do it again. He confided that he didn't want to go home and sit on the couch. He wanted to work. I ordered the cameras and giraffes to set up again, and I brought a smile to Jimmy's great face.

Another star who appeared on the tribute was Robert Stack, the actor. After the shoot, he showed me his gun collection, and I told him about the flintlock I had picked up in Yugoslavia and how terrified I was in meeting Marshall Tito. Stack told me that during the Second World War he and a fellow actor, Robert Young, were scared to death, themselves, because of all the anti-Nazi films they had made together. Both he and Robert Young were positive they were on Hitler's hit list.

At this time I began writing my first book, Playback. It came about because in December 1969 I was dating a movie actress who was a friend of the famed TV performer Shari Lewis, the ventriloquist who had partnered with a sock puppet named Lambchop. We were invited to Shari's home, and on arrival she said to be careful. Shari explained that she was capable of speaking out of both sides of her mouth. I asked her about Roone Arledge and the days when he started his television career on her show. Shari recalled him as the stage manager on her morning show back in 1960, but she didn't recall him ever producing her show.

Shari was a sharp lady. She knew that her puppet show had been a natural for early colorcasts. The camera coverage on her show was mainly a two shot of her and her hand puppet.

There were no quick moves that could distort the electronic colors if they had to repaint themselves on the surface of the viewing screen. Another thing was that the lighting for color had to be hot. It wasn't too bad for her sock puppet with a fleece head, but back in the 1920s, when television was only in the experimental and testing stage, the lighting was hot as hell. For their tests they used puppets instead of people, and—because of the intense heat—they could only use puppets with wooden heads to test their television transmission.

In England, Baird Television used a ventriloquist's dummy head named 'Spooky Bill'; in the USA, RCA used the wooden head of 'Felix the Cat'.

Shari's husband, Jeremy Tarcher, an esteemed publisher, asked if I'd like to get together on a book deal that would include the birth of the Instant Replay. Jeremy's idea was for me to author an insider's book that would cover the major sports being televised.

The book, 'Playback', became a reality and was published the following year, and the year after it came out, CBS aired Playback as a half-hour television network special with me playing me. In the book's introduction, Bill McPhail, the head of CBS Sports, explained the course he had decided for the Instant Replay to take, after he had okayed my initial airing.

McPhail had to okay the unheard-of request I made in needing one of the few New York studio tape machines to be hauled away so that it could travel down the freeway and be parked at my remote site in Philadelphia to do a sports experiment.

I always loved Bill McPhail for being one of the guys. Bill's first concern was being one-of-the guys for the viewers. Bill had always encouraged his producers and directors to use instant visualization to help his network viewers understand the exact 'why' of the 'what" that was happening in a blink of the eye. Bill favored anything that could help the home viewer understand what had transpired in a matter of seconds without the benefit of being able to see it again.

I always thought the bosses who followed him at CBS Sports were more interested in how many commercials could be aired. And their cold approach to anything creative was one of the reasons why I eventually quit CBS Sports. But that's another story for another decade.

But to get back to Bill McPhail, one visual effect that particularly delighted him was when I superimposed the strut of a wing over a flying skier to show that, as the velocity increased over the skier who had leaned over his skis, the air pressure passed quicker at the bottom of the skis than the air traveled above the skier's curved body.

I think Bill just got a kick listening to announcers like Art Devlin trying to explain Bernouli's Principle and relating it to why airplanes could fly. He might have used the same principle to explain the workings of a boomerang.

At the end of the sixties, in 1969, I had been living at a beach house in Malibu, but I had so many European assignments that I shared a summer lease in Nice, France, with my friend Jack Whitaker. The geographical location of my beach house played a strange role in one of my appearances on TV. That year, in August, 1969, Charles Manson, the guru leader, sent his followers out on a murder spree that killed seven people, including the well-known actress Sharon Tate. At a later time Vincent Bugliosi, the chief prosecutor, and I appeared as guests on the same "Mike Douglas Show."

After the show, Bugliosi and I talked about a surfin'-musician, Terry Melcher, who could have been the real target Manson was looking for that night. And I told Bugliosi that I was living at the time at 22114 Pacific Coast Highway next to the home of actress Doris Day where her son, Melcher, was staying and the scary thought was that he was probably not only visiting me that night, but probably sleeping on my couch.

Malibu, the scenic place to live, was no longer desirable for me. I moved to Beverly Hills and finished writing Playback (Follett Publication). In its finished form, it was a highly illustrated guide of how I directed the major sports over the previous decade.

Some things you remember well, and other things you don't. In the late '60s I directed the opening of the U.S. Air Force Academy in Colorado, but research provides me with no details to refresh my memory. I recall directing the opening of the National Cowboy & Western Heritage Museum in Oklahoma, but again research doesn't confirm it one way or the other. I recall directing a major rodeo in Tucson, but their research showed no signs of my being there. Strange! You see, I have this photograph showing me being strung-up by the rodeo's lynching party when they rode up on horseback to haul me off the plane.

A few amusing stories from this period, however, have

remained firmly locked in my memory; especially the one pertaining to the Kentucky Derby.

Churchill Downs called Bill McPhail and asked if he could help get a certain CBS star to attend the Derby. In the past, attending celebrities had included Babe Ruth, Jack Dempsey, John Wayne...but this year, they wanted the television talking horse, Mr. Ed. I told McPhail that I didn't think the president of Churchill Downs, Wathen Knebelkam, fully understood about the peanut butter and the nylon strings needed to make Mr. Ed appear to be talking.

I called Art Lubin, the show's producer in Los Angeles, but got his assistant. I asked if they'd be willing to let us fly Mr. Ed to Kentucky. The assistant gave a million reasons why not. Then I asked, "What if the horse was flown on his own private plane?" That got her thinking. But then I had to pass on the one condition that the plane's pilot had made. The pilot said that if the horse acted up he'd have to shoot him. The last thing the assistant said before she hung up was, "Shoot Mr. Ed?!"

My next Derby story comes at the end of the sixties, when Bill Creasy and I were using Eddie Arcaro as our analyst. We'd also included an injured Bill Shoemaker who was nursing a broken leg from being thrown from a horse during a race.

The night after the telecast, we celebrated in the hotel suite Aracaro shared with Shoemaker. The next morning, Arcaro called Creasy and me to come over. "They've kidnapped Shoemaker."

Sure enough, all of the doors were still locked and there was no way Shoe could have walked out of that suite. Our search ended when we saw his 2-1/2-size shoe lying on the floor. He had been wearing only one shoe. The other foot was in the cast.

Apparently when the party ended and the lights were being turned off, someone closed the oversized Murphy bed, not thinking that an injured jockey may have passed out on it.

My next Derby story comes via the mysterious Rod Serling. I got a call from an agency salesman, Larry Kent. He said he had started out handling Roy Rogers' merchandise and now he was helping pro football teams in selling team merchandise with their logos on it. And he wanted me to come up with something different in the way of a commercial for NFL Properties. So Hal Uplinger and I put together a commercial with the halting voice of Rod Serling doing the voice over.

Rod was known primarily as the creator of the Twilight Zone but was now using that fame to make the same money voicing a one-minute commercial as he did for working eleven months on a screenplay.

When Rod showed up, all 5 foot 4 inches of him, he immediately took his unseen script and placed it on the easel in front of his mike to look it over. His deep tan brought out the deep wrinkles in his face. Within five minutes he said he was ready to do a take. Rod read the copy perfectly on the first take, using a tenth of the studio time I had booked for the voice-over. I said it was a perfect reading. He asked to do it again, and a minute later I had another reading that sounded exactly like the first one. When I asked him why he did it a second time, he said he felt guilty taking that kind of money for so little work.

Before he left, he told me to bet the second horse on the second race the day of the Derby. I told him it was too early in the week and the entrees weren't in. He didn't seem fazed. He kept on chain smoking. I asked how much did he want me to bet on it. He said the bet wasn't for him, it was for me. Strange! We shook hands, and he left in a cloud of smoke.

Come Derby Day, I bet the second horse on the second race and it won. When Rod was told what had happened, he said, "That's amazing!"

The decade closed with me moving back to New York. My ex-wife had whisked my daughter out of the state without notice, to live in Connecticut. I moved back to Manhattan to pursue my visitations. On the flight I recall being as lonely a person at the end of the sixties as I was at the beginning of the decade.

Chapter Four

The Seventies

By 1970 six years had passed since I aired the first Instant Replay.

It was now a regular fixture, being used constantly throughout telecasts.

And it was 'being used constantly' because it was easier to do. The audio man, the tape operator, and the director didn't have to struggle with the original array of specific commands that I originally had to create to implement the Instant Replay. My original process was a very tedious process, and that's why there were so few replays on my first telecasts.

Look at it this way. In a Wright Brothers' plane, it was dependent on the pilot's physical efforts throughout the flight in order to control the plane. This continuous wrestling with the controls was so tedious that it made longer flights impossible at the time.

Well, the same kind of fatigue limited the first Instant Replays. Beeps had to be placed on the tape by the audio man. The tape had to be physically rewound to a certain point by the tape operator. And when it was played back, the director had to listen for the appropriate beeps to confirm the location of the recorded play on the tape's video.

My original working equation wasn't flawed. It had the same fate as any other invention once it's introduced. You expected it to be improved upon. Electronic circuitry replaced my three-man mechanical operation. The Instant Replay became a built-in feature of a telecast, but it was being achieved with so little hassle that the Instant Replay was no longer being hailed for its own identity.

As I've said, it was now 'built-in'. No one cared that there was a time when the Instant Replay didn't exist. Nobody cared or wanted to bring that fact out. Nostalgia is one thing in broadcasting history, but there is a place, too, for recognizing the role of the individual in pioneering a new way of doing things.

My contemporaries had no idea what I was striving to achieve. And once the Instant Replay became a reality, those same contemporaries began to treat the technique as if it had emerged automatically as an expected by-product of live transmission.

Before December 7. 1963, the Instant Replay was not only unknown, as noted; it was unforeseen. By 1970, the Instant Replay was seldom singled out as a conceptual breakthrough. The predominant thinking was that Live TV and the Instant Replay were a combination that naturally went together. Like pizza and beer or Tiger Woods and Gatorade 'Tiger'. Who cared how they came together? They were inseparable.

Yes, certain things do go together, like when I met Carol Blum. We went together like ham and eggs, me being the former, and we were married three months later.

A close friend, producer Stan Blum, no relation, had introduced us. Carol's maiden name was Hahn. She had come to the sports department from the news department where she had been an executive secretary. She originally started on the Ed Sullivan Show. These are Carol's words about her first meeting with Ed Sullivan in his dressing room.

"Mr. Sullivan was in full makeup, walking around in his boxer shorts. He said 'hel-lew' and that he was waiting for his trousers to be pressed. In the meantime, he wanted me to have all his cue cards changed.

"When I left his dressing room, I asked a key staff member, what should I do with all the notes Mr. Sullivan had dictated to me. I was told to chuck them. 'In ten minutes Ed wouldn't even remember he gave them to you.'"

Carol didn't find the Sullivan Show to her liking. She asked to be transferred to the news department where 'behind the scenes' would be more friendly. In fact, Jennifer, her five year old, at times would even sit on Douglas Edwards' lap. This was so much better than the Sullivan Show, where the producer wanted Carol to sit on his lap.

We both had five-year-old daughters, Tracy and Jennifer, and we'd go on to have Eric, a son together.

When I moved back to Manhattan I was directing a lot of games with CBS's number one analyst Frank Gifford. After one of the games, Frank asked me to pal around with him and Don Meredith so I could get a better feel of what Meredith was like off the field. Frank was right. Don was dynamite. And with this being his last season, he would be available as an analyst.

We set up a meeting for Meredith to meet Bill McPhail in Manhattan. But McPhail's only interest was to offer Don, a Dallas regional game contract for $20,000. McPhail's mind wasn't on Don Meredith but on the original golden boy of the NFL, Frank Gifford. Bill made it clear that he expected Frank to honor his remaining year at CBS rather than jumping ship to do color for ABC's Monday Night Football.

Afterward, I thought I'd be having lunch with Frank and Don to go over how things went at the McPhail meeting, but Frank had other plans. Now that he was unavailable, he set up a quick lunch with Roone Arledge It became an opportunity for Roone to offer Meredith ten grand more—$30,000 to do Monday Night Football. And, as they say, the rest is history. A year later, Gifford was free to join Meredith along with another of Arledge's additions: Howard Cossel.

As I was preparing to move back East, I received a call from two of my colleagues, Hal Uplinger and Steve Perry. They wanted me to help them out in producing "Duke Ellington and the Monterey Jazz Festival" as a live television pickup on 35 mm film.

Question: How do you do a live television show on film for theatrical distribution? One way was what Richard Burton had done in 1963, just before he left for Mexico to shoot a conventional theatrical film, "Night of the Iguana."

Burton had agreed to let Electovision shoot his Broadway performance of "Hamlet" as a theatrofilm. Basically, it was a television pickup filmed off a monitor. But the trick was to double the standard 525-line transmission in hopes of providing a clearer picture when it was blown up on the screen.

But it didn't turn out that way. The tech guys in my crew saw the film and told me that the close-ups of Burton were too dark. They said no one had taken into consideration that the theatrical lighting wasn't sufficient to provide the clarity needed for a higher definition kinescope recording. As expected, Burton pulled the theatrofilm two weeks after its release.

That was seven years earlier then when we were trying to do "Duke Ellington and the Monterey Jazz Festival" as another 'live' 35-millimeter theatrical film, and attempting to do it in a different manner. The plan was to have our television director, Norman Abbott, be able to 'cut' the live event on individual film cameras at the same time he was cutting the event with his four live television cameras. And to pull that off, four film cameras had to be slaved to the corresponding four television cameras so that the 'cuts' made by Norman could be marked directly onto each of the films for later editing.

Norman's direction was first rate, and the show was cut together in no time since all the edit marks were known. The end result had the high quality look of a theatrical film, but, as far as I know, nothing ever came of the project. I never found out where or when the film ever played.

Next came Super Bowl IV, played on January 11, 1970, in New Orleans, Louisiana. The AFL champion Kansas City Chiefs defeated the NFL champion Minnesota Vikings, 23–7, but as far as the telecast was concerned, I had a noise problem.

The noise problem was in my control truck that was underneath the double deck stands at Tulane Stadium. At the time it was the largest steel constructed stadium in the world and with my control truck parked underneath those metal stands, it sounded as if all 80,000 attendees were banging their feet above my head so as to prevent me from hearing Jack Buck do his play-by-play.

My analysts for Super Bowl IV were Frank Gifford and Pat

Summerall. The year before, I sat between the two of them in the stands at Super Bowl III in Miami, when Joe Namath upset the NFL Colts. We knew the next Super Bowl, number IV, would be drawing a huge TV audience. And it did. It was viewed by more people than watched Neil Armstrong walking on the moon the previous summer.

That game came with a lot of problems. The day before the game with the rehearsal for the stadium's pre-game show, a performing tiger broke loose from his trainer and pounced on my producer, Bill Fitts, who was so hung-over it must have been his worst nightmare. I helped pull Bill away from the animal. Fortunately he wasn't injured, but some of the crew seemed sorry that the tiger had been declawed.

When I went on the air, there was a pre-game feature already taking place on the playing field. It was a gimmick-race between two air balloons, one marked NFL and one marked AFL. But the pilot of the ship labeled AFL lost control of his craft, and it headed straight up and out of the stadium. The other balloon, the NFL balloon, crashed into the stands where it was soon ripped apart by the AFL fans.

And there was more. Pat O'Brien, the veteran movie actor, took the field with an introduction that honored his hundred screen credits. O'Brien proceeded to recite the words of the national anthem to the accompaniment of Doc Severinson's trumpet, but the public address system went dead and didn't come back until O'Brien was telling us about "the rockets red glare."

And there was even more. With the Super Bowl being in New Orleans, the promoters thought halftime an opportune time to recreate the Battle of New Orleans which ended the War of 1812.

From each end of the field came a cavalry charge. Horseback riders in period uniforms fired their muskets at each other as end-zone cannons boomed away. Unfortunately the horses weren't told about the cannons. The animals reared up and bolted, some dumping their riders on the field.

But the cannons kept firing until one of them misfired. We didn't know it at the time but a member of the crew sustained an injury that would eventually cause him the loss of his hand.

The game, too, was a blowout. The Chiefs dominated the Vikings despite the Vikings being a 13-point favorite. Kansas City beat Minnesota, 23 to 7. The game was a snore but at least it squared the Super Bowls between the AFL and NFL at two games apiece.

The stadium crowd was typical of how the crowd had changed since the inception of the Instant Replay. The problem came when the Instant Replay proved a game official wrong. There was no way I could ignore a stadium of fans chanting the word bullshit loud enough in Louisiana for even Bert Bell to hear it in his Pennsylvania resting site.

Perhaps the NBA's Pacers-Pistons Brawl in 2004 set the record for the most viewed replays in one game, as well as the most viewed by a police force. There were no serious injuries, but nine players and seven fans were identified and criminal charges were filed.

That leads to me to recall when my crew and I had our own direct encounter with the fans. The incident, I later read, was similar to one back in 1924 when the New York Giants were playing their football in the Polo Grounds. The game was a sellout, and part of the throng outside came up with an idea on how to get in. They dismantled a telephone pole and battered the admission gates open.

As for what happened to my crew, in 1959 I was directing an NFL game in Yankee Stadium. When the final gun went off, a drunken mob of Giants' fans poured onto the field and began rocking one of the wooden goal posts until it came down. The cops didn't intervene. They were happy to have the drunks unleash their emotions on the upright and not on them.

But four of the drunks hoisted the cross bar on their shoulders and marched around the stadium. As they headed out, they veered toward the rear of my remote truck with the goal post in ramrod position. My technical director, Sandy Bell, grabbed a couple of heavy-duty wrenches and handed me one of them. When the drunken stream of curses came close enough, we swung open the back doors before the ram-rodders tried to slam into the truck. I guess our offense was better than theirs, and they backed off.

By the '70s, more sporting events were being covered and with that came evidence that the crowds were becoming more aggressive and almost demanding to be seen on television. It didn't go unnoticed that we had been adding cameras to our telecasts. Some in the crowd began holding up cards proclaiming CBS Sports to be number #1. Those fans knew they'd probably get on camera sooner or later.

The '70s were also a period of great unrest, and some of the banners expressed confirmation of the Civil Rights Movement or opposition to the Vietnam War.

I think fans have always felt that certain rights were built into their attendance at the game. I was showing the Mohawks and Afros, along with the shaved heads painted in their team's colors and those weird hairdos air-brushed in rainbow colors. But I was careful not to show anyone heckling opposing players with curses or obscene gestures.

I also remember a time when the fans even turned on their own team.

This was back in the '60s when I was televising a San Francisco-49ers game from Kezar Stadium. San Francisco had lost a few in a row, and the crowd was pissed. I readied a camera in the tunnel to capture the 49ers leaving the field and coming through the tunnel back to their lockers. The only camera position I could get was shooting through a screen canopy that covered the exposed opening of the tunnel. I soon found out why the tunnel was covered. As the 49ers came into the tunnel, their fans let loose with a dangerous barrage of garbage and glass bottles.

A lot of that drunken behavior had begun with tailgating in the parking lot. If you look back in history you'll find there were drunken tailgaters at the Battle of Bull Run. The spectators parked their carriages on a hill so they could 'knock them back' as they watched the South take on the North.

My guess is that when MMLXX Super Bowl Deutschland is played in years to come, the same loutish behavior often witnessed during American tailgating will find little trouble crossing the seas and blending in with the hooliganism often displayed during European soccer.

But for now—let's think of the good old days when the crowds were only empowered with 'the wave'. It wasn't just the fans, though, sending a ripple in those early years. The players knew when the camera was on them, too. I did a lot of games where after scoring the player raised the ball over his head and threw it down into the turf as hard he could. For the record, the first spike in front of the camera was by Homer Jones of the New York Giants in 1965.

Let's move on to 1970. I remarried, with Chet Forte as my best man. He was then the director of Monday Night Football.

One night, along with Howard Cosell, Chet showed up at Rose's, a drinking joint which use to be down the street from CBS. I thought Cosell came along to challenge me to a game of knock rummy, since our good friend and keen historian Beano Cook had suggested the match-up due to our ability to remember all the discards. But when they began downing martinis, silver bullets, I knew Chet and Howard had more than playing cards in mind. The conversation turned to me jumping ship to ABC.

I ordered another round of martinis and told them that just a month earlier Roone, himself, had approached me on the matter at P.J. Clarke's—and that I'd decided to stay put.

Howard wasn't happy with turndowns. As we left the bar, he kept telling me that ABC Sports was the future. And then, when we passed the CBS building, he shouted to the upper floors, "Verna quits. That's right, he quits!"

That was Howard, always playing the role, blowing it out with his cigar smoke and acting the part he thought was expected of him.

While we're at it, a couple of years later, at Roone's request, I had lunch with one of his negotiators, the highly respected ABC lawyer Irwin Weiner. He was a pleasant man. We had a pleasant lunch, but that was it. I was staying with CBS.

In 1971 my first book, Playback, a guide to viewing sports on TV, had been published and I flew to Chicago to promote it on a popular TV talk show.

It was the "Fran Allison Show." Fran had gained her reputation in the forties when she hosted the puppet show "Kukla, Fran and Ollie," one of the first broadcasts NBC transmitted on their coaxial cable.

Fran was just like the other famous puppeteer, Shari Lewis—'quick as quick-silver'.

Fran read a passage from my book, which referred to a New York Times newspaper article written by Jack Gould and published on November 4, 1963. This was roughly a month before the first Instant Replay appeared on the Army-Navy Game, and the article claimed that the 'end-zone coverage' on AFL games was superior to the NFL side-angle coverage.

The column was in reference to the November 3, 1963, AFL game in which "Don Breaux of Denver uncorked touchdown strikes covering 70, 45, 43 and 27 yards." And that at the same game, "Daryle Lamonica countered for Buffalo with scoring throws of 74 and 35 yards."

The game had turned into an air battle that Buffalo ended up winning 30 to 28. For the record, let me note that I was able to reconfirm my memory of these events. In September of 2007 I contacted Michael Flansburgh of the New York Times Archive Department to verify the facts. I was actually able to download the column and was pleased to find that my account of the events was fully accurate. On Fran Allison's show, I explained that camera shots from behind the goal post would certainly provide a good view of those pass patterns, but I felt, as I still do now, that live game action should be covered with a press-box view and that end-zone variations serve better as videotape reruns played later.

Pointing out that Jack Gould's article had appeared shortly before I aired the first Instant replay, Fran asked if 'that article' and 'that game' led me to speed up my desire to make the Instant Replay a reality, and I said they had. As I noted in the introduction of my book Playback, the Times' article bugged me. I wanted to come up with something to show them that CBS knew how to televise a football game. But for the time being, I was fortunate that the mail from our viewers supported the press-box approach as the preferred coverage. That support was enough to have Bill McPhail decide to continue with CBS' sideline coverage and, for me, to push to come up with a way to replay that complementary video instantly.

Now, let's switch to a totally different subject: ice hockey. I was assigned as the director for several Stanley Cup Championships. And that meant I quickly had to learn why there were circles on the ice. Then I had to figure out the jargon used by the broadcasters, like "the Canadians are playing up high," and I had to be taught the rules, like why a goal had been disallowed because the scorer's skate had preceded the puck into the crease.

For me hockey was a fast and confusing sport. And for me it didn't matter if they played it indoors or out. One second a guy is stick-handling up the ice, the next second he's drop-passing, and then up comes another guy who slaps the puck at a hundred miles per hour at the net. I soon realized that hockey was a cameraman's sport. The better the cameramen the better the coverage. I had a good rapport with the cameramen in Boston, St. Louis, and New York, but forging a link with the guys in Montreal and Quebec was a problem. Many of the Canadians considered themselves to be the only broadcasters capable of using cogent camera shots, and I told them that such a claim was absurd.

My biggest problem with their coverage was that once a slap shot was taken, they would cut away to another camera fixed on the goalie. That sequence didn't work for me because it didn't always confirm where the puck ended up. A puck could carom. It could go in, around, or along the back of the net. So rather than switching cameras I had the cameraman zoom to the net. A fast zoom rather than a fast cut was how I handled it.

On my return to Montreal the following week, I found a newspaper clipping pasted above my chair. One of the local columnists had agreed with me on how I covered 'shots on goal'. Things were never the same after that. Let's say there was a Canadian chill in the air. I don't recall much about the games, but one incident comes back to me vividly. In the late '60s, Bobby Hull, the Canadian hockey star, was invited to work as a guest analyst with our play-by-play guy, Dan Kelly.

As usual, on the night before the telecast I went out for a pop with my announcers. But on this night some jerk came out of nowhere and popped Hull in the eye while he was sitting at the bar with me. The a-hole wanted to show his girl how tough he was, but what he really showed her was how he could be flattened with just one punch by Hull. The next morning, Bobby woke up with a shiner. Luckily the girl I was dating at the time, Miss Iceland, had enough fair-skin pancake to cover up the black eye on Bobby's pale face.

On the subject of ice hockey and Canada, there's some past history that I found interesting. The Canadians told me that in 1955, three years before videotape came along, they had filmed a live goal off one of their monitors in the studio. They claimed to have used a hot-processor so that the kinescope could be developed within thirty seconds and be available for the studio to play it back as an 'almost instant replay' about a minute later.

If we stay on the subject of 'almost instant replay' and go even further back to 1936, you'll find that the Germans were also trying an 'almost instant replay' when they mounted a film camera on top of a Fernseh remote truck that roamed the streets of Berlin, looking for news stories. When the film came out of the camera it traveled as a continuous band into the developing machine inside the truck below it. In about a minute, the film was ready to pass through a flying spot scanner so it could be electronically transmitted to their television station for airing.

And there were other sports that had attempted an 'almost instant replay'. Horse racing tried it back in 1941. They attached a lightweight binocular camera to each of the eight patrol judges' field glasses, so they could record eight sections of the race. The film was spliced and viewed by the stewards the following morning. This system was refined in 1945 when film cameras were installed in towers. But it still wasn't very instant.

It was in 1970 that my team came up with the actor John Forsythe, who was instantly likeable. John had just returned from Paris, where he'd shot the spy thriller "Topaz" for Alfred Hitchcock. John was itching to do live TV, but not anything dramatic. He wanted to do something that related to his passion for live horse racing, and he asked Hal Uplinger and me to give it some thought. Knowing that John had this great voice and crisp diction, we put together a package where he'd host some live features from Hollywood Park. To nobody's surprise, John's suavity and his upper-class elegance went hand in hand with the Sport of Kings. I recently visited with John at the Hollywood Turf Club. For a man going on 90, he was in fine spirits considering he had undergone major heart and eye surgery. When I mentioned to John that most of the friends we had in common had passed away, John smiled and said, "We still have each other."

In May, 1969, I began covering a two-year package of AAU Track and Field events that Marvin Sugarman Productions had sold to CBS Sports. If you don't know the name Marvin Sugarman, let me tell you this—if you had called Central Casting and asked them to send over a super-salesman they would have sent over Marvin Sugarman. We first met in CBS Studio 45 when I was visiting Jim Hirschfeld, the gifted director of Marvin's children's show, "Captain Kangaroo."

When Jim introduced us, it came with an unexpected downfall of ping-pong balls that had been dislodged by the lighting men working on the grid above us. These were remnants from an earlier show when the Captain had gone postal with his toy burp gun. I encouraged Marvin to ping-pong himself, suggesting that he venture to sports as well, a move for which he later thanked me, as well he should have, considering Marvin went on to sell sports shows to CBS, NBC and ABC for the next 20 years.

The package Marvin Sugarman had sold to CBS involved the 1969 and 1970 AAU Tack and Field competitions that took place in the U.S. and Europe. I alternated the direction with another CBS director, the late Bob Dailey, a great guy and a great director. We were very fortunate to have Lou Tyrell as our producer. Lou was a first-rate organizer who not only could handle our complicated telecasts but who could also control our drawn-out mix of announcers: Jack Whitaker, Ralph Boston, Dick Bank, and Bill Toomey. Not an easy job!

My assignments turned out to be mostly abroad. I hated leaving my beach house in Malibu, but I knew it would be best to base myself in a central location in Europe so that I could skip those weekly transatlantic roundtrips for the next two and a half months.

Jack Whitaker and I shared a two-bedroom, two-bath apartment in Nice, France. Our apartment was on the Promenade D'Anglais that stretches along the entire front of the town and overlooks the beaches along the Mediterranean. We were up on the 5th floor of a building so boringly quiet that I figured we were the only ones among the living. The beach was no prize either. For long stretches it was hard and pebbly and lacked depth, from the walkway to the water. When I had a chance, I was off to a sandy beach at St. Tropez, where the itsy-bitsy bikini was losing its battle to the topless bikini.

There was a major time problem in covering these events in Europe. The competitions were all held on a Saturday night and had to be edited as a complete package ready for transport and airing the next afternoon from Manhattan. The events would end as late as 9 p.m. and then I was free to go. But the producer had only five hours to edit the tape. By 3 a.m., and in pitch-blackness, he'd play back his finely edited package on a monitor sitting on the hood of his edit truck so that the announcers could use the headlights to read their copy. The package was then hand-carried on an airliner to Manhattan and then motorcycled to the CBS Tape Center.

My telecasts originated from Oslo, Malmo, Copenhagen, Helsinki, Stuttgart, and Warsaw. I had been to most of the cities before and knew, kind-of, what to expect. For instance, in Oslo I knew the streets would be empty at 9 p.m. on a Saturday night since most of the Norwegians would be in Dodge City, television-wise, watching "Gunsmoke." The big attraction was this guy James Arness, who played the sheriff. It wasn't until later that year, when I was at Vin Scully's home in Pacific Palisades that I found out Arness's real name was Aurness, a good old Norwegian name. Vin had bought Arness's Pacific Palisades property in California, which was nearby the home of the actor Ronald Reagan, the site where Vin and I would get together in the next decade and in another story.

In Malmo, Sweden, just across the water from Copenhagen, at the closest point between the two countries, I knew that I'd find American programs with subtitles—and none with dubbing. The subtitling was provided at the request of the Swedish viewers who wanted to learn English by watching the shows spoken in that language. In fact, in 1956, on the first night of Swedish television transmission, they aired a film episode of "I Love Lucy" in English as a special treat for their viewers.

In Denmark, there were fewer viewing hours on the tube because of the smaller population. Most of what was on the air was high-culture drama that could be produced inexpensively and yet provide the Danish viewers what they wanted—stories of people with common roots.

So it came as no surprise to me years later that the 1977 television mini-series "Roots" turned out to be a huge hit in Scandinavia. As you know, the series was based on Alex Haley's best-selling novel that linked him to his African ancestors. After the series had aired in the U.S., I had the opportunity to have lunch with the author at a celebrity function thrown by the trade paper The Hollywood Reporter.

Haley told me that it took ten years of research to trace his ancestral line to Kunta Kinte. Haley emphasized the nine generations of his family ties. What Haley left me with was the feeling that people always feel better when they know that they are part of a larger family.

Let's return to the AAU Track and Field Championships. I left off somewhere in Scandinavia so let's pick it up in Finland. I don't remember much about Helsinki except lying in bed and watching television, burning with a 104-degree temperature. I do recall watching the television series, "Peyton Place," which was just as popular in Finland as in America. I was told that the show provided the Finns a window to compare what they had with what they didn't have.

Another interesting fact is that in 1956 Finland was the first European country to introduce cigarette commercials on television. And in 1969, as I lay in my bed burning with a fever, I was looking at this penguin skating on ice smoking a cigarette. They were pitching Kool menthol cigarettes, the new rage in American filter cigarettes.

By the time I got to Stuttgart, Germany, my fever had cooled off. The hot item on evening television was the cowboy series "Bonanza." The German interest in western films went back to the days of silent films, when there was no language barrier in the movies.

During the sixties I also spent a lot of time in the south of Germany, in the Bavarian Alps, covering skiing events. One of those shows took place at the base of the Zugspitze, the highest mountain in Germany. Once in awhile there was a hot-air balloon floating through the sky as was the case when the event I was televising wanted to conclude with the town's mayor descending on a propane balloon to close out the show. But then the wind shifted, so I signed off the show with the mayor getting smaller and smaller, disappearing over the mountain range, with the site's police vehicles rushing to find him.

The last track-field pickup I had to direct before I headed back to Los Angeles was in Warsaw. The hotel bar was a downer. It was filled with women and money traders, each with offers I could refuse. When I moved away to sit by myself, the gypsy violinist must have figured that I was an American who was looking for some soul. So he went to the microphone and sang the latest American hit, "By the Time I Get to Fen—ix (Phoenix)"

I had never been to Warsaw before, and I felt it was important to do something more meaningful than throwing a Frisbee around with the crew before the shoot. I decided to go take the trolley to the northwestern part of the city, to the Warsaw Ghetto, where the German Nazis had killed thousands of innocent Jewish people. From 1941 to 1943 reportedly the population of the enforced ghetto declined from some 450,000 to about 70,000.

Even today, I can see those bullet holes in the brick walls made by the firing squads, and I still see those railroad tracks that took thousands of those heroic people to the gas chambers at Treblinka.

Recently, I contacted Mrs. Barbara Moszczyñska of the Warsaw Historical Society to help me recall the details of something that far back. Ms. Moszczyñska was kind enough to send me an old map. It showed that I must have taken either the 51 or 53 trolley since the last stop for each would have dropped me by the ghetto area and, on return, would have taken me back to my mid-city hotel.

The reason I was trying to remember the trolley line was because I had an encounter with the trolley conductor on the return back to my hotel. All the conductors were outfitted in the same municipal transport car uniform. But for some reason, this conductor was missing his official jacket. He had no jacket. The guy seemed to be embarrassed to be doing his job in his shirtsleeves. When I exited his trolley, he took a last look at the navy serge blazer that I was wearing. I felt badly for him. As I waved goodbye to him, I felt better, watching him clang his way down the trolley line, proudly wearing my blue CBS Sports jacket with its white 'eye' over his heart.

Let's move on to 1971 when my wife accompanied me on my European assignments. As newlyweds, Carol and I were fortunate to end up in the Italian Riviera for a track event taking place near Forte dei Marmi, the romantic resort where my boyhood hero, Guglielmo Marconi, had once courted his wife, Maria.

Fifteen years later, Carol and I revisited the Italian seacoast, and we found another connection to Marconi. While sitting on the terrace of the Hotel Miramare in Santa Margherita, she noticed an embedded wall plaque by my legs. It stated that it was there, in 1933, that Marconi had succeeded in being the first to transmit telegraphic radio and telephonic radio signals by short wave.

I should note that our second trip to the Italian seacoast took place after I had successfully transmitted both Bob Geldof's Live Aid and Pope John Paul's Prayer for World Peace, and we did this using multiple satellite transmissions and reaching record-breaking worldwide audiences.

More later about those spectacular events in the next decade, but for now let's go back to the 1970 Kentucky Derby won by the chestnut colt Dust Commander.

During the race the horse got bumped coming out of the gate and was taken inside along the rail. On the final turn he came out between horses and drew clear to the wire. I was anxious to rerun the race not only to show the horse winning again but also to give the home viewers another look at the long shot, Fathom, since it was being ridden by Diane Crump, the first woman to ride in the Kentucky Derby. Before the race, I had been cutting to Diane since the crowd kept staring at her as if she were some kind of oddity among the male jockeys. And now with the replay I could wrap-up the Diane Crump story. I showed her coming in 15th out of 17 starters.

But Diane Crump did bring something special to the telecast. She provided another angle on presenting the women's side at the Derby. She was a woman in riding silks, a relief from the females in the infield wearing shorts, pedal pushers, and even bathing suits—a relief from just showing ladies in the grandstand wearing all those ridiculous hats to get attention. Woodcuts of the early Derbies showed women in dress hats, but the modern tradition of wearing crazy, oversized hats began in the early sixties when I was adding more cameras within the crowd for my Derby coverage. For the record, Dust Commander did not win either the Preakness or the Belmont. The horse that came in 8th in the Derby, Personality, won the Preakness. And the horse that came in 3rd in the Derby, High Echelon, won the Belmont.

The following year, the 1971 Kentucky Derby had an even larger field with a sizeable twenty horses going to the gate. And a colt shipped in from the northern coast of South America won the race.

The horse was a long shot from Venezuela by the name of Canonero II. He was so lightly regarded in the USA that he was relegated to the mutual field—meaning he was an outsider who had been grouped together with other unlikelys as a single entity in wagering.

When the colt Canonero came from the back of the pack, he wasted little time in passing the other nineteen horses to the finish line. I cut to the Instant Replay showing Canonero closing ground with a crab-like stride due to his right foreleg being crooked. When I cut back to the crowd, they were still stunned.

I guess it never occurred to the horse with the crooked leg that he shouldn't have been able to withstand the rigors of the race. But then again, it never occurred to our expert commentators that the foreign colt had been training in three thousand feet of thin air and he had just now raced at only four hundred feet above sea level. Nor had it occurred to Chuck Milton, the producer, or myself to have a Spanish translator in the winner's circle, just in case. Nope! We were all dopes.

Neither the jockey, Gustavo Avila, nor the trainer, Juan Arias, spoke English, so when they pointed out that their horse liked gulping the thicker air of Kentucky, the viewers at home had to know Spanish to understand their explanation, to know why the horse had added stamina. They sure as hell didn't get it from me or my commentators.

When the Preakness came along, we not only added a translator but also a trainer, Frank Wright, who could also speak Spanish. And with that race Canonero proved he wasn't a fluke. He beat the same top rivals he had faced in the Derby, and he was now headed for the Belmont Stakes. I found it amusing that this big copper colt only cost $1600, which was less than my producer's bar tab.

I opened the Belmont telecast with the jubilant footage that came with Canonero's wins at both the Derby and the Preakness. There were lots of jubilant cheers in Spanish as Canonero went to the gate. But after the race, all was quiet. The Mariachi bands stopped playing. Canonero had finished out of the money, coming in fourth. The long shot, Pass Catcher, had denied Canonero II the Triple Crown.

But that's the way it went. The following year, it would be Riva Ridge who would win the 1972 Kentucky Derby and fail to win the Triple Crown.

Riva Ridge won that Derby, wire to wire, and he did it in such an easy fashion that he went to the Preakness as the heavy favorite. But things didn't work out. It came up raining in Baltimore, and the horse couldn't handle the muddy track. He was beaten by an unknown colt, Bee Bee Bee, who liked the off going. Riva Ridge did redeem himself at the Belmont on a dry track, winning by seven lengths.

I had bet on Bee Bee Bee as a winning long shot, then after the race I found myself to be a winner again. The well-known producer Woody Frazier had singled me out to direct his hugely popular afternoon talk show "The Mike Douglas Show," a show that was breaking ground by originating a week of programs from Moscow.

I guess Woody knew I had plenty of overseas experience and that my ego probably wouldn't let me say no. I ended up directing five shows in Russia where I not only had to switch my camera shots on an antiquated switcher, but I also had to call my shots in their language.

I was honored to get a chance to work with Woody, but there was a catch. I had to direct in Russian. Before leaving, Mike Douglas and I—along with our wives—took Berlitz lessons.

I learned to say 'szook' for 'sound', 'a svesh Chyan ee ye' for 'lighting,' and so forth. But during the show I had a translator standing behind me, in case I forgot the Russian words for my commands.

When I wanted to switch a camera, I had to figure which of the huge, knob-shaped buttons I had to depress hard enough to have it make physical contact with the electrical base of the switcher. I didn't have any problems until the fifth and last show when Mike got up and began singing the song 'Love Story'. I had the 'fo to ap pa RAAT' (the camera) close on Mike's face as he sang "Where do I begin To tell the story Of how grateful love can be?"

To dissolve away from Mike as he was singing, I had to manually criss-cross a double-lever arm. Not easy for a Yank trying to think like a Russian. Now before Mike was going to step away from his camera, I wanted another camera to cover the orchestra before he finished the lyric, "The sweet love story That is older than the sea." But I couldn't think of the word 'orchestra' in Russian, so I turned to the translator and said, "Quick what is the word for orchestra?" And she said, "orchestra."

I was a little late on the dissolve, but, all in all, the week's shooting was a great experience thanks to Mike Douglas' winning personality and Woody Fraser's amazing ability as a producer. When we returned to the States, Woody had me do a guest appearance on Mike's talk show. Mike's co-host that week was Peter Falk. Falk had just won an Emmy for his superb portrayal of the TV detective in "Columbo," so we had something to talk about. The series had been co-created by Richard Levinson, who had been my assistant director when I directed a live Passover Seder in the fifties.

During the show, Mike re-lived our experiences in Russia, especially recalling how we had taken our wives, Genevieve and Carol, to the "Bolshoi Ballet." He told how, when we arrived at the theater, we found a couple thousand people there, waiting for the ballet to begin. Mike knew our seats were somewhere up in the semicircular tiers of the balcony, but he didn't expect them to be in a center box next to the Royal Box where Premier Kosygin had just seated himself in the middle of his Soviet guard.

Now what Mike forgot to mention on his talk show was how, when the curtain went up, he went to sleep. He had never adjusted to the time change. At one point, Premier Kosygin leaned over to take a look at us. I nudged Carol, and she nudged Genn, and the three of us smiled back in unison.

After the show, we took turns trying to figure out what the Premier must have thought about the American television star who was sleeping through Russia's favorite ballet, Swan Lake.

On January 16, 1972, Super Bowl VI was held in Tulane Stadium. The game ended with the NFC's Dallas Cowboys defeating the AFC's Miami Dolphins 24–3. The telecast was expected to set the record for the top-rated one-day telecast ever. And it did, with 27 million homes tuning in.

The NFL provided a classy military pre-game show, with a Marine Drill Team, Army and Navy Corps presenting the Flag, the Air Force Academy Glee Club singing the National Anthem, and with eight F-4 Phantom jets streaking overhead. The pre-game show put everybody in a patriotic mood, and I reminded my announcers that Roger Staubach had served his country with five years in the military before he elected to join the Dallas Cowboys.

Dallas was a five-point favorite but Staubach led his team to a twenty-one-point victory. I recently spoke with Roger and reminded him of the big day he had some thirty five years ago and how he was named the Super Bowl's Most Valuable Player.

Roger shook off the praise and said, "I got the MVP because Duane Thomas wouldn't talk to anybody." That's Roger for you, all class. His reference was to his running back Duane Thomas who had continually shunned the press.

This was the Super Bowl that started their 'media day'. Players and coaches had been making themselves available the Tuesday prior to the game, but not Duane. He refused to answer any questions prior to the contest.

At the end of the game, Tom Brookshier began his interviews in the winning locker room. When Duane Thomas came to the mike, he was accompanied by Jimmy Brown, the ex-Browns' great, who as a favor to me and CBS was there in case he could help out in dealing with his non-talkative friend, Duane.

But not even Jimmy could help Brookshier out. Tom asked Duane a long question that finally ended with, "You're fast, aren't you?" Duane stared into the camera for several seconds and then simply said, "Evidently."

I'm also reminded of when Tex Schramm, the Dallas General Manager, lifted the Lombardi Trophy. When he was toweling off from being doused with champagne, he got a phone call telling him that his home had been burglarized while the game was being played.

In 1973 I covered Secretariat's Triple Crown Victory as he went on to win the Kentucky Derby, Preakness Stakes, and Belmont Stakes, making him the first Triple Crown winner in a quarter of a century.

Secretariat was a bright red chestnut with tremendous leg muscles that gave him an extra long stride, and it seems he also had an extra big heart. When he died, sixteen years later, they found his heart to be twice the size of other horses.

On Derby day I isolated Secretariat coming out of postposition 10. Leaving the gate, he dropped back last, then moved between horses entering the first turn, but then he started passing horses, one after the other, on the outside. The 'iso' was able to get extra close as he came into the stretch, and it was a good angle—with the horse being whipped right handed by jockey Ron Turcotte and with him drawing away from the one horse he had left to beat, Sham.

The Preakness had a small six-horse field. I had my iso back on Secretariat as he came out of the 3 hole. Leaving the gate, he dropped back last again, but this time he didn't stay there very long. He wanted to run and took the lead early in the race and won by an easy two and a half lengths.

At the Belmont, once again, there was a small field, six horses. Secretariat wore the number 'two' but came out of the one hole. He immediately went inside to battle Sham, who wore the entries '1A' for the early lead. The two ran neck to neck like two speed-crazy colts in a sprint race. They covered the first six furlongs, or half the distance, at a blazing 1:09 4/5. The speed was too much for Sham, but not for Secretariat. He was out to beat the clock. Without being asked, he widened his lead to twenty lengths on the turn, and then he kept widening his margin from there.

My cameraman on the finish line was George Drago. When Secretariat came into the last turn, George's lens was fully zoomed-out in order to keep the trailing horses in reference to the lead horse, Secretariat, all within his frame. But now, as Secretariat entered the stretch, George had to straighten out his camera and lose the foreshortening benefits that the turn into the stretch had allowed. He had to continue to pan to his right, and that meant losing Secretariat's relationship to the rest of the field.

George called out over his headset, "Whatta I do?" I told him, "Stay wide. Don't zoom in." I knew, from covering so many races, cameramen have a normal tendency to tighten up when they have so much empty space around the key figure in their frame.

George stayed wide and kept panning to his right until Secretariat crossed the finish line. Then I said, "Now pan back left, slowly, stay wide, and pick up the rest of the horses coming over the line."

It may sound easy to you, but you have to be a helluva cameraman to keep Secretariat's nose on the right edge of the frame while panning a camera of a very wide shot as the horse comes to the finish line, moving, as Chic Anderson said, "…like a tremendous machine." It was a great call. Chic usually did a low-key call, but with Secretariat's performance he was screaming like any other track announcer. He knew there were times that you had to boom your voice over the crowd, and that this was one of those times.

Six years later, I was a pallbearer at Chic's funeral in Evansville, Indiana. As I helped lift his casket, his call came to my mind. "He's moving like a tremendous machine."

In 1972, and again in '73, I was honored with an Eclipse Award from members of the media for my television direction of Thoroughbred Racing. And in 1973 I was nominated for an Emmy for my coverage of Secretariat's Triple Crown. But on that occasion I lost the Emmy to Jim McKay on primetime television. I still can't figure out why we were put in the same category.

I recall January 1974 and Super Bowl VIII. It was a match-up between Miami and Minnesota from Rice Stadium in Houston, Texas.

I was hoping to remember something memorable about that game, but there wasn't. The Dolphins creamed the Vikings. Miami scored from the five-yard line and one-yard line in their first two possessions, and they ran up 24 points before Minnesota finally scored in the fourth quarter. Miami beat the Vikings 24 to 7 for back-to-back Super Bowl wins.

I figured I'd at least get some good Instant Replays since Fran Tarkenton, the Viking quarterback, had been bragging to us all week that he would bust the game wide-open with his scrambling. It never happened. The only scrambling Tarkenton did was behind the line of scrimmage, while he was trying to unload the ball. Big Deal! Meanwhile the Dolphins went on to score the first 24 points of the game.

Ray Scott did play-by-play. Pat Summerall and Bart Starr did the color. They couldn't help the game, either. They were just as boring. After the first quarter the whole thing was a snore. About the only highlight was the National Anthem before the game, sung by the black country star Charley Pride.

In 1974 I worked with another black star, the great track-and-field athlete Jesse Owens—a man who had won four gold medals in the 1936 Nazi Olympics and single-handedly crushed Hitler's myth of Aryan supremacy.

Jesse was the best. We met in Philly when I was directing a popular sports legends show. Jesse had a chest cold that he found hard to shake. I'm sure his heavy smoking didn't help. But he never complained. He did the required multiple takes I needed to capture him from different angles.

I knew he was an inspiring speaker, so I wanted to capture him speaking on film. When I asked Jesse to address the students of a local high school, he was comfortable with the idea. He said he first became aware of the Olympics Games when Charley Paddock, then the world's fastest human, came to speak at his junior high school.

In '74 the auditorium was jammed to the rafters as Jesse delivered his message that individual excellence, rather than race or national origin, distinguishes one man or woman from another. That night at dinner I thanked him. It had been a tiring affair. I felt bad that I'd imposed on a man who not only ran faster and jumped farther than any person on the planet but who had also discredited Adolph Hitler.

Jesse kept his humility and waved off my apology with a laugh. To put me at ease, he told me how difficult it was for a star like him to make a living after the Olympics, how he wasn't offered any endorsement deals because he was black. He told me things got so bad he would get a hundred dollars a night to race a thoroughbred in a hundred-yard dash. He never lost, he said, because the starter shot the gun behind the horse's ear, giving Jesse a thirty-yard advantage at the start.

We had a drink, and he talked about the time the guys in his East Cleveland High School tried to outdo each other by racing on the school track. They didn't have the money to buy the bullets for the starter's guns, so they clapped two-by-fours together to make the sound of a gunshot. It seemed to be a defining moment in his life, one that showed he was determined that poverty would not deter him from his dreams.

During this time I also did a show with Howard Cosell when he hosted a half-hour film highlighting the football career of his friend Paul Hornung. At the time Howard was the most imitated voice in America. Even when Howard wasn't on the air he was pretending he was "telling it as it is." I thought I'd have some fun with Howard by writing some of his exaggerations into the copy he'd be using while questioning Hornung about his yearlong suspension from the Green Bay Packers for gambling. As I began typing, I wondered how the abrasive Cosell might handle the unsavory matter, considering Howard had been a major contributor in not only shaping the legend of Vince Lombardi but also in pimping the wholesomeness of the Packers organization with his TV special "Run to Daylight."

As I thought about Howard, the schmaltz came waltzing through my head. So I banged out some hooey on how Paul had forsaken those close to him. "Paul, what about your poor mother?" "Paul, how about Coach Lombardi? He was like a father to you! How could you do this to him?"

I had written that puffed-up copy as a gag to play on Cosell, the way Al Jolson's songwriters did when they wrote the corniest song they could dream up for Jolie to sing—a song about "Sonny Boy" and being forsaken. I wrote about Golden Boy and being forsaken. In both cases, the contrived joke backfired.

When Cosell arrived, he gave me his usual dead-fish handshake. His stooped figure strode quickly by me as he checked his hairpiece and asked about the lovely young woman I was with. I introduced him to my wife, Carol, and Howard proceeded to tell her that it was a pity he hadn't discovered her before I did. She laughed, but I held mine, waiting for him to read the hokey stuff I'd written. But surprisingly Cosell approved and said, "Okay Verna, let's do it!"

I gulped and rolled cameras. Speed! Action! Cosell swelled like a sponge in water. A river of words poured out of him as Howard effectively mixed his own caustic remarks with my mush. The outcome was a tractable story line of Hornung's life. The joke was on me. But then again, maybe I should have expected as much from Cosell, considering that the equally ego-driven Jolson sold a whopping three million copies of "Sonny Boy." Like Jolson, Cosell had his own brand of crapolla for turning schmaltz into something memorable.

Let's shift to the National Basketball Association. I've already noted that I first directed an NBA game back in 1957. Now in 1974, some seventeen years later, I found myself directing the NBA again.

My first significant memory was when Rick Barry replaced

Elgin Baylor as the analyst for Pat Summerall, who was making the game call. Like Elgin, Barry was also an NBA great. I've long been a big fan of Rick Barry. I always thought his comments were the most insightful of any analyst. But for some reason, management didn't rate him as highly. I never forgot what Jack Buck had once told me, that if the brass doesn't like you it doesn't matter how good you are.

In 1975 I worked quite a few games with Brent Murburger and Mandy Rudolph, the former great NBA official on the court and one of the best card players I've ever faced at a poker table.

Next I directed a half-hour show featuring another legend, Mickey Mantle, who, unlike Jesse Owens, prospered in his retirement, earning fees at card shows and business ventures. Jesse had ended his show telling kids to live the life he'd lived. But with Mantle, he always told kids not to live the life he'd lived.

When you're recording a living legend, you never know where or how the story should end. My plan was to play it safe by ending the show with Mickey visiting a children's hospital. I figured he could wrap things up by talking about his years of playing despite the constant pain from his succession of injuries. But when I explained the ending to Mickey, he went silent. Something was wrong. I thought it was a good idea. He didn't. I told him it would show his other side, the one where he'd overcome adversity and achieved greatness. Mickey said he couldn't do it. It would be too much of a reminder to him that his days were numbered. He explained that the males in his family were cursed by Hodgkin's disease in the bloodline and most died before 40. Mickey was 43 and counting.

Paul Hornung, who was the host of the series, explained to Mickey that a visit by him would mean a lot to the sick kids. The grace and courage he could display would be a reminder not only to those kids in the hospital but to all of those viewing that they should never give up. Mantle reconsidered. He went to the hospital, posed for photos, signed autographs for the kids, and it turned out to be a great day and a good shoot. For the record Mickey Mantle died 21 years later, at the age of 64 of liver cirrhosis.

That brings me to 1975 and directing Joe DiMaggio. Like anyone else who ever reviewed DiMaggio's footage, it was apparent that Joe never wasted a move. He seemed to glide from place to place on the playing field, so it seemed appropriate to have him moving rather than sitting for the half hour. Since the show I was to do with Joe was to be shot in an Atlantic City penthouse, I thought about having Joe move around the spacious upper-floor setting with a single camera tracking his normal fluidity.

The plane that had been chartered for the trip to Atlantic City was Gulfstream I. It seated 24. When I got to the plane, I shook hands with DiMaggio and sat down next to him. We were the only two passengers.

On takeoff, the plane wobbled. The pilot and copilot had opened their door to look back at their unannounced passenger, Joe DiMaggio. The co-pilot offered us coffee, but Joe took just hot water and then pulled out a single service envelope from his pocket. He might have just signed a contract to be a pitchman for a coffee maker, but he drank 'instant'.

I'd heard that Joe could be tough to deal with, so I let him start the conversation. I didn't want him to feel uneasy around me. Joe said he'd seen my credits on TV and had heard that I'd invented the Instant Replay. He looked me over. There was a generation between us. Joe was a powerful figure to Italian-Americans at a time when discrimination was still commonplace for giants like him and for little guys like me.

His somber face lightened up when I made it a point to connect the saloons we both knew. I ran down the list: Toots Shor's in New York, Frank Palumbo's in Philly, Duke Zeibert's in D.C., Skinny D'Amato's 500 Club in Atlantic City. Then I mentioned the Villa Nova in LA. I knew this was where he'd first met Marilyn Monroe, but I didn't mention that fact. Joe went silent. I said that I ran into one of his old friends there, the actor George Raft, a guy we both liked. Joe said he also had an offer to run a Havana casino during those pre-Castro days, but he turned it down.

When we arrived in Atlantic City, Paul Hornung explained to Joe how he would just prompt him to talk about his career. I explained to Joe that I wanted him moving around the penthouse as he answered Paul. Joe quickly looked over the floor marks set for the key lights and, in a blink, said he was ready to go. I rolled cameras, and DiMag set out on the course I'd staged.

Joe was a lean six foot two and he took big strides that looked good on camera. Amazingly, I never saw him look at any of the marks yet he hit them all with his left or right heel, dead-on.

It was a good show and a quick shoot, filmed pretty much in real time.

Hornung did a fine interview that ended with him saying that he had worn uniform Number Five in honor of Joe. DiMaggio was pleased and retired to his suite. The hotel had provided him with their best, a huge suite they'd finished refurbishing earlier that day. I figured Joe would be ordering up to avoid the autograph seekers. When he was still playing, his teammates said Joe led the league in room service.

As I returned to my room, the phone was ringing. It was Joe. He asked if I'd come over. He had a problem with the newly opened suite. When he opened the door, I found the suite was dark. He said they'd forgotten to put light bulbs in the sockets. So I called down, and we waited for them to send some bulbs up. It was like a strange dream of a child that had come true. Here I was in the dark next to the great Joe D., sitting side by side, just him and me, alone to the world, and with a conversation that would remain our own.

Before leaving 1975, I want to take you back to one of the most dramatic moments in sports—and especially sports on television. Back to July sixth, when just before 6 p.m., eastern, two horses went to the post at Belmont Park in New York. The "Match Race" was an extension of the then popular 'battle of the sexes' concept. This time it was colt versus filly. Both horses had gone through their two-year-old seasons undefeated. The colt was Kentucky Derby winner Foolish Pleasure, and the super filly was Ruffian. They hyped the crap out of the match-up. They strung up banners in the grandstands, gave out pins to the crowd with caricatures of either the filly or the colt.

I got saddled with a couple of producers whose job it was

to make up a series of animations as bumpers for me to roll in during the show. It was all a little too cutesy for me. I'd had enough hard experience to know things could go wrong, so I rehearsed my cameras and crew for an immediate call by me … "Split 4 into 2"…meaning that camera 4 would isolate either of the horses in case it didn't finish the race. That single shot on camera 4 would be inserted into camera 2's two-shot coverage of the race. It might have seemed heartless to my crew, but it was the groove I've always worked in…."What if?"

As the two horses paraded in front of the grandstand, the fans were cheering-on their choice, the filly or the colt. At the start of the race, the filly Ruffian took the lead, but on the backstretch she took a misstep and fractured her ankle. I immediately called out "Split 4 into 2," and a close-up of Ruffian was inserted in a box. Chic Anderson, the TV race caller, cried out, "Ruffian has broken down! This race is over!" The crowd was no longer cheering. They were horrified. When the jockey pulled her up, you could see that Ruffian had shattered her sesamoids—the small bones in her tendons—and torn up her ligaments, leaving her to run on exposed bones. By now the split screen had turned into a grotesque picture that showed her hoof dangling uselessly from her leg. I cut to the ambulance they used to carry her away to the equine hospital. Then I cut to the colt, Foolish Pleasure, crossing the finish line with no other horse in sight.

The creators of the event seemed to have bit off more than they'd bargained for, and they went as silent and as paralyzed as the crowd. I'd seen this before when the producers in the truck either froze or left the truck as if they were on a mission to right things. So I proceeded down my own path. I discontinued the use of all the cutesy devices or any shots that would remind the viewer that this was a made-for-television event that had let death beat the undefeated filly, Ruffian.

In the following year, 1976, the Kingdom of Saudi Arabia hired me to direct their participation in the Montreal Olympics. Fortunately I was teamed up with producer Hal Uplinger who was a great help in matching up my directing style to the Saudi way of thinking, like not mentioning certain things or not showing women in my crowd shots. I've been asked to explain my success in working in all these different countries with dozens of different crews. I've always said you needed a great deal of respect from the crew. I always made sure they knew that I was getting big money to do the event because I had a global reputation and I was expecting a top performance from them. The next thing I would do was to familiarize myself with the ability of the cameramen, the availability of lenses, and how I should communicate what I wanted and when I wanted it— and what words I'd be using in their language. Most times it was a little mix of their French, their Spanish or their German with my English. By giving them the courtesy of trying to learn the key words in their language, I always got off on the right foot. Many times their best cameraman were studio guys who were real arty. Art was not what I needed. Fast reflexes and focus were the ticket and I set pace by switching the cameras myself and eliminating their middleman. Not needing much sleep was another plus. I was never a great sleeper. Sleeping never took up a great part of my life. I directed a dozen Derbies and several Super Bowls after only a few hours of broken sleep. I guess being so awake kept my reflexes screwed up to a higher pitch.

After returning from the two weeks in Montreal directing Saudi Arabia's participation in the Olympics, I decided to move back to Los Angeles with my wife Carol, my daughter Jennifer, and son Eric. My ex had shuffled my daughter Tracy back to L.A. And my wife Carol suggested we follow so that I could remain an integral part of Tracy's life. It was a tough decision. But as fate would have it, an old friend, producer Jay Michaels, helped make it possible. Jay headed up Trans World International (TWI), along with Barry Frank, the noted sports-rights agent and packager since his early days at ABC Sports.

Jay offered me a package of shows that played on ABC-TV. It was the "Hilton Head Tennis Classic" hosted by Chris Schenkel and Pancho Gonzales. Amazingly, Jay and Barry produced and packaged not only legitimate events for TWI, which was the television division of IMG, but they also created clever synthetic concoctions that were played in front of made-for-television crowds. One of their creations was the primetime show "Celebrity Challenge of the Sexes" pitting Farrah Fawcett against Bill Cosby in a red-hot celebrity tennis match.

I used plenty of low-angle Instant Replays from behind Farrah as she ran around in her skimpy shorts. The shots were a big hit with the male audience. Maybe some of the shots may have been a moral failing on my part, but TWI pulled off a 49 percent TV Share of the audience.

TWI had also developed a series called "World's Strongest Man." Now on this show some of my low replays had me wincing, especially when they involved these huge men running around with these huge refrigerators strapped to their backs.

Of all the TWI shows, the weekly "Battle of the Sexes" was the most fun for me to direct. The format had the stars competing in a series of athletic events, men versus the ladies, to prove who was the superior sex. The summer events originated from Mission Viejo, an upscale town in southern Orange California. Vin Scully was the male host. Vinny brought the needed gravitas to make the television-created-event more credible, while Phyllis George added some sparkle as the female co-host.

The winter events were held at the Laurentian ski resort of Mont Tremblant, a couple of hours north of Montreal. While Phyllis was single at the time, Vin and I decided to lug our families up there to do some skiing and to have them help us run up our room service bills.

Following that, in 1976, I wrote and directed the pilot for a show I created called "Beauty, Beach, and the Bizarre." At first, Orson Welles fancied hosting it. Welles had figured out the beauty and the beach part of my idea, but he was only sort-of okay with the bizarre part, fearing that it might be like the theatrical documentary "Mondo Cane," which relied on shock exploitation and debasement.

My conception of bizarre was more on the strange side, like showing the proboscis monkeys swimming off the beaches of Borneo to catch fish. But Orson didn't want to wait for me to finish the script. He wanted to know it all now. So I moved on to Raymond Burr as the possible host. We met at the Musso & Frank Grill in Hollywood and discussed it, but the time frame didn't work out for Burr. The show didn't suffer, though.

Academy Award winner George Kennedy did my pilot. I was the only one to suffer. The pilot didn't sell.

In 1977 I created, and sold CBS, a winner-take-all show that pitted the top female professional bowler against the top female amateur bowler for the prize of $50,000.

Hal Meyers, a popular television producer for the Brunswick Corporation, put the package together. I think Bob Wussler, who was then head of CBS Sports, thought I was nuts when I put the bowling lanes directly on the stage of the Circus Maximus Showroom at Caesars Palace. But then again, Wussler probably thought I was screwy when I set up a basketball court on that same stage to televise an actual basketball game featuring the Harlem Globetrotters.

The bowling show was a hit mainly because the host was the charismatic Telly Savalas, who had won the Emmy the year before as Theo Kojak the bald New York City detective who had a fondness for lollipops. Telly and I were the best of friends even though I had turned him down on directing an episode of Kojak. Telly loved to gamble, and he loved the concept of giving a lowly nobody amateur a chance to cash in. That appealed to him, big time. The winner turned out to be the amateur. She got the $50,000. The loser, the pro, got nothing. After the amateur won, Telly couldn't have been happier. He gave the stunned amateur the check for $50,000 and asked her, "Who loves you, baby?" The loser, the professional bowler, got to talk to Ed McMahon. That was it. Nothing more. No appearance money. Nothing.

As expected, in 1976 Bob Wussler became President of CBS Television, and Barry Frank succeeded Bob as the head of the sports department, but they both got into hot water over a winner-take-all tennis tournament that wasn't so. Unbeknownst to them, the losers had received appearance money.

Later, in December, 1977, I was selected to produce and direct the very complicated global TV special, World Circus from London. I guess I got the assignment because they couldn't find anybody else stupid enough to do it. The show was being fed to a half dozen different countries, each of which had ponied up the budget, so I had to have a half dozen ringmasters. That meant that at the opening and closing—and in between acts—I had to isolate different cameras to serve the different feeds and languages. For the United States I picked my favorite announcer and lifelong friend, Vin Scully.

Big bites of the budget had gone to pay the performers, and there was barely enough dough to provide me the staff I needed to 'push the envelope' with the demands of all the separate language feeds. But I was fortunate that the circus had banked their finale on the feats of a courageous performer whose skills made the challenges I was facing look like chump change. The internationally famous aerialist, Karl Wallenda, would be walking the tight rope without a safety net. I never met a man so fearless. He was the founder of the Flying Wallendas, a four-person high wire pyramid, but in '74 Karl was freelancing as a solo act. He said he just couldn't retire. "Life is being on the wire. Everything else is just waiting."

Interestingly, the area where the circus was taking place in London had once been subjected to intense bombing during the height of the 1940 Blitz. The Londoners soon became known for their courage. The German 111 Bombers that were supposed to prepare the way for Hitler's invasion couldn't demoralize them.

Eventually, England struck a series of retaliatory raids with their RAF Wellington Bombers on a key industrial city in Germany, Magdeburg, the birthplace of Karl Wallenda, and apparently he wasn't easily demoralized either. This was the famous high-wire daredevil famed for developing the seven-person chair, performed without a net.

Karl, born in Germany to an old circus family, had begun performing when he was six, and when he was seventeen put together his own act with his brother, Herman, and his teenage girlfriend, Helen, who later became his wife. The group performed remarkable stunts touring Europe and later were discovered by John Ringling of Ringling Brothers.

Years later, during the rehearsals for the World Circus, Wallenda seemed to be remarkably composed during his practice runs. Vin Scully and I chatted with him before the show as he put on his white and green satins in the dressing room. I was envious of his competence and total control. Along with a hundred other people working the show, I'd stop in my tracks and look in awe at his crossing on a taut cable.

Before we went on the air, Vin and I asked Wallenda about the time he walked the tightrope across the top of Veterans Stadium between games of a baseball doubleheader and got a standing ovation from the Philly fans, who were not exactly easy to please. Wallenda said that the wind was his worst enemy and the fans knew it, and when he went from foul pole to foul pole, despite the dangerous air current, the crowd honored him for giving a hundred percent. That time everything went fine.

A month after the show we did together, in 1978, as Wallenda performed in Puerto Rico, a 30-mile-per-hour wind toppled him to his death off a cable strung between two hotels in San Juan. He was 73 at the time, and he'd lived a hell of a life.

The man had a quality that was expressed four years later by the writer Tom Wolfe, who came up with the right name for what Wallenda possessed. Wolfe called it "The Right Stuff." I didn't know what stuff was right in me, but I knew if that 70-year-old man had the guts to go up and walk on that wire, I had the guts to go sit in the truck and direct what was about to happen.

Earlier I tracked the birth of the Instant Replay, but now I'd like to bring up something that the visionary Marshall McLuhan said during a Toronto TV appearance on September 13, 1977. When he gave his definition of the Instant Replay, McLuhan referred to the world of speeded-up information, to the fact that the human attention span has become very small. He implied that the world's fast pace made people yearn for past values, for nostalgia. In fact, he said that the Instant Replay is a form of reviving the past. Let me add that, in the same year, McLuhan also made a special appearance in Woody Allen's great film "Annie Hall" in which Allen, playing Alvy, silences a self-impressed McLuhan expert standing in a movie line by pulling McLuhan, himself, out from the poster to tell the man, "You know nothing of my work!"

Let me point out that the McLuhan interview can be seen on my website: tonyvernaTV.com. Just click the word: EXTRAS to find it.

So in this case, I'm the expert, I guess. What about McLuhan's remark that the Instant Replay is a form of reviving the past? With all due respect to Professor McLuhan, I believe his reference overlooks an important element. I think the seeing-it-again aspect of videotaping, which certainly falls into the revival aspect, overtook him. The Instant Replay was created not just to relive the moment but to analyze the moment. A big difference!

1978, I combined the comedy of Soupy Sales with the Harlem Globetrotters. I had cast Soupy as the 'coach' of the Globetrotters. I was pre-taping a primetime special at Madison Square Garden, and I wanted to add some of Soupy's corny clowning to the Globbies' skillful trickery. Soupy played the role of the janitor who was mopping the floor of the empty arena where the team was practicing.

Sometimes, when you want an incredible shot, you don't have to fake it. Soupy Sales gave me two unbelievable shots. I had the ball get away from the players and roll the length of the court to where Soupy was mopping. The Globbies ask him to throw it back. Soupy knew he was to throw the ball in the direction of the basket so I could make the edit and put it through the hoop. Soupy threw it with all his might and—unbelievable—it went right it into the basket. We were all shocked. The Globbies fell over laughing. Great! That's a take!

I rolled again and had the Globetrotters ask Soupy if he could do it again. Again, Soupy knew I would make the necessary edit so he let loose. Yep. A second 'unbelievable'. The ball went in again. It was kind of spooky. For the record, both Soupy and Meadowlark didn't get the story right in their autobiographies. Each had a different comical version of this story. But the videotape will bear my account.

Also in 1978, when Pete Rose went from the Cincinnati Reds to the Philadelphia Phillies, I sold CBS the "Pete Rose Celebrity Roast" from the Dunes Hotel in Las Vegas. To MC the show I hired Milton Berle.

I wanted Milton to host since he had a built-in sense of liveliness about him. I met Berle at the Hillcrest Country Club in Los Angeles. As he began telling me about his joining the club when it cost only $275, the former actor/Senator George Murphy came by simulating a dance step. The famous comedian George Burns gave me a "Hello, kid," between cigar puffs, and another comedian, the legendary Groucho Marx, gave me a straight-faced wink and a nod as an okay to sit down at their round table. But before I could sit, Milton whisked me away and comically began paging a Mister Sinatra. I finally got to meet the 'inimitable voice' in person. Even though Frank Sinatra was being interrupted at lunch with his lawyer, Mickey Rudin, his 'old blue eyes' never left mine during his whole conversation that inquired about what I was up to, these days.

The TV show turned out to be a disappointment. Pete Rose seemed bored, and I was bored. Berle was great, ad libbing as the host, but the guest celebrities needed better written material to put Rose in the hot seat. All in all, though, meeting Frank Sinatra made the effort worthwhile.

Next I was asked to direct a primetime show for NBC, "The Rock n Roll" Sports Classic' created and produced by Bob Finkel.

Finkel was a brilliant producer who had the foresight to select the former Detroit Lions star Alex Karras, a big, backward, shy guy to host his cutting-edge marriage of music and sports with stars like Anne Murray, Lionel Ritchie, and Rod Stewart, performing and competing. The show really worked, on all levels.

1978 was a busy year that found me also directing "Celebrity Daredevils," a Bob Stivers' primetime special for CBS featuring the actor Christopher Reeve who performed various stunts on his glider. Chris was not only fearless, he was a super savvy guy. While he was in flight, he figured out that my two helicopters weren't getting close enough to shoot him in the cockpit. He hit his mobile communications to me and had me hover my choppers so that he could use the rising thermals of hot ground air to get close enough to my cameras. That's the kind of guts this guy had. He was a super guy who continued to show his courage right up to his death. The program was called "Celebrity Daredevils," and it also featured actor Chuck Connors, formerly The Rifleman on TV. Bob Stivers had created a spoof of a classic western fight scene, a comedic barroom brawl between the American cowboy, Connors, and the British comic Marty Feldman, known for his congenital wandering eyes. But the drag-'em-over- the-bar routines didn't work until Bob Stivers had me speed up the action to achieve the herky-jerky look of silent films. Then the scene took off.

In 1979 Bob Stivers had me do a pickup with Burt Reynolds and Carol Burnett as she presented him with the "People's Choice Awards" at Burt's playhouse, the Jupiter Theater. I had met Burt Reynolds a couple of years before when he showed up at the 1977 Sun Bowl in El Paso, Texas. Burt had once played in the Sun Bowl as a halfback of the 1955 Florida State Football Team. Now he was going to work the announcer booth as a guest analyst for the 1977 game between LSU and Stanford, which Stanford won 24 to 14. Come game time, everybody on my crew was still feeling the effects of celebrating the New Year, just a few miles over the border in Juarez, Mexico—everybody but Burt. He was so unbelievably popular that he couldn't leave the hotel until the police escorted him to the announce booth.

I also directed another hot sex symbol, Tom Selleck, when he was presented with the "People's Choice Awards." Bob Stivers sent me to do the pickup in Hawaii, where Selleck was doing "Magnum PI." Selleck was a major television star who was riding on the upper level of the business. But he was also modest and grateful. Like Burt Reynolds, I found Tom Selleck to be a big star with a small ego.

In 1979 I directed a "Celebrity Challenge Billiards Match" between Minnesota Fats and Willie Mosconi on the movie set of "The Baltimore Bullet." My producer, Jay Michaels, had a great feel for what should be isolated on the Instant Replays. On the playbacks, Jay would guide the announcers on their comments to illustrate such things as the strategy Mosconi or Fats had used to run the table. I always thought Jay could have been a heck of an announcer like his son, Al.

In the background of my camera shots, I could catch the two stars of the movie, James Coburn and Omar Sharif, who had been cast as gamblers. The two of them were looking at the competition between Mosconi and Fats who were real-life pros.

But, Coburn and Sharif were also the real thing in real life—two compulsive gamblers who, in fact, had appeared in various instructional gambling videos. The two actors were not only fun to be with, but they also provided me with a new experience. It was the first time I directed and made side bets at the same time.

In March of 1979 I was hired by Bob Stivers Productions to direct "All American Woman," a major beauty show that aired live on ABC primetime. It was a challenge to shoot an extravaganza like that live from Las Vegas. Vegas' stages weren't necessarily that large. I had 50 girls parading around the stage, dancing and singing to a 50-piece orchestra with tons of scenery, a half dozen cameras, plus stagehands and a load of circling hosts.

Bob Stivers was a shrewd producer who had a reason in picking his directors. He knew I had been juggling cameras and fans' sight-lines in sports stadiums for years. I followed Stivers' orders and planned the movement of my cameras' dollies and boom mikes so they didn't block the view of the live audience whose reactions were critical to the show.

Also in 1979 I came up with another idea. I created a live-on-stage series called "Weekend Heroes" that aired on syndication. That show was done in Las Vegas with my partner, Stan Blum, who produced the series. Paul Hornung and Jayne Kennedy were the hosts. What set "Weekend Heroes" apart from other shows was that people in the audience got to ask their own questions and got to ask them directly to their sports heroes.

In '79 and '80 I spent a lot of time in Las Vegas because I went on to become President of Caesars Palace Productions. I did this while I continued to produce and direct for CBS Sports. I had been selected for the position by Clifford Perlman, the Chairman of Caesars, and by his senior executive, Terrence Lanni, two of the smartest men I've ever met.

My work mainly revolved around coordinating with the television producers who wanted to shoot their shows at Caesars. What I remember most were the people, like Joe Louis, the former heavyweight boxing champion. Joe worked at Caesars as a greeter until his death in 1981. Shortly after he died, they erected a statue of him inside the hotel.

As I've mentioned, I directed the first sports event at Caesars when it opened. It was a boxing match and the greeter wasn't the 'Brown Bomber', it was a blonde Cleopatra weighing in at 40-20-37. That was back in 1966 and now by 1980 Caesars Palace had become a boxing and gambling Mecca. Heading it all up was the ever-thinking Cliff Perlman. Cliff always wanted more. He had a temporary auto track built in back of the hotel grounds. The 1981 Grand Prix Championship was decided on that track at Cliff's Caesars Palace.

That kind of spirit takes me back to the spirit of the entrepreneur Bill Rasmussen who came up with the idea for ESPN (The Entertainment and Sports Programming Network). Rasmussen created ESPN at a time when there was no real master plan for programming a 24-hours-a-day, all-sports network. I got a phone call from Bill and his son Scott. We spent hours at a bar. Bill was a fan of my work and wanted to meet me to find out what we could do together. He said he hardly had any programming, so I agreed to create a series of pre-taped, half-hour interviews "Sports Hotline," that would be produced by my company. After the handshake, I hired a former CBS Sports producer, Tommy O'Neill, as the producer and on his recommendation a new talent, Roy Firestone, as the interviewer.

I took a gamble and purchased a small mobile video truck that was sent around the nation. After fifty shows, Firestone moved on to do his own interview shows at ESPN with Bob Seizer as his producer. I sold the remote truck and took a loss.

Bill Rasmussen asked me to come to Bristol, Connecticut, to get the official word of non-renewal from the new guy just hired, Chet Simmons, who had been made head of ESPN. I'd met Chet half a dozen years earlier in his NBC office, when he and Carl Lindeman ran NBC Sports. At that time, Lindeman wanted me to jump ship from CBS so I could do some visionary thinking for NBC's Sports Department. I was tempted since I was a longtime friend of their top director, Harry Coyle. In the end I decided to turn down NBC's offer just as I'd turned down Roone Arledge's offer to move to ABC. Ah, yes! I was true-blue to CBS. And you'll see where that got me!

I topped off the decade of the '70s by creating yet another

show, "Battle of the NFL Cheerleaders," under the aegis of my own company. That competition went on for two years; a weekly show that I sold to CBS. All the NFL Cheerleading Squads competed except for the Dallas Cowboys Cheerleaders. Tex Schramm and his Cowboy Cheerleaders were in a league of their own.

I held the first competition at the Diplomat Hotel in Florida and, the second year, at Caesars in Atlantic City, just after its June opening in 1979. The cheerleaders proved to be very competitive, and Tom Brookshier and Jayne Kennedy proved to be the perfect hosts. The ratings were surprisingly high; so good, in fact, that the ingenious Eddie Einhorn, head of CBS Sports at the time, decided to air one of the episodes during the halftime of an NFL game. Then a strange thing happened—the cheerleader competition drew a higher rating than the game itself. I found it highly amusing. Pete Rozelle did not. He got the series yanked after its second year in 1979.

As we closed out the seventies, it was more than sixteen years since I'd introduced the first Instant Replay.

One thing that came to my mind at the time was that, while I hadn't made a dime more for inventing the Instant Replay, I sure had attracted a slew of people with other agendas, who wanted to bring me down.

Next the Eighties and the globalcasts that I hoped would change the face of television.

CHAPTER FIVE

THE EIGHTIES

Before I proceed with the eighties, let's go back to when I began directing live studio and field events in the fifties. That was when television had just grown out of its short pants and out of the novelty stage, when people would watch anything that was put on the tube. By 1953, studio productions were being formatted, and some of the directors of those studio shows became prominent while others who covered live remotes suffered short-lived careers. Why the difference?

Management found that their viewership increased whenever they aired a live remote. And they discovered it wasn't just the cameras leaving the studio but also the directors. Most of the studio directors were not the type to deal with the possibility of unforeseen happenings. Under the pressure, some began suffering recurring nightmares, like the one my good friend John Horstmann had in the middle of directing the 1952 World Series. Every night, John would have the same dream—that he couldn't find his remote truck and the telecast was going to begin with the Dodgers coming to bat and with him not in the control room. John quit the business, and the business lost a fine director.

Okay, let's pick it up in 1980. Seventeen years have passed since the first Instant Replay. The videotape recorders had made their way into the living room. How did that affect the Instant Replay? The home recorder allowed the viewer to go back and replay what just happened in the game. And when the infrared remote control came out, which was at about that time, it made it even easier for the guys on the couch to check out their own Instant Replays, instead of just relying on the guys in truck. Like any other innovation, it also took on a special kind of expectancy. In the case of the Instant Replay, it took on a sense of irretrievability.

And irretrievability is always basic to the power awarded a unique vision. The bell could not be un-rung. But—and this is a critical difference—the home viewers couldn't replay their own isolated cameras. They had to rely on the telecast. Isolated Instant Replays also help invigorate the call of the games since they provided the booth with a more active relationship with the game. They enabled one to analyze what the replays revealed—information that hadn't been seen during the regular coverage.

By November 1980, Ronald Reagan was President-elect and waiting to be sworn in as the 40th president of the United States. And CBS Sports wanted access to an interview with the President-elect at his home in Pacific Palisades, California.

Vin Scully made it happened. We all lived in Pacific Palisades, and Scully was a good friend of Reagan. It seemed to be a natural for Vin to interview the President-elect about the time when he worked as a sportscaster in the thirties at radio station WHO in Des Monies, Iowa and was known as 'Dutch Reagan'.

Scully had set up the interview at Mr. Reagan's home, and I tagged along with my video crew. The thought of taping at Reagan's home seemed to fit with this kind of informal interview, but when the Secret Service greeted us at the door, things didn't seem so casual.

Scully told me not to worry. He assured me that Reagan was a genuine guy and that he possessed a good sense of humor, which became evident when, on meeting me, the future President jokingly said that it was he who had invented the Instant Replay—back in April of 1934 at the Drake Relays when the 100 yard dash blew by him in nine-point-seven seconds [09.7] while he was in the middle of a live interview. He was forced to instantly recreate the running of the race as if it were live and the black star, Ralph Metcalfe of Marquette University, was just crossing the finish line first in a tight call.

Mr. Reagan's radio duties also included recreations of Chicago Cubs away games. In the 1930s, baseball teams would only broadcast home games from the park. Thus announcers like Reagan didn't travel with the teams for the away games. The games were recreated from a studio with a Western Union ticker providing the announcer with a bare-bones, running account so he could pretend that he was actually at the game.

Reagan told Vin of one of his recreations when the telegraph connection became so intermittent that he had to foul off a lot more balls than he usually did.

Many of us are familiar with stories about those radio recreations from the telegraph wire, but most are not aware that some of the recreations were done with information that was phoned-in. And that was because the studio announcer could get a lot more info from someone on the phone rather than from a telegraph operator. That's how they broadcasted the 1921 World Series between the Giants and the Yankees. There was no play-by-play direct from the field—the radio announcer, Tommy Cowan, was sitting in a studio in Newark. He simply repeated the phoned-in reports from a newspaper reporter sitting at the Polo Grounds, where all the World Series games were played that year with the home team alternating.

This brings me to a story during the first year of the Instant Replay when one of my analysts couldn't get the hang of picking up the action immediately after the play. I know this sounds crazy but there were some analysts back then who were frozen in their old ways. Often I would help them out by giving them the info so that they could just repeat it after me. I recall replaying a Rams sweep, and having said, "Number 65 Tom Mack, pulling for number 18 Roman Gabriel."

Unfortunately, the analyst's IFB was loose and my voice leaked out over his mike. Before we went off the air, phone calls were coming in asking: "Who is the guy telling the analyst what to say?"

In the days before radio, I often wondered how did people at home get their sports results? Let's say it's the 1918 World Series when the Boston Red Sox defeated the Chicago Cubs, four games to two. Most people, of course, got delayed news in their newspapers. The few lucky enough to know a telephone operator personally might be able to get 'instant' news.

The telephone operator would have probably first told them that they had just played the Star-Spangled Banner for the first time at a baseball game, in recognition of the men fighting in World War I. Information was passed on by the telephone operators, who now were usually the first to learn of new information, and soon their customers began expecting them to pass along what they heard—whether the latest game results or the latest on the deadly influenza epidemic, or word that the Braves' outfielder Larry Chappell, who was serving in World War I, had just died of influenza at his army camp.

For the record, the Boston Red Sox won the 1918 World Series, defeating the Chicago Cubs four games to two.

But for a minute, think back to how un-instant those days were. You're getting the latest on the World Series by listening to a telephone operator—not a well-known sportscaster—whose female voice is coming through a headset attached to your phone box, telling you that Babe Ruth will be the starting pitcher for the first game. Then maybe an hour later she calls to tell you that she heard it's pouring cats and dogs in Boston. And maybe later yet a different operator's voice comes through your headset telling you that the first game at Comiskey Park had been postponed.

And one other facet of these 'early days'—the faceless voice. In fact, in early TV, some broadcasts, some of which I directed, were also delivered by faceless, unidentified voices. Management didn't want many of their sportscasters or newscasters on camera because they thought they didn't suit the medium. Almost all of the European newscasters or sports reporters were kept off the screen so that the pictures could do the talking. Their Katie Couric or Bob Costas could walk the streets unrecognized.

Obviously, President Reagan and Vin Scully were quite recognizable, and both fitted the medium extremely well. No cue cards or time cues for these two pros. They could hit whatever it was on the dime.

I recall when I was breaking-in newcomers who lacked the

ability to ad-lib, to stand in front of a camera when they had to fill for long stretches of time without scrambling their thoughts. I would tell them about Bishop Fulton Sheen, who for years did a live half-hour, non-stop spiel on his "Life Is Worth Living" without the use of cue cards or prompter. His secret: "Always know where you are going to end."

In April, 1981, President Reagan was recovering from being shot in an assassination attempt. While he was recovering at George Washington University Hospital, the President autographed a photo he had taken with me. Even though his signature was unsteady, 'Dutch Reagan' kept his promise to me.

Another thing to pass on, before I forget it, about that 1921 World Series: when the games were over, Columbia University ran some tests on Babe Ruth and found he was born with preternatural gifts, such as his eyes being able to respond to flashing bulbs in a darkened chamber a fiftieth of a second quicker than the average person.

In the seventies, I was able to discuss the relationship of eyesight to hitting with the Cardinal's great Stan Musial, while we were filming a show together. Musial had ended his career with a .331 career batting average; so, after mentioning Babe Ruth's extraordinary vision, I pointed out that when Ted Williams took his armed forces physical they found his superior eyesight to be one out of a hundred thousand.

Then I told Stan the Man about my conversations with Joe Di on the subject and how Joe told me that he and his brother, Dom DiMaggio, had such poor eyesight they almost couldn't enlist into the Navy during World War II. Musial didn't make much of what I was saying. He said his eyesight was just normal, nothing special.

I never met Babe Ruth or Ted Williams but I did meet men with exceptional eyesight, such as they had, during my short stay at West Point. In fact, when the first astronauts were making a number of observations from space, identifying regions of India and Tibet, it was first thought that their ability to see those areas was due to some kind of atmospheric magnification, but then they realized that these West Point guys had terrific vision with some even scoring 20/12 on their NASA tests.

One of them was Al Worden, a former classmate of mine at West Point. In 1971 Al had piloted the command module of Apollo 15 while his crewmates James Irwin and David Scott were on the moon's surface. I should mention that NASA Mission Control transmitted the results of two preseason NFL games 74,650 miles into space—the Bills beating the Saints and the Cowboys beating the LA Rams. The scores were sent to the three-man Apollo 15 crew as they approached Earth for their splashdown.

Several years later, after the Apollo 15 Mission, I had a chance to meet up with Al Worden, thanks to my good friend Stan Blum. I knew Worden from his days at The Point to be a cool guy, but it was hard to grasp him being shot off this planet by a rocket taller than a football field and then being sent orbiting behind the moon.

At one point, orbiting the moon, Worden found himself on the dark side and some thousands of miles further out in space from the other two astronauts walking on the moon ; the farthest for any man without having any communications whatsoever with planet earth. Al didn't make much of the fact, but he explained his mind-set to me, and that was that he had made peace with everybody and everything before he left the planet.

Under slightly different circumstances, it was the same fatalistic approach I ended up with after I was pressed to leave CBS Sports after serving them for thirty years. But before I get to any of the unpleasant experiences involved in that transition, I want to give you a clue to what led up to it. What was my first sign that the CBS tide was turning against me? And that was when I wasn't assigned the 1980 Super Bowl. I used to get that assignment on a regular basis—so when it didn't come, I knew I was being screwed with. After the game aired, I thought the situation had corrected itself since the coverage of the 1980 Super Bowl was so bad that the producer, Terry O'Neil, in his book, The Game Behind The Game, cited the poor coverage by quoting the Sports Illustrated review of the game:"The CBS crew … missed a more basic aspect of big-game coverage: reaction shots…When Los Angeles's Frank Corral missed an extra point attempt, he surely must have reacted in an animated fashion. We did not, however, get a quick glimpse of him after the miss... On none of Terry Bradshaw's three interceptions did we see an isolated replay of one of the NFL's most animated quarterbacks reacting to his misplay."

I should point out that Terry O'Neil was brought in as the Executive Producer of NFL telecasts by Van Gordon Sauter, who had now become president of CBS Sports.

I didn't get along with Van Sauter. Sauter's first words to me were a killer. He said that he didn't like that I also had a contract with Caesars Palace. I explained that I had the right to do so contractually. His response to that was to look away—so I asked him why he had a problem with that. Van Sauter puffed away on his pipe and finally claimed that it really wasn't him. He said that it was the CBS lawyers. And he said "CBS lawyers" like I should shit my pants at the sound of it.

Van Sauter never told me which CBS lawyers or what the problem actually was. Then it seemed like the handwriting on the wall was getting even larger when Van Sauter assigned Terry O'Neil to head up the football telecasts. In fact, even my friend the announcer Jack Buck warned me about O'Neil, asking, "Do you think you can take him?"

Now with the 1982 Super Bowl coming up, O'Neil had already decided that John Madden would get the color assignment, and that he, O'Neil, would be the best choice to produce the game, and that the director assignment wouldn't be made until the end of the season so that he could award it on merit. Once I heard that remark, I became suspicious. And I became more suspicious when O'Neil told me that he had selected me to direct the 1982 Super Bowl even though the NFL season was only at the halfway point. O'Neil told me—"Keep it under your hat."

What was going on? This came from the guy who said he would wait for the end of the season to make the assignment —so what was this about? Could it be a setup? Why did I have to keep it 'under my hat,' unless he didn't want the word out? What if his plan was to change his mind, so as to leave me looking like the unsuspecting fool? What if he was thinking that the best way to undermine my 30-year-tenure at CBS would be to have me decide to save face and quit on my own accord so that he could get rid of me, thereby ridding himself of his main obstacle in changing the producer-director relationship, whereby the producer would control the Instant Replays, instead of the director?

In all my years as the live director, I cued the talent, took all the camera shots, matted graphics, and chose the replays. But now I felt that O'Neil wanted more control, more glory; he wanted to take over some of the director's duties, especially in controlling the replays. And, to make matters worse, all of O'Neil's thinking was just hunky-dory with Van Sauter. I told both of them that it wasn't okay with me. I filed a grievance with the Directors Guild of America, but whatever decisions were made by the DGA came only after O'Neil had victoriously taken control of the Instant Replay and well after I had, indeed, left CBS.

As far as the play-by-play assignment for that year's Super Bowl, O'Neil had told Vin Scully that the choice would be between him and Pat Summerall at the end of the season. Once again, that decision would not be made until then because O'Neil wanted to make it on merit. But that didn't turn out to be true, either. Something else was going on. The decision to pair Summerall with Madden was announced well before the season ended. Why would O'Neil do this? He certainly must have known that Scully wouldn't take that kind of crap and would bolt after his last commitment, the 1982 NFC Championship Game.

Before I finish the story of my CBS exodus, let me take a second to comment on that Championship Game since it has a special importance in the history of the NFL.

The 1982 NFC Championship would become known as 'The Catch' because the 49ers wide receiver, Dwight Clark, made a sensational, leaping grab to win the game. It was the 4th quarter and Dallas had a 27 to 21 lead with four minutes left to play. Joe Montana and the 49ers were pinned back on their own 11-yard line. Then Montana led San Francisco down the field to the Cowboy's 6-yard line. Now, with third and three and 58-seconds left on the clock, Montana went to the air, and Dwight Clark made an impossible catch to win the game. I couldn't wait to see the Instant Replay—and to see how the hell Clark could catch that ball.

The Instant Replay rolled back showing Montana scrambling out of the pocket to his right, the side closest to the camera, with Dallas' defensive end Larry Bethea closing in on him. Montana leapt into the air and let one loose over Bethea's outstretched arms. But the ball is thrown so hard and high that it looks like Joe had deliberately thrown it out of the end zone. But that wasn't the case. All of a sudden, up comes his wide receiver, Dwight Clark, like a shot out of a cannon, and catches the ball on his fingertips.

It was not only an amazing TD, but it also provided some great close-ups of Bill Walsh, Joe Montana and Dwight Clark. And, of course, there was the mandatory cutaway shot of the dejected Dallas cornerback, Everson Walls, who had been unable to soar up to cover Clark.

What was just as surprising was that in the post-game show we found out that the TD play, the one that coach Bill Walsh had sent in, 'Sprint Option Right', was designed to be executed in exactly that manner—either Dwight jumped high enough to catch it or it would sail over everybody's head and out of the end zone, leaving Joe Montana with another down to try to score.

With that victory, the 49ers were on their way to Super Bowl XVI. But I never got the assignment to direct that Super Bowl, even though Terry O'Neil had promised it to me, reaffirming that my direction was superior to the other director he had in mind, the one he had criticized on CBS's previous Super Bowl.

But it seemed to me that this other director and his producer were determined to take out anyone who stood in their way from their being teamed with Summerall and Madden. I didn't have an agent to huddle-up-with, as they did, with management. Plus Terry O'Neil was making it crystal clear now that it would be he, not the director, who would be in charge of the Instant Replay. The Instant Replay wasn't 'Tony's baby' anymore.

In the fall of 1981 Neal Pilson became head of the sports department.

I didn't get along with him either. I had run-ins with Pilson from the day he arrived at CBS Sports as a 'bean counter' some five years earlier.

As I mentioned, I had created and sold a few shows to the sports department. I found some of his 'bean counting' on those deals with me not pleasant. And now in 1981, with Pilson being the head of the department, I thought it best to put some distance between me and the New York office he was running. It appeared to me that he looked at televised sports solely as a means for him to put a numbered amount of commercials into a numbered amount of events.

I asked to be assigned to the West Coast games and events. Pilson countered by offering me 10 assignments for the whole year, a seventy five percent drop. I told him I wanted to push new frontiers and it seemed that I was being pushed out the door. When he asked who was pushing me, I moved closer and said, "I'm looking at him." Pilson walked away saying, "I don't care what you think."

That was the last slap in the face I was going to take. So it was down the elevator and out the door. But when I left CBS I also left Caesars Palace. And the reason was because I felt tainted by the suggestive remark that Van Gordon Sauter had made. Let me explain. Being an Italian-American, I felt that the suggestion that the CBS lawyers had reservations about my association with Caesars could damage my career. It was hard to ignore the glaring and suggestive connections that could be made by that shitty comment. Perhaps some would even think that my being an Italian-American with connections to Caesars Palace added up to a suggestion that I could possibly fix the outcome of a game.

As absurd as that was, and no matter what the true intent of the remark was, the bell had been rung, and I wasn't going to be able to un-ring it.

The remark was pure horseshit. I have no idea how a TV director could affect the outcome of a game. Plus, I disliked any allusion on the guys at Caesars. The brass at Caesars always treated me with respect. There was no horseshit there. No one ever lied to me. No one ever asked me to do anything but my job. But as I said, the bell had been rung and the notion that I could be a dago/wop with Vegas ties had been put out there, intentionally or unintentionally.

I met with Terry Lanni, a top executive at Caesars. I told Terry that I thought it would be best if I moved on, and he let me do as I wished. Terry Lanni was a first-rate thinker. I wasn't surprised that he eventually became the CEO of MGM Mirage, the company that now dominates the Las Vegas Strip.

As I left the CBS Sports Department and Caesars Palace Productions I may have entered a new stretch of my career—but I made sure the strength of my life's accounts would continue to rest in the intertwining of my parallel careers.

For starters, I headed off in a new direction, traveling to Buenos Aires, Argentina.

I had to get over my CBS/Caesars trauma, so I took a couple of months off to write a movie that popped into my head, Algebra I Murder II. The script was a whodunit with a small budget, so small I was asked to check out Buenos Aires as a possible shooting location for the movie. It seemed like a good idea to produce and direct in a country which was known to have a strong culture that embraced the thinking that a low budget can also 'make you more creative'.

On landing in Argentina, I decided to treat the survey trip as a form of mental foraging, like opening the refrigerator just to look around without removing anything.

On arrival, I struck up a friendship with a German-Argentine businessman living in Buenos Aires. He confessed, "I am particularly worried about my colleagues who have disappeared."

Next I checked out the private school where I considered enrolling my son while I was shooting. The school was well guarded. A little too well guarded. The professor confessed, "We have many American children here, and there is always a possibility of kidnapping for ransom."

While I was going over my script with a local film crew, outside the window I could see a political march of women coming down the street with a sign that read: "We are the Mothers of the Disappeared from Buenos Aires."

I wanted to grab my bag and head for the airport, but since I had committed to my investors I needed a solid business reason, not an emotional one, for why I shouldn't do the film there. I found the excuse I needed when I tried to secure the completion bond that would be needed to guarantee that the film would be completed or the guarantors would have to repay all sums invested by my U.S. investors.

Before boarding my plane, I phoned the U.S. and told them that obtaining the completion bond would not be a problem but collecting it would be. If the guarantors didn't keep their end of the bargain—good luck in taking them to court down there! (For the record, the movie wasn't made but twenty-five years later I rewrote the script as a blog novel.)

In 1983 I get a phone call from Roone Arledge. He was now President of ABC News, and he asked if I was available to direct a live debate between Paul Newman and Charlton Heston. The actors were going to take opposing sides on President Ronald Reagan's Star Wars Defense Missile Program. Which, I should note, became a hot international topic of debate again some twenty years later in 2007 when Russia objected to the Bush Administration's attempt to expand bases for the Defense Missile Program into Europe.

It was controversial for different reasons back in the Eighties, and I was a little hesitant, but I firmed-up my reluctant 'yes' when I heard Roone say that Av Westin would be producing. Westin was a big-name news producer who was humble enough to recall starting out as Ed Murrow's copy boy on the 17th floor at 485 Madison Avenue. This was back when the radio guys were the ones occupying the larger portion of the L-shaped workspace, leaving the less prominent, shorter side for the television guys.

Paul Newman and Charlton Heston were both 58 years old, and both were famous, graying actors. The two had once been close friends and fellow Democrats, but Heston had shifted his political beliefs to the Right and changed his registration from Democrat to Republican.

I greeted the two actors as they entered the ABC studio. I had met Newman before, so I wasn't surprised that he showed up at

5' 9", but when Heston sauntered in, he was an easy 6'3"—shit, I thought, this could look like a real "Mutt and Jeff" act on camera. I had to figure out a way to televise this so Moses wouldn't win the debate simply because he towered over Cool Hand Luke.

I thought it best to 'even the two up' with a split screen close-up that would give them the same distance in headroom from the top of the frame. I went up to the control rooms to discuss using a split screen with Arledge and Westin, but neither of them was there. The only guys in my control room were ABC wannabes with their mean-looking faces dragging because they didn't get this plum assignment.

I rehearsed my cameramen on how to simultaneously slip from a 'full frame close-up' to slide the actor's face to one side of the frame so that I could dissolve to the split at the right moment within the give-and-take—rather than having to punch up the combined-split as a single shot. As I readied for air, Av Westin called me up over another headset. He was sitting next to Roone in a New York control room.

On air, the actors went non-stop as they debated the wisdom of either reducing nuclear weapons—or building a new Star Wars shield. It seemed to me that Heston was more informed than Newman, but, then again, Reagan never took the Star Wars shield beyond the experimental stage.

During the telecast the only time a voice came out of NY it was that of Av Westin telling me to stay on the split screen.

When we went off the air, Westin put Roone on the phone. Roone was pleased. He said that the split screen had worked well since it also included each of the actor's reactions at crucial times. I joked with Roone about how much money he was now making, and as we said our goodbyes, he added that he'd like to use me on the 1984 Summer Olympics to be held in Los Angeles, and I took him up on it.

I ended up directing the swimming events that were being held at the Swim Stadium, a newly constructed, open-air facility next to the Coliseum. The first thing I recall was getting great crowd shots since there were thousands of Americans in the open stands who kept cheering on the US swimmers who were dominating the Olympic competition. Of all the swimming events, the one that remains most in my mind is the 200 Meter Butterfly that featured Michael Gross of Germany, who was nicknamed "the albatross," because of enormous wingspan.

In the past, I had used an underwater camera to capture the butterfly swimmers undulating like dolphins. But the angle I wanted for Gross was head-on, above the water, to show him propelling his body forward and out of the water, lifting his head up as he pulled both arms out of the water and swinging them forward with a massive 7 1/2 feet reach. In super slow motion it was an amazing shot.

For the record, Michael Gross of Germany lost the gold to Jon Sieben of Australia. And I won an Emmy to add to the one I had for directing NFL Football.

On July 13th, 1985, Bob Geldof 's Live Aid raised more than $100 million to help combat poverty, famine and disease in Africa.

Echoing that global breakthrough, twenty years later, on July 2nd, 2005, Live 8 took place as a series of concurrent concerts across the world to highlight the continuing problem of global poverty. They've said that "Live 8" was "Live Aid" for the Internet Age, since it used the Internet as a tool to bring together a global community.

Let me take you through "Live Aid," Geldof's television event that started it all. At the time, 1985, it was hard to believe that anyone could pull off a sixteen-hour live telethon using satellites from around the world. In the US, Bob Geldof turned to Michael Mitchell, president of Worldwide Sports and Entertainment. Mitchell brought on Hal Uplinger as his co-executive producer. It was their job to sell this idea—and the scope of this idea—to Europe and the rest of the world.

To put on the event, Geldolf relied on two mega-promoters, Harvey Goldsmith in England and Bill Graham in the US. Wembley Stadium, in the north of London, had been signed up as the European venue, but when the Meadowlands Stadium in New Jersey dropped out as the U.S. location, Geldof thought about using JFK Stadium in the south of Philadelphia. I approached my sister-in-law Anna Verna, who was the councilwoman of that district. Anna immediately saw the benefits of having

Philadelphia involved with this humanitarian effort and brought about a meeting for me with Mayor Wilson Goode.

After the mayor gave his permission to use JFK Stadium, the promoter of the U.S. venue, Bill Graham, immediately came in, shook hands, and held a press conference in City Hall. No sooner had Graham begun than he was peppered, then shelled, with questions by the newspaper reporters regarding his lack of booking black artists on the bill. The matter was resolved when more black rock stars were added to the program. But then a couple of other major problems developed. Geldof had the USA covered only by the cable channel MTV. I was asked to arrange a meeting with my contact at Orbis Communications. The syndicator agreed to bring in more than one hundred stations across the country.

But Geldof still needed a U.S. Network to carry the show, so I set up a meeting with John Hamlin at ABC-TV. Harvey Goldsmith joined Geldof and me, and a deal was hammered out whereby the local stations would terminate their coverage three hours before ABC took over the prime-time coverage with Dick Clark hosting for his production company.

In London, Geldof had arranged for the BBC to feed Europe and beyond. In the U.S., Mike Mitchell had arranged for our satellites to feed the USA and beyond. So, in effect, it was both the BBC and the US that transmitted to the rest of the world.

Bob Geldof explained in his book 'Is That It?' that many artists wanted to be on during syndication and not during U.S. primetime, because this was the time their band would get the best worldwide audience. Geldof eventually got so fed up with these pressures that he agreed to all requests and that decision forced me to tape some of the live acts for a delayed airing on ABC.

Earlier that week, I got a call from Harvey Goldsmith in London. Mick Jagger and David Bowe wanted to ask me—what if—while Mick was singing in Philly could it be timed with David singing the same song in London. I explained the problem of sound delay to Mick and David when using satellites. They got a laugh when I suggested that unless they did "Row, Row, Row Your Boat" they'd better record their song. Which they did.

"Dancing in the Streets" became a hit music video.

"Live Aid" ran sixteen hours. ABC's John Hamlin wanted me to direct the musical acts, but I told him it would be impossible since I had to control the World and Syndicated Feeds. The U.S. musical acts were directed by Lou Horvitz, a top director and a former cameraman of mine, and by another talented director, Sandi Fullerton.

A dozen more directors were employed to cover the overseas acts. For those interested, all the facts about "Live Aid" are covered in my book Global Television (Focal Press) along with diagrams, charts and rundown of the six television feeds along with their satellite schematics. Or you can view some of the material at the website: tonyvernaTV.com.

There are also many stories in the book, including the one where the DiamondVision screen helped bail me out when Paul McCartney's microphone went dead as he was singing "Let It Be." McCartney was in London singing at the piano when the Brits lost sound. I tried to persuade the director to walk-in a microphone, live on the air, and make a moment of it. But he and his producer didn't think it 'proper'. They were going to have someone crawl under the cameras with a new mike. I couldn't deal with that nonsense, so I cut away from Sir Paul to shots of the audiences in both stadiums and put it on the massive DiamondVision screen. The kids knew all of the words, of course, and began singing louder when they saw each other from opposite sides of the Atlantic. It no longer mattered that we couldn't see or hear McCartney. We saw and heard his fans who sang loud and clear in what seemed to be a tribute to him. Strangely enough, my cutaway coverage was praised in the Press as if the 'bloody' thing had been planned.

When Harvey Goldsmith accepted the TV award in England, he gave me a special thank you for staying at the controls for the entire telecast. Yes, it was a long day for me. I had televised two sunrises and two sunsets on the same program from a truck in South Philadelphia. It was the same site where, a dozen years earlier, I had introduced the Instant Replay.

Now let's move on to the following year to May of 1986, when Bob Geldof created another show he called "Sport Aid" to help raise funds for African relief. Sport Aid actually used more technology than "Live Aid," even though it only lasted two hours. It used an extra satellite, bringing your total to 14.

I decided to direct this far-reaching, worldwide program from a control room in New York even though the U.S. wasn't carrying the program. I needed NBC's Studio 8-H as my control room. It had enough monitors for me to view the thousands of runners from twelve countries. And the facility was capable of providing me with an audio setup where I could communicate with the dozens of producers and directors from around the world who were providing updates of their races. For those interested in a more elaborate explanation of "Sport Aid," all the facts can also be found in another of one of my books, Global Television.

I think many television students will find it interesting to learn how we arranged for the anchor, Rolland Smith, to be ready on a second's notice to jump in and be fully knowledgeable about the location so that he could provide a timely commentary.

Timing was key. It was critical to show the winner of each race crossing the finish line. In my control room, it got really confusing, to watch those runners racing in all directions on all the monitors. To make matters even more difficult, sometimes I'd be covering the finish of one live race with a post-race interview in broad daylight when I needed to undercut the finish of another live race coming in from the other side of the globe in the dark of night.

I was able to close out 'the two-hour run from around the world' with a nice touch, thanks to a satellite view of the Earth taken by Tom Van Sant, a gifted conceptual artist. Tom had captured a present-time image from the GOES-6 Satellite stationed 22,000 miles above our planet. It was an exceptional visualization.

My involvement with "Sport Aid" began in May of 1986, and it was during this time that I had an unexpected and very distinguished visitor in my control room. Tom Van Sant had brought along his friend, Richard Feynman, the now late Caltech physicist who had shared in winning the Nobel Prize in 1965 for his work in quantum physics and whose Feynman Diagrams on particle behavior played an important role in development of the atomic bomb.

When Feynman died several years later, at age 69, science author James Gleick quoted noted scientist and author Freeman Dyson of the Institute for Advanced Study in Princeton, N.J. "He [Feynman] was the most original mind of his generation."

And this is the guy who had just walked in on me.

Feynman was curious about how I would handle transmitting feeds from seven countries on the fourteen satellites—and how I'd be able to tape one winner crossing his or her finish line at the same time I was airing others crossing live—a situation, which, as I've said, actually happened. Feynman found it really interesting that I was using satellites not just for relaying programs but also as a director's tool by intercutting one nation's feed for another nation to comment on. Even today, I remain honored that a genius-intellect like Richard Feynman was curious about what I was trying to achieve.

In 1987 I was honored that Omni Magazine chose me as one of the '14 Great Minds' to predict the future. I was joined by Carl Sagan and George Will. Pretty good company, I'd say. Plus they had my prediction follow directly after that of Bill Gates. They probably did that because we both stressed the way the digital age was going to change communication, including TV. Gates stressed storage capacity and how it would affect our personal lives. I stressed how the digital age, along with ion and laser technology, would come together 'someday' to allow televised images to be transmitted onto a 'contained cloud of ion gas'. And how you'd be able to walk a 360 around a football game being projected holographically in the middle of your living room.

In 1987 I also joined forces with the renowned producer Graham Lacey to aid in his syndicated special, "Christmas Around the World." The program was a musical celebration with artists singing Christmas songs from around the world. Lacey brilliantly produced the event live on stage and, in turn, it was beautifully directed by Matthew Crouch of the Trinity Broadcasting Network. The only assistance I could lend was when Johnny Cash showed up to do his Christmas number with plans of singing it over a pre-recorded musical track.

That was a problem since the set had been designed to have the orchestra as the backdrop at all times. 'The Man in Black' took center stage, and when the lights dimmed he looked even more so. The musicians readied themselves in the orchestra section, relieved to know that I told them to just 'fake it' when Johnny sang to his recorded track. The only mike opened was the one in front of Johnny's sad face.

Cash never looked back at the musicians as he sang nor did he acknowledge anything but the lens on the camera. He sang, shook hands, and was out the door, leaving me thinking, here was a man who was either truly at peace or someone who was half dead.

1987…was the year I created what singled out for me my greatest TV production. The Instant Replay will live forever, but it was a concept and a technique. Pope John Paul II's "Prayer For World Peace" was the message that used the medium as no one else had ever used it before.

I was and am very proud of having had an ability to use television to accomplish one of Pope John Paul's goals—to communicate with people around the world to bring the world together in a meaningful fashion. I created the program without commercials, so the money had to come from somewhere. Thankfully my co-producer Paul Dietrich had the right contacts and got the job done. In Paris we met with Baron Bic, the notable pen manufacturer, and in the Netherlands we met with the members of the Lumen Foundation.

To open the live global hour, I thought it appropriate to have Mother Teresa appear on tape to deliver a short message and then to dissolve live to the exterior of the Basilica of Saint Mary Major and begin the program. I had developed a fondness and respect for Mother Teresa. I had met her when I filmed her being interviewed by producer Graham Lacey for his special "Christmas Around the World."

While I was filming the interview, Mother Teresa received a phone call from one of her nuns in Calcutta, India, and even though she retreated to the rear of the studio, to speak in privacy, I couldn't help but hear her repeatedly saying, "Throw it out the back window." When she returned to the set, she looked at me, knowing she had been overheard, and explained that the nun had just received an unexpected gift of new furniture and carpeting for the convent and that she told the nun to throw it out the back window into the alley below so that the poor could have access to it. Their vow of poverty did not allow them to have such worldly possessions.

Now for the "Prayer For World Peace," Paul Dietrich had spoken to Mother Teresa and she agreed to appear on the program. When I phoned her in New Delhi, she explained that she was traveling to Poland and that it might be very difficult to tape a piece in Krakow. Mother Teresa must have known what she was talking about. When the tape arrived from Krakow, it was practically unusable. The two cameramen assigned by the Communist-run television firm were only interested in making her audio distant and her camera shots inappropriately close. It seems even back then there were those interested in muddying up the purpose of this great lady's life. Fortunately I was able to cut and remaster the piece into a usable thirty seconds to open "Prayer for World Peace."

The program I created for John Paul II called for linking the Pope with sixteen countries around the globe while he—and the parishioners in churches on all five continents with five different languages—recited the Rosary, a devotional prayer, together. Actually, parts of the ceremony were conducted in eleven languages, but the Our Fathers and Hail Marys were recited in just the five languages—English, French, Spanish, Portuguese, and German. I arranged it so that the Pope could both see and hear the parishioners, and they could see and hear the Pope. To me, that was part of the power of the prayer; to be able to bring them all together.

The program was blessed from the start to have the assistance of Cardinal John P. Foley at the Vatican. At the time Rev. Foley was an Archbishop, and was best known for delivering the English commentary during the Midnight Mass from St. Peter's Basilica on Christmas Day.

The Archbishop knew of my production successes with "Live Aid" and "Sport Aid" and had the faith that I was probably the only one ready to undertake such an endeavor in global transmission. Let me say this up front: without Archbishop Foley the program would never have aired. It was only with the aid of the Pontifical Council that we were able to line up countries around the world to take the telecast.

But we didn't have a US Network to carry the event. Paul Dietrich arranged a meeting with Gene Jankowski, president of the CBS Broadcast Group. I hated to bother Jankowski at a time when he was busy cutting jobs at CBS by the hundreds. To make the story short, Jankowski, said "No." He wasn't going to open the spigot and let the religious word flow. Nor was he inclined to lend a hand. In my mind I thought, "Screw you. Yes I Can."

I decided the best way to blast a hole in this luddite's decision was to line up as many CBS O&O's and affiliates to prove that Jankowski was behind the times and didn't know what was best for the CBS stations. Many of the strongest stations in each market jumped at the chance, and in some markets more than one station made airtime available in what had now become my own 'ad hoc network'. I had a combined 'viewer potential' that was not only greater than what CBS could have offered but also provided programming for its competitors to up their ratings by airing the special against the CBS affiliates that hadn't signed up. The idea I created turned into the most viewed program in the history of television at the time. More than a billion viewers viewed the one-hour live telecast worldwide. The program was so amazing that it made the front page headline in many newspapers worldwide, including USA Today.

On "Prayer For World Peace," in addition to the prayer itself, we had the incredible live shots of the special pilgrimage in Caacupe, Paraguay, with 100,000 parishioners. In Czestochowa, Poland, the Pope's home country, we saw Mother Teresa, who had been taped earlier, sharing the prayer in Polish—live with the Pope.

Let's analyze some of the hurdles I had to overcome to make this program happen. Once in Rome, I hit a major obstacle with RAI (Radiotelevisione Italiana), the primary Italian television broadcasting system. RAI sent over several executives, in expensive suits, led by the late Vittoro Bono, to pay me a visit at my hotel. Signor Bono told me that the Vatican was 'RAI's beat' and guys like me didn't just come over and do programs there. This confrontation presented a major problem—but I didn't let on that they had me pinned to the wall.

I needed RAI to do the pickup since I couldn't transmit the program either over Europe or out of the European Continent without the telecast being done by an EBU (European Broadcast Union) member. Archbishop Foley and I weren't going to give up. The Archbishop, now a Cardinal, didn't like the state-run Italian network saying 'no' so coldly, especially since they were supposed to work out such problems with his Pontifical Council for Social Communications. But RAI had made it very clear to me that this was their turf and that I should pack-up and go home. It wasn't going to happen. Arrivederci!

But I didn't go home, and that left them wondering. My wife and I lingered at the Excelsior Hotel on the Via Veneto, the same hotel where my mother and father had honeymooned. My office contacted the EBU, seeking an alternative. As the days went by, I busied myself in writing a twenty-page contract between the Vatican and the global company I worked for, Global Media, which was headed up by Ian Watson along with entrepreneurs Jim Slater and Paul Temple. As days crawled by, my wife Carol and Archbishop Foley encouraged me to believe in my motto: Yes I Can.

At the end of the week, I got an okay from the United Kingdom Independent Broadcasting which was also an active member of the European Broadcasting Union. And that meant I could put the cameras I needed in the Basilica of Saint Mary Major to cover the Holy Father and be able to transmit the feed over and out of Europe without the approval of the Italian Network.

But now came the hard part... the really hard part! I wasn't allowed to direct from Rome. I had to go to London and call my live camera shots in Rome from there. That meant that the live cameras in Rome were on the monitors in my London control room. And that also meant, even though I was in England, I had to call the St. Mary Major camera shots in Italian. To steady camera one that was back in Rome, I had to call out "Firma

Uno." When I wanted the Italians to punch up camera one, I called out "Uno." If I wanted to steady camera two, it was "Firma Due"...and so forth. When I wanted to zoom in on the Pope, I called out, "Più vicino sul Papa."

And of course, I still needed to cut away to the other cameras around the world as the faithful responded to the Holy Father's prayers when he offered them up in their language. If you look at a recording of the live show, you can see the Holy Father, at times, checking on what was happening by looking down to where I had hidden a monitor. Originally, I was told that I could not put any TV monitors in St. Mary Major. I fought back. I had to have monitors, especially for the close of the program, when the Pope would leave the Basilica, and had to be able to see all the countries waving at him as one. But the Pope's assistant, Father Mariano, had said "No," and that was final. When I persisted, the priest walked away uttering "basta," meaning 'enough'. But I didn't want to hear "basta." I wanted to hear "si," so I asked the rector of St. Mary's if he would approach the Pope and have His Holiness make the decision. The next day, I was told that the Holy Father had granted my wish.

Once I had used my Yes I Can philosophy to get monitors in the church, I began working on my What if? philosophy— What if the Pope was praying in one of the five languages and the satellite feed with parishioners responding in that language went down? If the Pope was praying in French and the satellite feed went down from Lourdes in France, I had back-up satellite feeds from both Senegal and Quebec, where parishioners were also praying in French. And if all those satellite feeds collapsed at once? I put microphones in strategic locations within the Basilica where the Pope was praying. I had planted the mikes in the groups I had set up, praying in each of the five languages.

And part of the mechanical magic that let me make the Pope's wish come true was the use of quads, which I probably should have mentioned with Sport Aid, cause I used a 'Quad' to make that video possible, too. In the case of Sport Aid, we had live injects from twelve cities, but we didn't have the budget to satellite them all individually into my control room. The 'injects' from many of the countries came into London as quads containing four inject locations as a single signal.

For Prayer For World Peace we were dealing with eighteen locations, so I used four quads that were put together in other countries and then fed to me, If I was going to take the people praying in Fatima, I would call the quad that had Portugal in it. Let's say Fatima was in the lower left of Quad #4, in the third quadrant. Then I called "Q4-3," meaning to punch up the 3rd feed in Quad 4... and bang!—Portugal would be on the air. At the close of the live program I put all four quads on the screen at the same time, so when the Pope exited the Basilica we could see all of the sixteen cities praying along with him at the same time

The other technical magic I remember was the mix-minus pattern. Let me explain what it was and why the need for it. We had to do that with the audio so the Pope could hear the parishioners and the parishioners could hear the Pope. If we ran all of the audio, including that of the parish currently responding to the Pope, there would have been feedback and all kinds of weird noises, so we had to set up the audio cables so that each church could hear the other churches and the Pope but not their own responses.

Let me bring out something that happened on my way to do this show. Before flying to Rome, I stopped at Washington DC with Paul Dietrich. We were invited to have dinner with David Brinkley, Sam Donaldson, Jim Lehrer and some other heavyweights.

They were interested to know how I was going to pull it off. Our conversation never dried up. Most of the questions came from Brinkley—a highly skilled interviewer. He wanted to know how I was going to get the Pope to do a rehearsal. I said the Pope didn't do rehearsals and he didn't take time cues. I said I'd be standing in for the Holy Father and I would rehearse my cameras by having them follow me through the Basilica. When I was in doubt which way the Pope would go when he had a choice, I would go to the right. I was told that the Pope always goes to his right.

Sam Donaldson wanted to know what my vision was regarding the future of global television and news broadcasting.

I told him I wasn't sure. I don't think Sam liked my answer and the fact that he had to draw his own conclusions.

The meaning of the program was not to show what technology could do.

A rosary could be done on film and that suggestion had been submitted to me before. Filming a rosary was an old practice that no longer worked in new settings, but the idea began milling around like an unfinished tune in my head— and one morning I woke up with the live global idea. I basically envisioned the form of the entire production.

I woke up my wife and told her of this multi-satellite program I had just conceived for the Pope to do. Carol looked over at me and said, "You don't even know the Pope!" Right she was, but 90 days later the program was on the air.

I explained to David Brinkley that I was worried about my control crew. Nobody had ever really seen such a live blitz from around the world. I explained how I couldn't take the chance that the spectacle could slow down my video tweakers who had to ready the feeds that were coming in as quickly as possible.

Jim Lehrer was intrigued about the method I was planning to use to overcome the possible problem of my control room staff slowing down when they became fascinated by all those live feeds coming in, one after another, from around the world. This was my plan. I had spliced together an hour tape that simulated what I was hoping to bring about. The footage contained similar locale shots from the various countries, and I edited them in the order I hoped to be cutting to live.

Then the part that Jim Lehrer liked—that I planned to run that tape over and over until my crew became so fatigued that all that would be on their mind was to do their job and get this pain-in-the-ass program over with.

When I said goodbye to the famous newsmen and thanked the hostess of the party, I left for Rome, but I didn't know I'd end up directing the program from London. And while "Prayer for World Peace" and my other global shows were going on, I was also working on my second book, Live TV, Focal Press, commissioned by the Directors Guild of America. It was a great book to pull together. It was a chance to connect with dozens of top professionals in their field and have them tell how they did it.

My field interviewer, David Leaf, did a fine job in his travels to record the comments of the directors, producers, writers, and talent—everyone in news, sports, music, and special events. It was also interesting to learn the various ways various people had worked their way into the business.

William T. Bode got to edit the 2,000 transcribed pages of interviews. The book covers the Oscars, the Emmys, the Grammys, the Tonys, Telethons, plus some great interviews with pioneers like Pat Weaver. My favorite account was and is the one by Steve Allen because his account capsulated the whole purpose of the book. Steve told how seeing Edward R. Murrow's special on the plight of farm workers, "Harvest of Shame," so affected him that he not only researched the problem but also wrote two books about the subject. And while he was doing that work, he encountered two other people —men he'd never met before—writing about the same farm worker problems. The catalyst was that the other two had been inspired by the same program, Murrow's "Harvest of Shame." As Steve Allen said, that story dramatized the power that television can have. Most of the shows may be mediocre, but once in a while one program can spark changes that affect lives. And there's still a fair amount of live TV around—news, sports, coverage of disasters like hurricanes and earthquakes.

Those environmental factors led producer Hal Uplinger and Momoko Ito, a renowned consultant for the NHK Network in Japan, to have me direct "Our Common Future," an idea getting a lot more emphasis in today's world of overpopulated, underfed, under-medicated areas of the globe. The program aired just before World Environment Day, June 5, 1989. And we did both a World Feed and a Syndicated USA feed, so we had the challenge of fitting live acts into both shows. We had a ton of musical talent—John Denver, Kenny Loggins, Melissa Manchester, Diana Ross, Phoebe Snow—and then-eight-year-old Korean violinist Sara Chang. Not to mention the hosts—Lisa Bonet, Bob Geldof, Sigourney Weaver, Anglica Houston, and the late Christopher Reeve.

As usual, we used the star-power to lure viewers to the program's message. One song, "Spirit of the Forest," was dedicated to the show's theme. It featured Donna Summer, Olivia Newton-John, Ringo Starr, Mick Fleetwood, and Brian Wilson. I got some pretty good names for the Public Service Announcements on the show, too. The UN asked us to use heads of state, so Uplinger and Ito rounded up the first President Bush from the United States, Canada's Prime Minister Brian Mulroney, China's Prime Minister Li Peng.

Another factor that was particularly interesting was the new technology that NHK was experimenting with—using its new High Definition Television cameras to televise the program back to Japan. The Japanese technicians attached their HDTV camera electronically to my cameras, so that my camera cuts became theirs.

And that's how I ended—and we now end—the 1980s, looking ahead both technically and in terms of programming to the '90s.

CHAPTER SIX

THE NINETIES

We ended the Eighties looking forward to the rapid development of new technology. It was certainly rapid for me in 1963. When I was 29 years old, there was no such thing as an Instant Replay. Two weeks after I turned 30 there was an Instant Replay.

I've been asked how do you feel today about that, as compared to what I felt back then? The Instant Replay in 1963 was in black and white, and it was aired without the benefit of slow motion or high definition, but it still achieved what I wanted it to achieve. The Instant Replay today is capable of an image five times sharper. It's in color, and it has the benefit of super slow-motion plus its high definition capabilities are a natural for improved officiating. And my hope is that Major League Baseball comes around in the same manner to help out the officials on games that could determine a club's season.

When I started in television in 1953, technically, in that year alone, there were so many shows that had been kinescoped that one hundred million feet of film were consumed. I didn't have any inkling that someday programs would be recorded on videotape, but Pat Weaver did. He was NBC's visionary executive and when he heard about videotape, he went down to the electronics company called Ampex to see what all the fuss was about. He recalled entering a room called 'the-run-for-your-life-room' because the operator could face a situation where the fast-speeding tape would break off the reels and whip-around the room.

In England, they preferred to film their shows to get a better quality than going quick-and-dirty with kinescopes. At that same time, however, the English began using a teleprompter that BBC engineers rigged up after one of their presenters, Peter Dimmock, had seen one being used in America.

And personally, as long ago as it was, I still remember the day when Irving Kahn showed up in Philly to demonstrate his teleprompter. And let me give you one more pre-teleprompter fascinating-fact: Before Don Hewitt got his hands on a prompter, he tried to talk Douglas Edwards into learning Braille so that the newscaster could keep his eyes on the camera lens at all times. And, if that sounds strange, let me tell you how another TV star solved the problem of eye-contact. I ran into it when I was directing some live commercials with Dick Clark, in his pre-Bandstand days. Clark was doing a local show in Philly called "Barr's Diamond Theater." Instead of using cue cards—which could draw his eyes away from the camera and his viewers—Dick used an earpiece prompter that was wired to an audio tape recorder. On the air, Clark displayed his 'Instant Memory' by simply repeating the copy he had recorded just before going on the air.

And on the same theme, Heywood Broun once told me about another star, Henry Fonda, the acclaimed movie and theater star, who had a memory that was so focused that while Fonda was on stage, performing, Broun could actually give Fonda a running account of the Giants baseball scores from the wings, no matter how involved Fonda was in performing. Broun used his fingers to relay the score that he had just heard on a stagehand's radio, and then he followed his fingering of the score with a thumb up or down if the Giants were winning or losing.

Broun was also one of many who criticized NBC's Harry Coyle and me for using the centerfield camera because it made it easier for the opponents to steal the catcher's signs. But Harry and I had often explained that hometown spies were commonplace in the scoreboard, and even in 1951, they found the Giants had a guy with a telescope in the scoreboard.

And that brings us to present times and the New England Patriots breaking NFL league rules by secretly videotaping the defensive signals of the rival New York Jets. All I can say is that if the viewer were ever tipped-off before the play, then it would take the magic out of the Instant Replay. If the viewer became aware of what was going to happen, then the rerun would be like standing behind the magician and the effect would be lost.

"Earth 90" was another show I directed for the Japanese Broadcasting Corporation (Nippon Hoso Kyokai), or NHK. The show was produced in fine fashion by Hal Uplinger, Momoko Ito, and Joi Ito, but it turned out to be a very dicey globalcast for me. My control room was parked outside the Brooklyn Academy of Music in New York, and that meant that the USA Concert, which was being hosted by singer Debbie Gibson and newsman Rolland Smith, could be piped directly into my truck. But the other two live concerts were satellite feeds, from Tokyo and France, and since those satellites wouldn't be available until an hour before going on the air I was facing some possible major holes in my three-hour live global telecast.

To cover the 'What if' on the French satellite feed—in case Olivia Newton-John's performance went down, I had a backup taped of Richard Marx, performing "Help" by the Berlin Wall. Plus, I also had a couple of live options: cutting to Gilberto Gil, who was performing live in Brazil, or cutting to the musical group Alabama, performing live in North Carolina. To cover the 'what if' on the Japanese satellite feed, in case John Denver's performance went down, I pre-taped John and the rest of the Tokyo performances the day before. To cover the What if on the New York Concert, in case we had problems there, I had stockpiled performances by Crosby, Stills, and Nash, the Vienna Children's Choir and Julio Iglesias's concert from Jones Beach. For those interested in how all the emergency, stand-by scripts I had written were coordinated, please check out my book Global Television.

I'd also like to point that our live TV audience had no idea what was supposed to happen. The audience knows only what happens. So my emergency scripts dealt with addressing a clean, polished presentation no matter what. One of the built-in complications I had was that NHK had attached its High Definition Cameras to our Standard Definition Cameras so that its HDTV Feed could be sent back as an experiment to Japan; but that, in turn, limited the cameras' mobility.

And since the NHK people were edgy about the language difference and because they weren't yet accustomed to producing that many globalcasts—what they did was to set up a camera to cover my control room so they could see and hear me at all times.

I also set up a back-up system to be sure that John Denver was protected from any mishaps caused by the stage crew in Tokyo. In addition to having the ever-present Interrupt Feedback so that I could talk to John directly in case of an emergency, I set up a video feed from Tokyo so I could see John's teleprompter copy. I would have caught and avoided any possible language mix-up by talking directly to John, in his ear, about a potential problem.

Let me say a word about John Denver. They don't come any better. Just being able to kid around with John, who was some 6,000 miles away, made the whole experience one I will never forget. In that show I used the big screen differently from the way I used DiamondVision on, say, "Live Aid."

This time I put a smaller version of the big screens directly on the stage, as part of the setting. In New York I had two screens suspended on either side of a huge "Earth 90" Globe. Because the screens were suspended, I could have them there when I wanted them or have them pulled up out of sight. I used them to show close-ups of the New York performers, so that the wide shot also had the close-ups within it. I used them to let the New York audience see live performances from Tokyo and other locations. I used them to show video of the "Earth 90" Globe to reinforce the show's theme. I even used them a few times to carry Public Service Announcements being sent out on the air. And because there was an eight-second delay between John Denver in Tokyo conversing with Gilberto Gil in Rio de Janeiro, the dual screens were especially effective to help bridge the time-lapse in their conversation by using a slow pan. Again, imagination was needed to help the viewers forget the limitations of my technology.

When I saw "The Old Man and the Sea" in 1958, I wasn't thinking of Spencer Tracy sitting in his boat in a water tank behind a blue wall in Soundstage No. 16 at Warner Brothers. Nor did I question the moment when the big fish was able to drag Tracy out to sea by the magic of the first chroma key being used on a movie.

Creativity inspires. I approached Brooks Graham, my West Coast EIC, about installing a chroma key flat behind the announcers in the booth so that they could appear to be standing in front of the playing field instead of that plain wall in their booth.

What comes to mind when I think back on all those effects, what comes to mind now, is the uninspired in-the-round set used in Fox's broadcast of the 2007 Emmys. The set didn't offer any sense of marrying the latest use of the latest television technology to the film industry's latest accomplishments. Nor did the set do anything for the art of stagecraft since 'Emmys-In-The Round' demanded 'in the round blocking' rather than 'proscenium blocking' on a round stage.

When I saw how limited this one-angle approach was going to be, I stared away, thinking that a merciful God would have restaged their coverage for them. I also got to thinking back to the sixties, when Abe Saperstein told me about a show in Prague that had tricked his eye. He told me how the Czechs had projected a film behind their actors performing on the stage. Their background was, in reality, a curtain of vertical vinyl slats that, in effect, became a porous chroma that allowed the live male dancers to reach into the movie screen and pull out the females as their dancing partners.

Unlike the Emmys of 2007, the Czech Theater of 1960 understood the importance of marrying the imaginative art of stagecraft to the tremendous strides made by their film industry.

Then I got to thinking way back—to 1898, when the stage production of "Ben Hur" used a moving, painted cloth as the background behind the eight real horses which were pulling two chariots, while running on treadmills that had been installed in the floor of the stage. Visual magic, like beauty, is in the eye of the beholder—and in the creative minds of producers and directors.

With that thought in mind, let's go to Ted Turner's "1990 Goodwill Games," a series of 23 shows over 17 days that took place in August of 1990. I was hired by Bob Wussler, who was, at the time, the Executive Vice President of the Turner Broadcasting System. Bob and I had a long friendship, and through the years we shared the same instinct for innovation.

Wussler introduced me to Ted Turner, who was quick to tell me that I didn't work for him, that I worked with him. To this day I am still in awe of this man's remarkable and visionary career. Wussler encouraged me to take chances, to be creative and to use the satellites not only to send out the show signals but also to bring in the live injects from around the world in support of Turner's vision that there are no 'foreigners'.

With that goal, I began using the overseas satellites to set up on-camera interviews between, say, the winner of an event with his mother in Russia, so we not only linked the two countries but did it in a closer, more emotional way that people might remember long after the show.

To further that approach, I included an inject from the Russian space station MIR. And with the help of Vladimir Pozner, a major TV personality in Russia, we were able to have a live interview with the two cosmonauts Gennady Manakov and Gennady Strekalov. To prove that the two of them were floating in space, Larry King asked the two cosmonauts to do a back flip. And they did.

Let's go back to the beginning. Ted Turner allowed me, as the executive producer and executive director, two years to prepare for his "1990 Goodwill Games." And all the while I couldn't wait to work with the laser-sharp Larry King. And that experience eventually turned out to be such a delightful time that it still sits high in my memory bank.

There were twenty-three shows over seventeen days, and the days were consecutive—with no breaks. I had to get the whole team ready ahead of time because once the marathon starts, there's no chance to pause and reflect. It was show after show, day after day. The first thing I did was to develop a series of Program Overviews with the help of my head writer Brian Brown. Thanks to Brian, there was an Overview for each show. It detailed events and locations and participants and even sketched out some potential reporting by our team—Larry King as our anchor and co-hosts Hannah Storm and Nick Charles. Each Overview ran from about 25 to 50 pages. It was a huge effort, but we had to do it that way—one Overview for each show and one at a time. If we'd compiled a book, it would've been huge, and all the people we sent it to were working professionals off doing other shows. No one had time—or inclination—to read a book a foot thick.

So Brian and I wrote one Overview at a time and mailed it out. The Overviews were also needed to develop the Operation Manuals that were put out by the supervising coordinators, Rex Lardner, David Raith and Barry O'Donnell. The Overviews were also needed for Turner's CFO, Paul Beckham, who headed up the whole operation. Beckham was on an extremely tight budget. Coverage of NBC's 1988 Olympics cost a hundred twenty million dollars. Beckham had a twenty million dollar limit. It was reported that Turner ended up losing forty million. But that didn't stop Ted. He went on to do the Games again in 1994.

Just before the games, I had to fly to Washington DC to direct the first President Bush, George Hebert Walker Bush, in a series of public service announcements that would be played during the Games.

At the White House, I had them run the copy on the teleprompter for the President to review. I was concerned that the copy had too many informal contractions that could be debatable for use in formal—presidential—speech. But the President thought the contractions were in common use. He got on camera and did the series in one take. When I returned to Seattle, I told Ted Turner that the President was amazed that Larry King could also anchor an international sports event. We smiled and went off to have a drink.

Turner Broadcasting was responsible for the television

coverage—some 500 hours of international sports events. There were some fourteen remote locations in the Seattle area, ten connected by fiber-optic cable, four coming in via satellite downlinks. For a complete account of the production and scope of "The 1990 Goodwill Games" you can check it out in my book Global Television, Focal Press. The book has gone out of print, but it is still available at the public library.

The book didn't come out until 1993, because it took a couple of years to pull together all the stats and budgets and photos from all the global shows we've been discussing. When it gave birth, it came in at more than 300 pages.

The world moves on. "Live Aid" morphed twenty years later into "Live Eight." The shows I wrote about in 1993 are ancient history to today's kids—but, as they say, "The past is behind. Learn from it."

The world moved on, and so did my mind. I had always been curious about various worldwide beliefs that an object, action, or circumstance not logically related to a course of events could influence the outcome of those events. So I created a show "Superstitions Around the World." The pilot was quickly financed in France and shot in London. In Paris, it was agreed to cast the likeable European actor Georges Corraface as host of the show. Corraface was still on cloud-nine from playing opposite Marlon Brando in the movie "Christopher Columbus: The Discovery."

With superstitions you must give both sides of the story. On one side, I presented those who firmly believed in the ominous significance of their beliefs—and on the other side, I gave equal camera time and a paycheck to a debunker who would discredit their claims. In short, the pilot didn't sell, despite the debunker's crossing of his fingers in hopes that it would.

Let's move from Paris to Tokyo. The producers Momoko Ito and Joi Ito had requested my assistance with their booking and the shooting of Ray Charles, the multitalented blind black musician, for a live performance during a concert to be held at Japan's NHK Hall. The only help I was really able to provide was during Ray's rehearsal, when I saw Charles' drummer moving his chair to a new spot so he could see Ray's feet. I recommended to the Japanese director that he should change his camera moves so that the equipment didn't block the drummer's sightline to Charles' feet. Ray moved his body to the music, but it was his feet that provided the deft accompaniment that the drummer needed to pick up the right tempo.

And then—cue the fireworks—in 1995 I received one of the greatest honors in my business: The Directors Guild of America's Lifetime Achievement Award for Sports. That was a very special occasion—very formal. Tony Danza formally presented the award to me. And what I'll never forget is how Anthony Salvatore Iadanza took time out to go into the audience and say hello to my sister Helen who had always been the wind beneath my wings. I don't know if inventing the Instant Replay was the main reason I was chosen for the award. It was certainly a factor. This was 1995, and by then the world had thirty years to see how the instant part of Instant Replay had changed the way we watched sports.

It's been amazing to see how it's still changing things with the advent of high definition. And that takes us into not just another decade but to another century—the 21st Century, the 'Digital Century' filled with iPODs and Blogs and Podcasts and more cell phones than Alexander Graham Bell could have imagined!

There is one loose end before we move on. I mentioned earlier that I had created "Superstitions Around The World," the show that included the seeming powers of certain people and events. I've often wondered if the show should have included Chuck Milton, a producer on many of my NFL game.

During a Chicago Bears home game from Soldiers Field, in the early seventies, Milton exhibited a strange ability. It was the fourth quarter and the Bears were trailing with no time outs when Milton leaned over and pointed out an exit on one of my monitors. It was one of the openings by the corner of the end zone. Milton had a feeling that the door of that exit would open and that a black dog would run out of that exit and onto the field and delay the game. Sure enough, out came this dog running like he was trying to get away from Michael Vick. While they tried to catch the dog on the field, I asked

Milton how he knew it was going to happen. He had seen it happen before when the Bears were out of timeouts, and all of a sudden this mystical feeling had come over him, that it could happen again.

On that amazing note, let's go from the 1900s to the 2000s!

CHAPTER SEVEN

21ST CENTURY

I should mention that I closed out the nineties by inventing a portable video and audio device called the Scannor, a handheld unit that could store and play back video while still being able to continue to record while doing so. The recorded information could be manipulated in regular, slow motion, or still frame. It was a portable device initially intended to be carried by football officials so that they could review the action while remaining on the playing field. It was first shown to the sharp executives at Fox Sports, David Hill and Ed Goren who were quick to see its limitations. The invention was shown to the NFL but the size of the screen, as Fox had noted, was a key drawback. Plus many of the replay challenges were in need of several camera angles to figure out the correct result. I had previously signed over the invention to Scanz Communications but, after some disagreements, I accepted an out of court settlement.

My next project, kind of a follow-up on the billion-viewer worldwide "Prayer for World Peace," was the creation of an Internet Globalcast. Entitled "A Vatican Christmas," this featured holiday choirs from around the world celebrating the season together. The program became possible solely because I had partnered with Stan McHann, a brilliant engineer whose vast background with computers and video streaming made it possible to spread the Christmas message on a shoestring budget.

With the cooperation of Archbishop Foley at the Vatican, Stan was also able to transmit the Midnight Christmas Mass celebrated

by Pope John Paul II from St. Peter's Basilica—live and worldwide over the Internet from his office in Bozeman, Montana. This transmission was accompanied by the musical performances submitted from many choirs around the world. Stan had written all the arrangements so that one choir in one country could segue to another choir in another country as the sung the same hymn. Going from one to the other visually and with a perfect sound match—was a great experience, and it made for a great globalcast. Someday I hope to revive the Christmas celebration on the Internet and possibly offer it as a DVD release.

In 2003 the Instant Replay celebrated its 40th Anniversary. Now with the digital changes, the Instant Replay process that once slowed down NFL officiating got a whole new digitally-fast life for the 21st century.

Lindsey Nelson thought the Instant Replay would go on forever.

The influence of the Instant Replay was noted again when the Sports Illustrated 50th Anniversary Issue picked Instant Replay as number eleven on its list of 'The 20 Great Tipping Points' of the previous fifty years. And hats off to S.I., they got the essence of the invention just right. They said it helped the viewer see what actually happened once a complicated play went by so fast you couldn't be sure what happened. And they pointed out my reason for struggling so hard to create the Instant Replay—because it gave the broadcasters something to show while the teams were getting ready for the next play. It was the answer to filling dead time between plays. What also impressed me about the Sports Illustrated's analysis was that they also stressed that Instant Replay was not just a technical breakthrough but a conceptual breakthrough. Once TV had the Instant Replay, it could show home viewers something the people in the stadium couldn't see. It gave the TV viewer an advantage. Of course, we should note, too, that since the Instant Replay the sports stadiums have for some time been using their huge screens for playback.

Here I should mention my invention the InstantFootballer—a computer widget that lives on your screen so that you can stay connected to a live football game while you're working away on your computer. To spare those of you who may not want to tackle the four explanatory passages that follow, I'd suggest checking out the five-minute video available for viewing on my website: tonyvernaTV.com, under the section: Extras.

The InstantFootballer widget is a template that automatically tracks the 'Game Ball' during a live football game and exhibits it as a rendering on the exact yard line where the ball is being spotted during a live game. The visualization of the ball's movement appears on a rectangular strip, or grid, at the bottom of a computer, cell phone or other electronic device screen, along with accompanying data. The visualization self-activates after each and every play, and eliminates the need to click off and visit a web site for an update. It's always there during a live game. Whenever the subscriber desires, he can just glance over to see what happening in the game… right now. Presently, there are no such Eye-Catchers of a live football game for those immersed in the Internet or on a cell phone.

But the InstantFootballer can now provide an early radar warning of an upcoming hazard, such as a 'fumble', by showing the ball-image tumbling on your screen widget.

I intentionally created the widget as a 'stand alone' device that would not need to accompany a live telecast, broadcast, or web-stream. There are no cameras, memo fields, or image processing, nor are there any electronic images, such as the first-down lines, painted on the field.

The InstantFootballer was also created to allow fans who are not watching a game to be socially networked with one another—to provide a 'shared experience' by a 'media invention' that never existed before—to allow legions of fans to communicate because of this live screen widget.

On that happy note of communication, let's turn to our final chapter, our "Coda," to add any thoughts about the years of this decade that are still to come—or about anything that may have been overlooked.

Chapter Eight

Coda

We've come to the last chapter, and before we get to the issue of careers and how to get them—which I know you want me to stress—I have asked my researcher and lifelong friend William T. Bode to conduct this chapter as an interview.

BODE
I'd like to cite some research I've done regarding how others were able to hide or alter the truth about who actually invented the Instant Replay. I've poured over the false claims made over the years and I found they were made by two methods: one based on deception, the other on misinformation.

First, let's deal with the claims based on misinformation. This was and still is being achieved by obscuring the factual basis of the invention of the Instant Replay. These deceptive claims are accomplished by selective use of history. One claim, for instance, subtly implies that ABC and AMPEX came up with and developed the idea. This claim is an Internet submission by a communication professor.

In 2002 Steven E. Schoenherr posted an article, Television Instant Replay. In the article he says that in 1966 AMPEX developed the 'instant replay' videodisc, doing so at the request of ABC's "Wide World of Sports." He also notes that in 1965 CBS had been using a 'freeze-action' videodisc, a disc developed by MVR Computers and capable of only short-action sequences in normal motion. After describing the technical development in

AMPEX's videodisc recorder, he summarized that the use of this AMPEX HS-100 color video magnetic disc recorder—in March 1967 at the U.S. Ski Championships in Vail, Colorado—marked "the beginning of instant replay on commercial television."

That's it. No mention of you first using the Instant Replay in December 1963, and no mention of the hundreds of Instant Replays in football, basketball, horse racing, hockey—every sport—during all the years after 1963. That's simply misinformation cloaked as fact.

But let me go on to the second category of claims—blatant deception, which at times is no more than an outright lie wrapped up in circuitous language. This is the saddest part of the whole Instant Replay story. I'm sure our readers hate lies as much as I do, and they hate it even more when people hide lies by screwing with the language.

And what I've discovered is that all these claims based on deception, such as screwing around with dates, relate one way or another to Roone Arledge's claim that he was the one who created the Instant Replay and how he was the one who changed the way we view televised sports.

VERNA

When ABC celebrated its 40th Anniversary, Jim McKay said—on the air—that Roone invented the Instant Replay. When I asked him why, he wrote me back, saying that he just read what was on the teleprompter. I should note that another broadcaster, Bob Costas, refused to read such Instant Replay misinformation on his prompter and instead phoned me immediately to alert me.

BODE

In his autobiography, "Roone," in a single paragraph, Arledge admits that you were the first to use the Instant Replay but still claims that he was the one who invented it. If he created the damn thing, why didn't he use it? Because to air an Instant Replay you had to be the director in the truck!

What Arledge had achieved earlier was the airing of a halftime highlight in slow motion, but it was aired from a studio control room some twenty minutes after the play had happened.

VERNA

That's right. Nothing instant took place on that game. It was a delayed halftime highlight in slow motion. Arledge wasn't trying to do something between live plays. How could he? He had never even directed a live football game.

The innovation of Instant Replay demanded three undeniable factors. First, it had to be done by the director who was calling the shots during the game. It could only be executed by the director who has immediate control. And that could never have been Arledge. He never directed a live football game. Period.

The second factor was that a videotape machine had to actually be on location. Bill McPhail, the head of CBS Sports, gave me permission to truck one of those early giant studio tape machines from its home in the New York Center and travel it ninety miles to South Philly. The machine had to be there so the game director could control it. And that let the third factor come into play.

I needed to commandeer the recording machine to do something it wasn't invented by AMPEX to do—to immediately playback something and allow it to hit the start of the previous play within seconds and on-the-dime so as not to clip the start of the next play. AMPEX didn't invent the first videotape machines to do instant replays. The machine had no built-in brainpower to accomplish such a task. It did not come with a manual that told you how to do an Instant Replay. It was unforeseen!

BODE

But you gave that ability to the machine by using audio instead of video.

VERNA

Because the videotape machine wasn't geared to produce Instant Replay, I created a timed-tone tracking system whereby the video machine's audio cue track could accept a series of timed-tones inserted during the live action of the game—and done in such a manner that I could hear those tone variations while the viewers at home would not hear them.

BODE

We should make clear that these original AMPEX machines were built primarily for playing back shows in different time zones around the country. As you've said, these early machines were never marketed as being able to do instant replay. The concept was unforeseen at the time. The machines lacked not only the circuitry to do that but the machines also weren't invented with any controls to stabilize the video within a time reference a live director could calculate. And that meant that you had to come up with your own method of controlling the functions of the tape machine. "You are machine. I am director. Do what I want you do to!" How'd you make the video machine behave?

VERNA

I knew we couldn't control the video, so I conceived the idea of using audio tones that I could insert on-the-fly during the live action of the game. The conception of an audio-alert was needed so that I could hear the state of the tape's playback distortion as it rolled back through its heads while trying to reach the right speed for synchronization. By analyzing the audio tones we inserted I was able to calculate exactly what the tape was doing during the lengthy eight to ten seconds of indecipherable video hash it was transmitting.

BODE

It was like radio controlling television—like the past controlling the future! And for all his claim of having "created" the Instant Replay, Arledge couldn't come up with that combination of inventions until you aired your replay, thus showing his ABC staff how it was done.

But the real sadness of Roone's claim is that it wasn't the only inaccuracy he spread about himself. If it were just his claim about the Instant Replay, people might be able to say you were nitpicking at Arledge's record of accomplishments. But it was a pattern with Roone. In his ABC biography he even got it wrong about his days at college.

VERNA

You're referring to the Internet article by Shira J. Bass, Class of '93, as she identifies herself.

BODE

Right. In her article, "Spanning the World," of February 2, 2004, she talks about Roone's upcoming autobiography. Ironically, she says he's avoided reading other people's books about his career "because the inaccuracies [in them]" bother him too much.

VERNA

But I remember she points out that "some of the inaccuracies, such as that he was president of his class at the College and that he majored in business have made their way into various official ABC biographies."

BODE

As if Roone didn't have the power to have his ABC biographies 'corrected'. The man was President of ABC Sports and the President of ABC News. He could have had anything he wanted in his ABC biographies, and he did; witness the Jim McKay statement about the Instant Replay. Roone's autobiography made all these claims—including that he'd created the Instant Replay—apparently because he wanted his biographies to make those grandiose—if false—claims. Why? Who knows? Seemingly the man wanted credit for everything he could persuade people—especially the news media—to accept.

VERNA

And, as you pointed out, it had to be a quirk with him because of all his actual accomplishments. Come on, how many people get to be president of both the Sports and News Divisions of a major network! I can only think of two, Roone and his buddy Jim McKay's son, Sean McManus.

BODE

One of my hopes is that the bloggers who created the Rathergate episode will go to plnews.com and tackle this Roone

Arledge scandal, first to get the facts out and, maybe just as important, to show how these phony claims of his covered up Roone's real genius. His real skill wasn't creating new projects. It was perfecting projects better than other people.

VERNA
Witness his making a smash success out of "Monday Night Football" after CBS had tried and failed.

BODE
Right. And I think Roone's real genius was in casting people. I know how important and difficult casting is and can be. His casting got people like the late Jim McKay on "Wide World of Sports" and Ted Koppel on "Nightline." And the same for all of his projects. It's just sad that he wasn't secure in his real talent and had to try to reach out and grab credit from other people.

VERNA
You said there were two points. What was your second point?

BODE
The second point was the way he and his associates went about deliberately not correcting their lies. With the help of my Liberty, North Carolina library I looked into some technical terms used in debate, and the closest I've been able to come is called circumvention—avoiding the issue in the hope that it will go away. The technique Roone and his associates used—and are still using—is to acknowledge that there is a question about accuracy but never to go beyond acknowledgement to actually arguing the point, the issue.

VERNA
You're going to have to be more specific than that.

BODE
All right, I'll tell you about the one I've been involved in personally. When Arledge's autobiography, Roone, came out,

I wrote to the publisher HarperCollins. Their representative acknowledged receipt of my letter and said he would refer the matter to the Arledge estate with a promise to "respond to you more substantially" as soon as he'd consulted representatives of the estate.

Never heard back from either publisher or estate.

VERNA
That was 2003.

BODE
And counting. When we got within shouting distance of finishing your biography, I wrote again—in July 2005—asking for any decision or decisions from the estate.

VERNA
And no reply.

BODE
Silence. This is the technique they inherited from Roone. You acknowledge there's a problem, but you don't discuss the problem.

VERNA
And you ran into the same verbal roadblocks when you tried to correct the issue in the obituaries after Roone's death.

BODE
Exact same pattern. I wrote to half a dozen or more of the media sources—big ones, like ESPN, Sports Illustrated, CBS News—even Columbia University. Every one of them credited Roone with introducing 'innovations' including the Instant Replay. Never heard a word back from any of them. Never saw or heard a correction.

VERNA
And you said there was a second pattern inside that pattern.

BODE

Yeah. We should have called this chapter "The Case of the Terrible Twos."

The second pattern is the virus effect, where one usually reliable source—like ABC biographies or the obits in any of those media—prints the lie and then other people copy it because it's from a "reliable" source, so the lie spreads like a virus from one "reliable" source to another.

VERNA

And you know this because....?

BODE

Because of the language. Adding "English teacher" to my credits has served me well. Let me just quote for you from two of the obits—one from WRL.com, Capital Broadcasting, and another from Sports Illustrated.

From WRL.com: "He introduced innovations taken for granted today, including the use of slow motion, freeze-frame, instant replay, hand-held cameras and the placement of microphones on the field."

VERNA

And from S.I.?

BODE

Almost verbatim: "He introduced innovations taken for granted today: slow motion, freeze frame, instant replay, hand-held cameras...."

It's the virus effect. ABC's biography offered up a lie. Other people copied the bio. Other people passed it on. "Introduced innovations."

By the way, CBSNews.com used exactly the same words. You'd think if anyone knew the truth about when the Instant Replay was first introduced it would be CBS News and Sean McManus.

VERNA

Well, on my website, www.TonyVernaTV.com we'll post the sources these people could have and should have gone to verify their source or sources—whatever they were—so that our readers can get the articles from Barry Horn in the Dallas Morning News and from Joe Starkey in the Pittsburgh Tribune-Review.

By the way, Starkey has an article on the Ice Bowl game in 1997—Dallas Cowboys and Green Bay Packers—the game that inspired Jerry Kramer to call his book Instant Replay. And in all fairness, you have to remember these people who got caught up in the Arledge virus are news and sports writers, not TV people. They lack the perspective that differentiates Roone from me. He and ABC Tech Robert Trachinger did introduce slo-mo in the half-time replay, and all those replays helped solve his problems as a producer to fill the half-time show with interesting stuff. But I was a director. I was the one on line, having to fill the time between the end of one play and the start of another.

I was under the gun a million times in every game, looking for the way to show the viewers what had happened and to give my commentators video that would show that. As a producer, Roone needed the replays. As a director, I needed the Instant Replays. That's why I went out and figured out how to do it. I didn't just want it. I needed it.

BODE

And you got it. And some of us bless you for it and some of us curse you for it.

VERNA

Yeah, but wait a minute. See, that's another reason Roone didn't invent the Instant Replay. He wasn't in the control room calling the shots.

It had to be a director who invented the Instant Replay. We were the ones calling the shots. We were the only ones who could coordinate all the audio and video involved in making "Instant" possible and workable. Getting in and out of Instant Replay isn't the easiest thing in the world. It's a hell of a lot easier now than it was in 1963, but it still takes a director's skills to pick which players to isolate, to pick which shot to go with, when to go to it, and when to get out of it in time for the next play.

It had to be a director. If it hadn't been me, it would have been another director, not a producer, not a lab-bound engineer.

BODE
But as it turned out, it was you, on December 7, 1963, and anything else is a damn lie. Case closed. End of story. End of sermon. A-men.

VERNA
Now let's turn to the action you want to cover: careers that your readers may be working for and how to get there.

First, let me stress how competitive work in television is. Whether you want news or sports or entertainment, six dozen other people want the same job—and don't want you to get it, or even near it.

BODE
When I was in New York when my script was on Studio One Summer Theatre, I remember telling you I felt like there was always someone holding a knife two inches from my back. I was really in a hurry to get back to Philadelphia.

VERNA
So, of course, it's gotten even more competitive now. It's the nature of the beast. But let me remind everyone—and it's only a reminder because everybody knows it—the whole world is more competitive.

There was a story on National Public Radio recently about the job of Street Cleaner in Paris. To get the job of Street Cleaner in Paris, you not only have to attend classes and take a test, you have to write an essay!

BODE
The thought of it touches my English-teacher heart.

director ordered—how could one human mind constantly absorb so many visual images and choose them, often with only seconds to choose, to make them create a story that seemed to effortlessly flow onto the single TV screen viewers were watching? And how could all of the technicians keep up with the untold story that— most of the time—couldn't be predicted ahead of time? It was that sense of curiosity.

VERNA

It's a three-W world—the WorldWideWeb of the Internet that keeps opening doors and windows that no one knew existed. Start YouTube and two years later tons of people begin posting videos every day.

And it's not just video, of course. The economic expansion in India and China are directly linked to the computer and its potential. As we noted, every TV program, every TV station not only has its own website but plugs that website endlessly because that's where the viewers are going, where the audience is. So in terms of careers for the future you have to imagine where our world will be a decade from now. It's about as exciting a time as has ever existed.

BODE

Joseph Campbell's admonition: "Find your bliss." Figure out what means something to you and follow that light where it leads you.

VERNA

I've always gone for the challenge. It's part of the pattern. Look at me. I'm in my seventies. I've done the Sports and the globalcasts, and now I'm up to my ass in writing a Civil War occult novel, Beyond the Blue and the Gray.

BODE

And translating that personally again, before we finish this I'd like to thank you personally for letting me share so much of your bliss. You called on me for "Live Aid," "Sport Aid," and more. You got me to Seattle for Ted Turner's "Goodwill Games." You got me to London for "Prayer for World Peace."

VERNA

So you were following your own bliss in the context of someone else's.

BODE

And that can be a career path, too. Find an imaginative creator like Tony Verna and tell him, "Hey, I can help with that project!"

VERNA

So want it, train for it, get inside the door where the job listings are posted; then look for ways to advance your career—and/or find someone whose bliss you want to be part of.

BODE

So as we come to the end, one last question. How would you like your tombstone to read?

VERNA

Tony Verna
Son of Italian immigrants
Invented the Instant Replay

Timeline

Chapter 1   December 7, 1963 Birth of the Instant Replay

Chapter 2   1950-1959

1951   Attend U.S.M.A. (West Point)
1952   Attend U. of Pa. (Penn)
1953   (June) Start at WCAU-TV
1953   (Nov) Promoted to TV Director
1954   Acting...Various roles
1954   (Oct) Edward R. Murrow
1955   (Feb) Alexander Fleming
1955   Local games: Phillies and Eagles
1955   (July) Grace Kelly
1955   Several—CBS Game of the Week with Dizzy Dean
1956   CBS/NFL Red Grange, Jack Buck, Chris Schenkel.
1956   Several—Friday Nite Fights...Jack Drees
1957   The Big Idea...Rob Reiner's grandpa...Carl Reiner's dad
1957   Local NBA Eastern Conference Final...Boston/Phila.
1957-59   Hired gun...e.g. WBBM, KRLD
1958   Acting...Phila. Police Department Training Film
1958   NFL...use of VTR during at halftimes
1959   Nelson Rockefeller—Governor of NY
1959   NFL Commissioner...Bert Bell dies in the stands

Chapter 3   **1960-1969**

1960   (August) Rome Olympics…freelance
1960   (Sept) Sign Contract with CBS Sports
1960   Eddie Arcaro Bio
1961   Roger Maris…Mickey Mantle—Yankee Stadium—
        Lauderdale
1961   CBS Special…West Point and the Naval Academy—Jim
        McKay
1962   Marshall Tito—ski jumping—Yugoslavia
1962   Private plane hits tree Grossingers – Catskills
1962   Live theatrical aquatic show "The Theater Of the Sea"
1962   NFL Championship—Vince Lombardi
1962   London: CBS Soccer Brazil vs. England at Wembley
        Stadium.
1963   CBS's "Harlem Globetrotters" in Rome—Abe Saperstein
1963   Private plane makes emergency landing—Wisconsin
1963   Opening of NFL Hall of Fame Chris Schenkel
1963   Freelance:Televisia: Charreada Rodeo—Mexico City
1963   (Dec-7)…Instant Replay invented
1964   Kentucky Derby, Preakness, Belmont
1965   Seaplane crash…air balloon race Catalina Island, CA
1965   "English Derby" Fred Friendly, Chas. Collingwood, Dan
        Rather
1965   Jumping Championship—Garmisch-Partenkirchen,
        Germany
1966   Move to Los Angeles
1966   Wild West—Gilligan's Island
1966   Freelance:Televisa Mexico—24 Hours of LeMans Race-
        France
1966   Caesars Palace first sports event—USA USSR Amateur
        Boxing.
1967   Art Linkletter Productions—Roy Rogers and Dale Evans
1967   CBS Pro Soccer Jack Whitaker, Danny Blanchflower
1967   Figure Skating Championship—Vienna, Austria
1967   Freelance: 4 Star Pilot Tom Harmon
1967   Oahu, Hawaii—Duke Kahanamoku
1967   Ice Bowl

1967   Las Vegas—Liberace
1968   Created:"Jogging Short" Rocky Marciano, Jonathan Winter
1968   "Musical Hoedown" Roy Rogers, Dale Evans, Christy Minstrels
1968   Super Bowl II
1969   "Marciano Tribute" Ali, Jimmy Durante, Robert Stack
1969   AAU Track and Field—European Continent
1969   Rod Serling Commercial
1969   Move back to Manhattan

Chapter 4   **1970-1979**
1970   "Playback" book (written in 1969)…released
1970   "Playback" airs as a CBS Network Special
1970   Duke Ellington—"Monterey Jazz Festival"
1970   "Billiards Special"—Mosconi, Minnesota Fats, Omar Shariff
1970   Super Bowl IV
1971   Fran Allison Show—Chicago
1971   Stanley Cup Championships—Canada—USA
1971   John Forsythe—Hollywood Park
1972   Freelance:"Mike Douglas Show"—Moscow, Russia
1972   Super Bowl VI
1972   Created:"Instant Quarterback" freelance short…John Unitas
1973   Created:"Day at the Derby" freelance short…Heywood Broun 1973 Rod Serling Commercial
1973   Triple Crown—Secretariat Kentucky Derby, Preakness, Belmont
1973   Created:"Hambeltonian" theatrical short United Artists
1973   First Sports Emmy on Prime Time. Lose to Jim McKay
1974   Super Bowl VIII
1974   Jesse Owens
1974   Howard Cossel—Paul Hornung
1974   NBA Championship
1974   Mickey Mantle
1975   Joe DiMaggio

1975   Match Race...Foolish Pleasure—Ruffian Tragedy
1975   Saudi Arabia Freelance for Montreal Olympics
1976   Move back to Los Angles.
1976   Freelance: TWI-ABC-TV "Hilton Head Tennis Classic"
1976   "Celebrity Challenge of the Sexes" Farrah Fawcett—Bill Cosby
1976   TWI "World's Strongest Man"
1977   Created: "Beauty Beach and Bizarre" George Kennedy-
1977   Created: "$50,000 Challenge" Telly Savalas - Las Vegas
1977   Arthur Halley—Roots
1977   Sun Bowl in El Paso, Texas—Burt Reynolds
1977   London..."World Circus" Vin Scully—Karl Wallenda
1978   Soupy Sales—Harlem Globetrotters—Madison Sq. Garden
1978   Celebrity Daredevils, Christopher Reeve—Los Ang.
1978   NBC-TV—Primetime—Rock n Roll Classic
1978   "Pete Rose Roast" with Milton Berle (Sinatra)—Las Vegas
1978   Jupiter Theater, Fla. Burt Reynolds—Carol Burnett
1978   Tom Selleck—Hawaii—"People's Choice Award"
1979   "Celebrity Billiards" Mosconi-Fats Omar Sharif -James Coburn
1979   ABC-TV—Primetime Pageant—"All American Woman"
1979   Created: "Weekend Heroes" Paul Hornung—Jayne Kennedy 1979 President of Caesars Palace Productions
1979   Created "Sports Hotline'—ESPN—Roy Firestone
1979   Created: "Battle of the NFL Cheerleaders" Tom Brookshier

Chapter 5   **1980-1989**
1980   Ronald Reagan—Vin Scully Interview
1982   NFC Championship Game. "The Catch"
1982   Contract ends with CBS Sports
1982   Contract ends with Caesars Palace
1983   Buenos Aires, Argentina "Algebra I Murder II"
1983   ABC News: Paul Newman—Charlton Heston Debate
1984   ABC Summer Olympics Emmy Swimming
1985   Live Aid (worldwide) Bob Geldof

1986   Sport-Aid (worldwide) Bob Geldof
1986   Richard Feynman
1986   David Brinkley Jim Lehrer Sam Donaldson
1986   Created: "Prayer For World Peace" Pope John Paul II
1987   Live TV Book (commissioned by the DGA)
1987   "Christmas Around the World" Mother Teresa—Johnny
        Cash
1987   "Omni 14 Great Minds Predict The Future"
1989   "Our Common Future" NHK Japan

Chapter 6   **1990-1999**
1990   NHK "Earth 90" NYC Paris Tokyo John Denver
1990   Ted Turner "1990 Goodwill Games"—Larry King
1990   White House President George H. W. Bush
1991   Japan—John Denver
1992   Earth Day— Freelance
1993   Global Television Book released
1994   Created: "Superstitions Around The World" London
1995   DGA Lifetime Achievement Award—Tony Danza
1996-99   International consulting services

Chapter 7   **21st Century**
2000   Consultant Millennium Telecasts
2001   Consultant Japan "NHK Concert"—Ray Charles
2002   Created Vatican...Christmas
2003   Director...Internet TV Game Pilot
2004   Author..."Beyond the Blue and the Gray"
2006   Author..."Algebra I Murder II"
2007   Invention..."INSTANTFOOTBALLER"

Chapter 8   Coda

The Coda presents sample patterns on how others have advanced their careers in the industry. It also recaps how others were able to hide or alter the truth about who actually invented the Instant Replay.